"Pam brilliantly unfolds the value of your own self-worth not only as God sees you but as He longs for you to see yourself. Every person should read, implement, then recommend to others."

Ron Pratt
National Event Planner
LifeWife Christian Resources

"Excitement! Joy! Inspiration! Each of those words describes how I felt as I poured over *Will the Real Me Please Stand Up*! Pam grasps biblical truths and brings them to our hearts in fresh, insightful ways."

Debbie Taylor Williams
Speaker, Author *Pray with Purpose, Live with Passion*

will the
real me
please stand up

Cynthia

It has a joy to
know and love you
over the years! May you
be blessed as you come to
know yet more and more
your immense value to
Christ the King.

Your are loved !!!

Pam

will the *real me* please stand up

by Pam Kanaly

TATE PUBLISHING & *Enterprises*

Published by Tate Publishing & Enterprises, LLC
127 E. Trade Center Terrace | Mustang, Oklahoma 73064 USA
1.888.361.9473 | www.tatepublishing.com

Tate Publishing is committed to excellence in the publishing industry. The company reflects the philosophy established by the founders, based on Psalm 68:11,
"The Lord gave the word and great was the company of those who published it."

Book design copyright © 2007 by Tate Publishing, LLC. All rights reserved.
Edited by Tracy Terrell
Cover design by Janae Glass
Interior design by Stephanie Woloszyn

Published in the United States of America

ISBN: 978-1-60462-240-9
1. Christian Living   2. Spiritual Growth
07.10.12

Dedicated to

Jason and Sara

To dedicate means to give up wholly or earnestly. It's with great passion that I wholly and earnestly give up to you the lessons I learned and the spiritual maturity I gained as a result of us being a single parent family from 1986–1991. May the riches of who you are in Christ serve as your greatest joy, and may you forever hunger and thirst after righteousness.

I love you immensely,
Mom

Acknowledgments

I believe the success of a testimony, a life, or even a book is only as great as the encouragement and prayer force behind it. It's with sincere gratitude that I thank those whose passion for the content in *Will the Real Me Please Stand Up* brought about its completion through fervent support and prayer power.

I thank Tate Publishing and the entire production team for their gracious insight and dedication in the completion of this book.

To my family I extend a word of thanksgiving: to Rich, my husband, thank you for the love and unselfishness over the last year in providing the atmosphere at home to work on this project. To my children, Sara and Jason, I express my gratitude for your love and prayers. To my step-children, Ryan and Amber; my daughter-in-law, Beth; and son-in-law, Jess, thank you for granting me a significant place in your lives. To my only sister, Vicki, thank you for serving as a testimony of God's healing power and faithfulness.

To my friend and co-founder of *Arise Ministries*, Shelley Pulliam, thank you for daily editing this manuscript bringing profound insight and cheering the cause.

To those who helped lay the foundation, I thank David Thomas, pastor and professor at Oklahoma Christian Schools, whose review of the manuscript enhanced sound doctrine, and to Gary Payne whose initial advice concerning the book contract served as a valuable benefit. To Michael Scroggins, thank you for your insight in the graphic design of the fountain, and Cindy Prince for your excellent suggestions.

To my long-lasting friendship with Debbie Williams, thank you for the Christ-centered life you have set before me since college days.

To Rene George, Linda Catania, and Jim and Gay Cunningham, your faithfulness in prayer for me through the years have helped to birth this book, and to Nena, Geraldine, Helen, and Mac, blessings to you.

To the *Arise Ministries* prayer team: Connie Cook, Joanna Gregg, Phyllis Hartman, Diane Loesel, Ann Nelson, Shelley Pulliam, and Kelly Weir, your Thursday gatherings from 4:30–5:30 provided the energy and wisdom to accomplish God's work.

To the *Arise* Board of Directors: Donna Alexander, Kim Bearden, Gail Carr, Brad Goad, Cindy Jefferies, Susie Delano, Rich Kanaly, Ann Nelson, Shelley Pulliam, Keith Tracy, Larry and Lydia Travis, and Kelly Weir, I express my appreciation for the wise counsel you have given concerning God's direction for the ministry.

To my *Monday Night Group* of couple friends: Jon and Sherri Cook, Rich and Cindy Jefferies, John and Diane Loesel, Gary and Shouna Olson, Larry and Lydia Travis, thank you for your weekly encouragement, and a special thanks to Larry and Lydia for the use of your lake home for the solitude needed in completing the book.

And to all the readers of *Will the Real Me Please Stand Up*, I extend my desire that the Spirit of Almighty God will bring you into an awareness of how valuable you are to Him through Jesus Christ.

Table of Contents

Foreword

How many times have you been asked the simple question, "Can you tell me a little bit about yourself?" And on the surface it sounds like a very easy question that would presumably have a very easy answer, unless you actually wanted to go beyond the surface. So often in today's society our identity is linked closely to our family, the family we grew up in, our job, our salary, our house or apartment, the zip code we live in, the car we drive, the brand of clothes we wear, the size of our bodies, and even the color of our hair.

Think about that question again, "Can you tell me a little bit about yourself?" Well, I work at so and so. I live in that neighborhood. I have a brother and sister, each with one child. I just took a vacation to the mountains. I have two kids, one dog, and a cat that I'm not that thrilled with, but my kids like it. And my hobby is trying to get in at least six hours of sleep at night, to do it all again the next day. Yes, that is the answer. But it is also the surface answer. We seem to want to hide behind these easy answers. It's a safe place to be and, quite honestly, many times those answers meet the person's expectations asking the question.

However, to look beyond the surface, you have to actually think about who you are inside. You need to look at how you came to be on this earth, not just in a biological way, but in the spiritual sense from the beginning of time, why did God plan to have you enter this earth on that certain hour of that certain day of that certain month of that certain year. When you think about the question in those terms, it takes an entirely different perspective. It goes beyond just the here and now; it goes all the way back to the beginning. And not just the day of your birth, but all the way back to the beginning of time. Wow, now that's beyond the surface. That truly answers the question from a whole new perspective. And that is when you begin to recognize who the "real you" truly is!

My dear friend and sister in Christ, Pam Kanaly, has poured her heart and soul into looking at the question for you beyond the surface. Who are you really? What is your true background? What is your purpose for being on this earth? And does it really matter to anyone?

For several years, I've watched and heard Pam speak on "identity in Christ" and so often those talks are at a conference or church and restricted by limited time. And when the Lord placed on her heart to write a book such as this, the rivers of truth began to flow. As you will see, the river is like riding the rapids. There is great joy and excitement. There is a bit of fear and trepidation. There is constant moving. And at times you feel like you are being bounced around. But the reward is getting to the point of realization that comes with the fact along the trip; God was with you the whole time and that is the safest place to be.

In Scripture there is passage after passage that speaks directly to who the "real you" is in Christ. There are stories of others who have traveled similar paths though the surroundings and transportation might have been quite different all those centuries ago. The God who created Abraham created you. The God who gave his Son that you might live is the one who has given you life.

You have the opportunity to take a stand. Now you will probably be sitting or lying down when you actually read this book, but if you allow the Spirit of God to teach you through the truth that is revealed in the following pages, you will not only be able to stand up and say "This is the Real Me," but you will be able to soar on the wings of eagles and never be the same again. So as you read, get ready to stand, and when you stand, get ready to soar.

Brad Goad
Pastor to Singles and Single Parents
Second Baptist Church, Houston, TX

Introduction

If any man be in Christ, he is a new creature.

2 Corinthians 5: 17

For a number of years, God has given me an insatiable desire to see myself the way He sees me, not as others see me, or the ways I often see myself. As a result of my quest for truth, He's pulled back the veil and allowed me to envision *in part* my illustrious new creation in Christ Jesus. I'm astonished at His delight in His children!

In *Will the Real Me Please Stand Up*, God will unfold 100 facets of your new creature status. Though you'll enjoy reading through the book, I believe you'll most benefit from its content by reading one or two entitlements a day and answering the follow-up questions in the accompaniment guide *Let's Go Deeper*. In the study guide, you'll discover that your six basic needs for security, purpose, value, service, comfort, and hope, all find fulfillment in the "100 I Am Blessings."

May God richly bless you as He opens your eyes to the magnificent wonder of the new you!

Part One

My Spiritual
Ancestry

Chapter One

My Authority

It was the mid 1960s. I sat in the living room of my house at 2417 Duncan Street waiting for my favorite television game show. Not an evening passed by that "To Tell the Truth" didn't find me glued to the screen along with millions of other fans. Would I pick the one who had testified by an affidavit to be the authentic truth teller? As the game unfolded, three contestants graced the stage, all posing to be the same person. For example, they might all agree to the personage of Dr. Benjamin Cosh, a celebrated college professor. After the three supposed characters of Dr. Cosh took their seats, a panel of judges interrogated the players hoping to expose the liars and determine the actual person. After an allotted time, the panelist chose who they thought was the *real* university lecturer. But the best part of the game came at the end when the moderator would direct, "Will the real Dr. Cosh please stand up?" Each contestant would purposefully prolong the suspense by popcorning up and down until the *real* Dr. Benjamin Cosh proudly stood to his feet. The celebrity panel would clap waves of bravo to the two contestants who sometimes tricked them by fraudulently assuming the character of the one true individual. And as for me, I either jumped for joy because I had intuitively guessed correctly, or I sat there stunned by the polished deception of the imposters!

What was it about "To Tell the Truth" that made it one of the most enduring television game shows of all time? And why was the nation mesmerized for over twenty years by a silly game show that found suspense in stealing another's identity? Or was it simply a fun-loving matter of congratulating the real person for his amazing individuality and celebrated story? Whatever the case, I learned at a young age the concept of identity, that is, we all have a distinctiveness of character and personality that comes from somewhere.

On the game show, individuals testified night after night of their identity's source. "I'm Dr. Cosh, a renowned teacher," whose significance came from his career. Or the next evening, another would confess that her identity came from a dangerous feat, "I'm Meggie Alperno, a stunt woman for cyclist daredevils." Everyone's identity and sense of purpose was tied to something: either to his popularity, performance, prestige, profession, position, or pompous power.

How about you? Where do you get your identity? What defines you as a person? What catapults your core being? In other words, if you were hopelessly shipwrecked on an island all alone without family and friends or the accolades of others, stranded without the need to impress by your updated fashion, stripped of the enjoyment of your favorite hobby, or abruptly vacated of that inside drive to make money, or have a great body, or be the best underwater photographer in the world, who would emerge? Did you know there's a real you in there? In fact, William James interestingly assessed, "When two people meet there are really six people present. There is each as he sees himself, each man as the other person sees him, and each man as he *really is!*"[1] Do you know *the real you?* God deposited an authentic you. Can you imagine going your whole life being another you? Talk about being an imposter!

Friends, when it all comes down to it, one day at death you and I will be stripped of all the fluff that wraps itself around the *real you.* Will the real you please stand up? Do you know the *real you?* I'm afraid for most people in this busy world of building relationships, establishing a career, providing financially for ourselves, raising children, finding a mate, or chasing our illusive dreams, such an examination finds itself snuffed out by the urgency of the moment or the fear that if you dis-cover the God-impregnated you, it will somehow confine or limit your desires of what you want to do in life. Oh, friend, no one wants you to meet your ultimate potential more than the God who put it there! The question is, "Will you let Him show you who He made you to be?" Who is the real you? Most humans don't realize they've been chasing the wrong you until later in life.

For example, take my new friend I met yesterday. She mourned, "Pam, It wasn't until I was forty-four years old after the Oklahoma City bombing that I realized my Ferris-wheel life had lost its thrill. I felt empty, tired of gliding through life going around and around. I thought, *What's the purpose? Why do I feel like such a failure? I don't even know who I am. My life hasn't turned out the way I had planned. I live in a hollow world.*" And then she added, "Until I found Jesus Christ and started the journey of living my life from His perspective did I find myself."

Or how about Rich, my husband. He's a phenomenal man. If there were a male pageant for the most humble and gentle-hearted man in America, he would win. Like me, he's in a second marriage. We've been married over sixteen years. He spent the first half of his life building a career, raising a family, and establishing an honorable reputation. Though he was brought up in a Christian church, it was not until later in life that he received Christ as His Savior and began to investigate who He was as a new creature in Jesus. Many of his previous years fell to the wayside in making an impact in the Kingdom of God and letting His God-given talents be used to bring God glory. He recently admitted, "Once I realized my position in the Lord through salvation, I was set free from the guilt of sin and performance in trying to please God. I rested secure in the knowledge that I was whole and complete in God's sight forever. Now through the gift of redemption, I am forever a son of God. Having this knowledge has given me a firm foundation in the challenge of blending a new family and trusting God to repair broken hearts."

My life is yet another unique testimony. I grew up in a godly Christian family with my only sister, Vicki. She was the student council queen, and I was the cheerleader type. We attended church every Sunday morning,

Wednesday night, and attended Training Union on Sunday evenings. I grew up in the church, attended Kanakuk/Kanakomo Christian camps for years, traveled to the other side of the world in college as a summer missionary. I knew Jesus! I knew the Bible stories: Moses and the parting of the Red Sea, Daniel and the lions' den, Elijah and the whirlwind with his chariot. I knew God had a plan for me. I knew I was to only marry a Christian. I knew the rules about being faithful in a marriage. I knew that teaching a Bible class in church would require time in studying His Word! I knew the role of a godly wife! I knew the love of a mother with her babies. I knew! I knew! I knew! But what I didn't know was who I was in Christ, and when the bottom fell out of my life when my first husband left me following ten years of marriage, I looked at myself in the mirror and said, "Who are you?" It suddenly dawned on me: I wasn't the "To Tell the Truth" cheerleader, or "To Tell the Truth" missionary, or "To Tell the Truth" wife, or "To Tell the Truth" mother, or "To Tell the Truth" Bible teacher. To tell the truth, who was I?

Beloved friends, here's the heart of my book, my life, my God: if you don't know who you are in Christ, you don't know much! (I don't care how many Bible verses you've memorized.) Knowing Him and who He says you are is the most substantial and magnificent gift you'll ever uncover. It's only as you discover His identity that you find your own! When tragedy hits, and it will, seeing yourself the way God sees you is the only remedy for rising above a life that's brought you heartaches you didn't ask for and life situations you can't restore. Viewing your purpose and identity from God's standpoint hurls you into the domain of the supernatural where God's presence and comfort abides. Actually, I've been a follower of Christ for over forty years, but it hasn't been until the last number of years

It's only as you discover His identity that you find your own!

that my eyes have been opened to the expansive life, the existence that thrives far beyond circumstances that couldn't be fixed, broken dreams that couldn't be mended, physical ailments that couldn't be cured, disappointments that couldn't be repaired, hurtful words that couldn't be erased, or tragedies that couldn't be reversed. I'm obsessively passionate about this topic of who you are in Christ because I know it's the golden key to *everything* in life you've always wanted. You were created to know the wonderful you God formed in your mother's womb. Consider the role of your mother. She carried in her tummy God's design of a magnificent human being. Do you believe in that person she carried? Yet, apart from granting Christ permission to live His life through *that* person, or your spirit, you will never, never find the real you, God's you!

It is my prayer that in *Will the Real Me Please Stand Up*, the Holy Spirit will roll back the covering over your heart, allowing you to become acquainted with your immense value to God. I've noticed in my own life such a revelation has come through five stages. Maybe you're like me. Sometimes you see a truth in the Bible about who you are in Christ, merely reading it, a verse like Ephesians 1:18 where Paul prays that "the eyes of your heart may be enlightened...so that you may know the riches of the glory of His inheritance in the saints." You only glance over the thought because you don't understand it. Then the Holy Spirit leads you into a deeper step where your intellect grabs hold of it, and for a second, you begin to taste what it means. From there, the newfound thought enters a phase of meditation where God's Spirit begins to unfold how each word relates to one another, and for days you connect your mind to its application, seeing the truth from God's perspective. And finally the Spirit links this divine knowledge to your heart, where the revelation of the *living* Word becomes a permanent deep reservoir of illuminated insight that brings the real you to life! Such a process births a transformation conforming you to the image of Christ. And that's what I pray these entitlements will do in your walk with Him, that as the Spirit leads you from the written word, to the mind, to mediation, to the heart, and then to revelation, you will emerge into the glorious fullness of who you are in Christ Jesus. Glory to God!

It's a true fact, one in which I must remind you. One day, my friend, you and I, along with every manmade creature, will give an account of our lives to God. I wonder if my Creator, my Maker will look at me, His creation, and compare it to the creation He envisioned me to be. I know I fall dreadfully short some days, but broadly speaking, the bottom line question is this: What will God say when He looks at you and me and asks, "Who were you on planet earth?" And "Why did I put you there?" And He might continue the dialogue, "Did you use the natural talents and spiritual gifts I gave you to accomplish My ultimate purposes?" After all, herein lies the *real* you! If you did, then you will hear the Master say, "Well, done, thy good and faithful servant."[2]

It's for people like my new friend who questioned her identity after the Oklahoma City bombing, my husband, and my own story that I wrote *Will the Real Me Please Stand Up*. And it's for someone else, too, my mother. I have highlighted in my Bible a most precious passage. It's dedicated to my mother, Melba Martin, who entered the Lord's presence January 25, 2005. Psalm 73:25, "Whom have I in heaven but thee?

He's made my mess His message.

And besides thee, I desire nothing on earth. My flesh and my heart may fail, but God is the strength of my heart...I have made the Lord God my refuge, that I may *tell* of all Thy works."

Tell, tell, tell. It's my life mission, to tell of His mighty deeds in my own life and how he repaired a million broken pieces and put them back together in a different fashion that I might be a present day witness of His awesome goodness and mighty power. He's made my mess His message. He's graced me with the eyes to see the beautiful creation I am in spite of my not-so-perfect past. I praise Him! I exalt His wondrous name! I can't help but tell, tell, tell! I want the world to know, my friends to know, my family to know, and most of all, my children and their spouses, my step-children and their spouses, and my grandchildren to know who they are in Jesus Christ, the Restorer, the Healer, the Lover of their souls!

As a follower of Christ, who are you? It's the most significant journey of a lifetime in discovering that answer. Are you ultimately a product of what you do (teach or perform perilous stunts) or is what you do a product of who you are? I believe the basis for all achievement, maturity, and fruitfulness finds its source in discovering the magnificence of who you are, specifically related to your identity in Christ. Such a realization lays hold of the foundation that forms your belief system, which drives your thinking, emotions, and behavior, and ultimately opens the floodgate to explosive Christian living.

When you received Christ as your savior and He came into your life, He didn't come empty handed. He unrolled a red carpet legacy, an exquisite inheritance, indeed, His finest wealth passed down to you as a rightful heir of His expanding Heavenly Empire, gifts not only for eternity, but magnanimous resources empowering you to live in His God-ordained purpose *now*! Do you know what benefits you received? As a believer, are you enjoying the heights of God's bountiful liberties or are you living beneath your privileges? What a shame to have been granted an entitlement deed to all God's prosperity and never cash in on your spiritual birthright.

Embracing who we are in Christ reminds me of a toy sponge flower. When Sara, my daughter, was a toddler she was captivated with bath time. Her fascination came to life when I'd hand her a package of what looked like pills, yet tucked inside waiting for the water to dissolve the outside coating was a crunched sponge flower waiting to unfold its true self.

Many believers' enjoyment of the Christian life reminds me of a sponge flower. They spend years reading their Bibles, attending church, going through the routine of doing "the Christian thing," yet tucked inside remains a sponge flower waiting to unfold. How is it that many have missed the unveiling message of who they are in Christ? It's what every soul longs to know. It's what Christ longed for you to possess. And until the flower of the *real you* releases its beauty, you will continue to live in a crunched position of spirituality.

Who are you in Christ? What blessings has God stored up for you and all those who have received Him as Lord and Savior? I can assure you, what He has stored up for you now outglitters, outclasses, and far outshines anything you could muster up on your own efforts and talents. Yes, He's given you human talents and giftedness, but if it's not being put to use by His power and for His prestige, then you've tragically cut yourself short! He gave you those gifts to do exceptionally and profusely beyond what you could hope or imagine. What a shame to settle for rhinestones when He gave you diamonds!

Do you know the diamonds you've received as His follower? Look at the cycle of the blessing for both you and God. He gives you grace gifts bestowed for the purpose of not only your satisfaction and the blessing of others, but also for the pleasure it brings to Him in blessing you with His finest treasures. And in return, your thanksgiving and praise to Him brings honor to His Kingdom.

Here's a tongue twister relaying the same concept. Are you ready? "Do you enjoy the joy of being enjoyed by Him as He sees you enjoying what He gave you to enjoy?" I told you it was a mouthful, but think about it. Or let me restate it in a more simple fashion. The *real you* can only find true purpose when the God who made you is releasing His joy through you, which actually gives Him joy as He sees the pleasure it's bringing you. It's then that the real you finds the freedom to come out and play in God's highest realm of fulfillment, which in turn brings Him great delight. It's actually a beautiful cycle: God handcrafts in you an exceptional blueprint that only you can carry out. When you lay your sketch or life plan before Christ and ask Him to complete the draft and fill in all the corners, nooks, and crannies,  He begins to formulate through you a structure that not only gives you the highest pleasure known to your earthly existence, but it brings Him the honor due

You are a divine container of God's finest attributes.

His name, the praise due His goodness, and the glory due His reputation! When you give Him glory, He just boomerangs it back to you! And the glorious cycle continues: honor to honor, praise to praise, glory to glory! It's a spectacular cycle! It's astoundingly wonderful! Knowing and living in the *real you* is too marvelous to be true.

In this book, *Will the Real Me Please Stand Up*, you'll unwrap God's endowment package of who are you in Him, claims establishing your genuine identity, blessings you received when you gave your life to Christ and received your new nature. You're not who you think you are, friend! You're much, much more! You are a divine container of God's finest attributes. In this book your eyes will be opened to your precious and rightful possession of God's most generous dowry. He is Jehovah God, the vast and powerful "I AM!" And as His son or daughter, He's passed along transforming "I am" benefits, rightful allotments that come as a result of your salvation, 100 of them find enlistment in these pages, a reference I'll continually refer to as "The 100 I Am Blessings," entitlements or virtues such as: "I am a Light of the World," "I am Enriched in All Speech and Knowledge," "I am Inseparable from His Love," along with ninety-seven more!

Like a Christmas Eve child, I can't wait for you to discover who you are in Christ. Knowing who He says you are in Him releases heaven's power and vision and thrusts you far into the realm of spectacular living! Why settle for the cheap trinkets of this world when He has prepared fulsome gifts for those He loves! Celebrate the truth! Partake in the pleasures of His benevolent goodness. Let the *real you*, the person who encapsulates the life of Christ, awaken to someone inside you've never known before. You are astoundingly attractive to Him. In fact, the Bible says *you* are His glory! He's enraptured by your beauty! He's bowed over by your desire to live for Him! And He's waiting to lavish you with His purest grace. It's time to let the *real you* step into the infinite and inexhaustible affluence of what God has entrusted to you and all those who have found their identity, purpose, and core impetus in Jesus Christ alone.

Who's your authority?

When I speak of the *real you*, I always mean the one *God* designed, the one in whom He wants to indwell. With that being the case, let me ask the *real you* a question: if you're going to stand *up*, you're going to have to examine what you're standing *on*. What and who is your ultimate authority on which you stand, that voice that serves as the foundation that defines the way you live, the beliefs you hold, and the values you pursue?

I about fainted. While writing this book, a friend of mine put a copy of Oprah's monthly magazine on my front porch. In bold letters on the front cover it read, "Will the Real You Please Stand Up!" What? How could this happen? Oprah stole the title of my book! Should I call her and discuss the matter? Or, after reading the article, should I continue my conversation with her by shedding light on who the Bible says reigns as "The Source" of all power and authority, the One in whom originates every man's true identity?

In the article, the magazine highlighted Hollywood stars who *finally* figured out who they perceived themselves to be in life by trusting their own instincts. The author of the article applauded their uniqueness and the avenues they found in creating their own self-discovered niche. Celebrities like Chris Rock praised Prince for his self-generated ability "to reinvent himself." Actress Nilaja Sun pronounced that her faith came from her own experience. In other words, her belief system came from what her circumstances had taught her about herself. And it was Harvey Fierstein, Broadway actor, who compared peoples' faith in an actor's ability to one's faith in God's performance of His ordinances in the church. He strangely noted, "When people come into the theater, it's an act of faith no different from a sacrament in a church."[3] Will the real me please stand up? Obviously they are trying to find the real me, but according to God's Holy Word, they have grotesquely missed the mark!

Friends, discovering the *real you* comes out of this one question: who is the authority for what you believe and what is the platform governing the way you think? What's the foundation that forms your morals? What marks your boundaries for defining what's right or wrong, true or false, good or evil? What verifies the authenticity of what you consider divine truth? And most consequentially, who's the source that defines your niche? I've found that people generally gravitate to one of three sources in search for truth: their conscience, their culture, or their Christ.

The Conscience

The conscience is a powerful tool. It's the place where people search for the most sought out commodity today: peace. We somehow feel that if we finally find peace within, then we've also found the real me.

But consider this, if your car is broken down, would you take it to the dentist? Or if your watch quit working, would you take it to the doctor? No, when something is broken you take it to the manufacturer. Life is no different. If there's no peace and you're looking for the real you, go to your Maker, the one who manufactured your very embryo. Who is your maker? Is it simple enough to say that God is the maker and leave Christ out of the picture?

Paul spoke to the false teachers at Colossi who tried to relegate Christ as a much lesser person in the chain of deity, especially concerning the topic of who made the material universe. He rejected their blasphemy stating, "For by Him (Christ) all things were created, both in heaven and on earth, visible and invisible, whether thrones or dominions or rulers or authorities, all things were created by Him and for Him. And He is above all things, and in Him all things hold together."[4] He simply stated that Jesus was God, having been the agent through whom God created the physical world. And John confirmed, "All things came into being by Him (Christ) and apart from Him nothing came into being that has come into being."[5] And the writer of Hebrews added that Christ, the Son of God, the One appointed heir of all things "made the world."[6]

At the beginning of Creation God said, "Let *us* make man in our image."[7] Who's *us*? Having been the first evidence in the Scripture to the doctrine of the Trinity, God speaks of the three-fold Godhead: the Father, the Son, and the Holy Spirit, as consulting about man, the Crown of Creation, knowing His created purpose served as a devotion to all three. With that being the case, if one is looking for the real me, how can he possibly find him or her by going to the dentist? Or the car shop? Or seeking for him outside the One who made Him? Finding the real me and God's peace that's often identified through our conscience can only come through the One whom God put inside us at salvation, Christ's Spirit, the One who critiques our life, leading us into the discovery of our true identity. While it's correct that you were given an inborn moral code at birth serving as a compass to what's right and wrong, if the needle of that instrument is not under the influence of the Holy Spirit, then misguided direction is sure to follow in your heart. To think that your natural conscience, apart from Christ, is a wise guide in discovering the real you is as ridiculous as going to grocery store to find a new organ for your upcoming heart transplant. The Bible says that the conscience is our inner testimony of what's right or wrong; however, because of sin, the heart and the conscience remain tainted.

Jeremiah confirmed the condition of man's predicament apart from God. He stated, the "heart is more *deceitful* than all else and is desperately sick. Who can understand it?"[8] Deceitful? Who me? Who you? Yes, apart from Christ, God's Word says your heart is polluted, insidious, anguished, and tracked for destruction. God disclosed in Genesis 8:21 that the intent of man's heart has forever been evil since his youth. So how can the real you, the you that God made, stand up and find true peace if His Spirit is not in you?

Often you'll hear someone say, "Just follow your heart!" Oh, no! Please don't! The heart, the conscience of man, is corrupt in its fallen state apart from the indwelling presence of God's inborn nature. Out of a man's heart springs his will and behavior, and apart from Christ's indwelling Spirit, the heart is assured to deal in treacherous rebellion with the issues of life. Such a heart is shady, depraved, and engraved with the pollution of sin, indeed, the perfect soil for the establishment of all the false idols man so easily inserts above God: the love of money, possessions, status, fame, power, success, and achievement. So, carefully consider your conscience, that inside voice. If it's empty of God's Spirit, it's a destructive guide, and the *real you* can never find its way out!

The Culture

Unfortunately, most of society lays prey to Satan, the god of this world, and the regime he continually propagates against God's Kingdom of Light. You don't have to look very far to be coerced into following what the present culture defines as truth. Its falsehood bellows out of highway billboards, seeps through the TV screen, and splashes its fraud across the covers of magazines, all of which we can't help but trip over in the checkout lines of the grocery store. The world's anti-Christ values engulf us. No wonder people have a difficult time finding the real me. The world's evil system is everywhere, flashing in neon lights. I saw a bumper sticker the other day that reeked with the world's attitude: "Happy about nothing, so let's party about everything." Society's unremitting pull incessantly demotes Christlikeness and promotes a likeness that seeks to conform us to licentious behavior and self-exerted freedom. It adulterates: "Buy into the culture's values based on its standard of appearance, fortune, and notoriety. It's here that you'll find exotic gratification, contentment, wealth, and satisfaction. Come on! Join the *in* crowd!"

Such an approach to life clashes with how Jesus instructed people to choose the *narrow* crowd, a pathway directly divergent to what the popular, present day society defines as truth. Christ warned: "Enter by the narrow gate, for the gate is wide, and the way is broad that leads to destruction, and many are those who enter by it. For the gate is small, and the way is narrow that leads to life, and few are those who find it."[9] In essence, He appealed to the truth that the first step of following Him in obedience and discovering the real you involved a revolution in one's self-will to surrender. The gate is narrow in that few decide to take it. It's not a popular gate, but it's the true gate.[10]

Choosing His path is an invitation to shun the present fallen society, leading to inexpressible abundant living. He was saying, "Today, friend, I confront you with a choice: My way or yours. Every way but Mine leads to the same fate: ultimate destruction and eternal separation from Me."

On Mount Carmel the prophet of God, Elijah, asked the people of Israel the same question God asks His people today, "How long will you hesitate between two opinions? If the Lord is God, follow Him, but if Baal, follow him."[11] If the real you is ever going to stand up and enter into the inheritance promises of God, some part of you must take the first step and get off the fence and deny the impotent imposters that keep you from fully turning over your entire life to the one true God. To compromise your allegiance is to limp or totter in your ways, thereby, cutting off the full-fledged supply of spiritual blessings He has waiting for you.

Beloved, the reason many Christians fail to experience the abundant life is not because of a *willingness* problem but a *wavering* problem. The Bible says, "The double minded man is unstable in all his ways."[12] How long will God's people hobble between a lethargic, half-hearted devotion and an obsessive, full-hearted commitment?

What God was saying was this, "Make a radical decision in whom you will serve. If Jesus Christ is My Son, then follow Him with an undivided heart. Quit living with one toe in the world Monday through Saturday and the other toe in the church pew on Sunday. Either renounce Me and embrace your false god, or abandon him forever and enthrone Me as Lord." By definition, a Christian gives up the right to live like he or she wants to live. Jesus Himself clearly defined the harm of living for oneself or being emotionally attached to

How long will God's people hobble between a lethargic, half-hearted devotion and an obsessive, full-hearted commitment?

this world. "You adulteress, do you not know that friendship with the world is hostility toward God? Therefore whoever wishes to be a friend of the world makes himself an enemy of God."[13] The rebellious believer who has an illegitimate relationship with the world is in conflict with His Creator, and the real me will never surface.

So examine your heart once again. Are you living under the sway of an ungodly conscience or immersed in the world? Will you allow the real you to come out?

Christ

Who is this God, Jesus the Christ? And on what premise does He possess the position as Lord "over all and in all and through all?"[14] Is Jesus Christ truly God? On what authority is that so? It was God Himself who placed on Jesus the power of His own name, "I AM," granting Him divine association with God's essence. God said, "I AM," meaning, "I

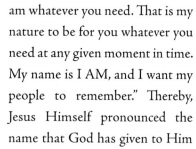

The only way to know the real you is to know the real way.

am whatever you need. That is my nature to be for you whatever you need at any given moment in time. My name is I AM, and I want my people to remember." Thereby, Jesus Himself pronounced the name that God has given to Him in John 8:58, "Truly, truly I say to you, before Abraham was born, I AM." In one breath, Jesus proclaimed His eternal preexistent deity by claiming to be the ever-existing God. Jesus is "the exact representation of God's nature."[15] So who is Christ, you ask? And on what authority does He qualify as a trustworthy source?

Jesus Christ is God incarnate or Jesus of Nazareth having come to the earth anointed by God as the divine messenger and redeemer of all humanity. *He is the way!* Jesus is not only a way, but He is *the* way. The only way to know the *real* you is to know the *real* way. Jesus is the One true God, and God proclaimed that access to Him came only through His Son. The Bible avows that Jesus Christ is the *only* door through which Heaven's glory appears, and it is Christ alone who bridges the gap between man and God.

> And Jesus made known, "I am the way, the truth, and the life. No man comes to the Father except through me."
>
> John 14:6

> And Paul exhorted, "For there is one God and one mediator between God and man, Christ Jesus."
>
> 1 Timothy 2:5

And John comforted, "And the witness is this; that God has given us eternal life, and this life is in His son. He that has the Son has life, and he who does not have the Son does not have life."

1 John 5:11–12

And Jesus decreed, "Unless you believe that I am He, you shall die in your sins."

John 8:24

And Paul heralded, "And there is salvation in no one else, for there is no other name under heaven that has been given among men by which we must be saved."

Acts 4: 12

Jesus is the only way *to* the Father because He is the only one *from* the Father. Good works, sensible philosophies, or religious ceremonies all fall short in assuring the real you eternal life.

Jesus Christ is the Son of Man, the present authority having died on the Cross for man's sin and having been raised in the power of His resurrection. *He is the power!* Because of Christ's resurrection, the real you possesses the same might. The word *power* translates dynamite. You've been granted Christ's potency to detonate the strongholds of any temptation, addiction, or resistance that blockades your growth in your new identity. Jesus' resurrection blasted forth absolute victory over both the physical and spiritual realms. There is nothing that lies outside your ability to overcome any adversity because you inhabit the identical power that raised Jesus from the dead! You are girded up to do mighty feats through His enablement that gives you superhuman strength, having been "strengthened with power through your spirit in the inner man."[16] You have God's fortitude to defeat temptation, lead a holy life, and fruitfully proclaim the gospel. It's yours for the taking; however, you must seize it. The capacity to experience this heavenly generated momentum depends on a moment-by-moment choice: either grieve the Holy Spirit with sin by cutting off your surge of Christ-empowered vigor, or yield your mind to His Word, giving way to full-throttled power. Heaven's divine energy awaits the real you!

Jesus Christ is the Rock, the immovable bedrock that will uphold the righteous in the day of adversity and secure eternal placement in the Day of Judgment. *He is the foundation!* Will the real me please stand up? No other story in the New Testament better pictures the fate of those who choose the right authority to build their life upon than the parable in Matthew 7. It's about the wise man, the individual who dug deep in order to build his house on the solid rock, Jesus Christ, and His teachings, versus the foolish man, the individual who built his house on the sandy surface of his opinions, pursuits, and standards. Both built a house of quality material with a seemingly sturdy plan; however, only one acknowledged the true way of salvation. The wise builder, a believer and a doer of the Word, acted upon his belief and built his life on the divine revelation from God. The foolish builder built his house on the sand, either representing the individual who merely believed *about* Christ yet failed to place his full trust *in* Christ or he rejected Him all together. Yet when the storm of testing and trials came, both men's foundations found exposure. The wise man's house remained, for it was built upon Jesus and obedience to Him, while the foolish man's house disintegrated, having been built upon disobedience to God's divine blueprint. God's Word is true: "No man can lay a foundation other than the one already laid which is Jesus Christ."[17] Friends, Matthew 7:27 tragically states the foolish man's outcome: "and great was its fall." The bottom line is this: eternal life is not based on one's church or credentials, but on Christ, the solid rock, and those who reject the Son of God forfeit eternal life. Jesus Christ stands as God's absolute foundation, and upon Him every man's destiny will fall.

But ultimately, *Jesus Christ is* the Alpha and Omega, the Beginning and the End, the First and the Last, the One who will bring creation to its final goal throughout all eternity! He is the Sovereign Almighty God! As His followers, we've been gloriously placed under His allegiance: a proclamation calling us to submit, repent, obey, praise, follow, rejoice, and ultimately glorify His holy name. So what will you do with this command? Dwight Edwards provokes, "The commands of God are not suggestions, or helpful hints, or practical advice but rather royal decrees, the king's rightful demands upon His subjects. To disregard or disobey them would be high treason against the heavens."

Will the real you please stand up? Will the real you solidify the sole authority of life? Will the real you yield to the One True God?

Chapter Two

My Salvation

Everyone comes from someone. I'm not much of a genealogist. My cousin, Betty Jean, holds that prestigious title in our family. Through much research on her part, I discovered I'm a D.A.R., a Daughter of the American Revolution. Joseph Martin, a war general in the 1776 war against Britain, serves as a progenitor in the Martin Family Hall of Fame. Does that make me famous?

But as a follower of Christ, I have another lineage, just like you. Its origin goes back to the Garden of Eden where it's indirectly tied to the first man that ever walked the face of the earth, Adam. You and I share this descent together. Adam was brought to life with the divine breath of God, granted a perfect fellowship with His Creator, stamped with His Father's image, and the first human inhabitant engaged with a free will. And it was God Himself who directly talked to him as he maintained the fertility and productivity of the Garden. Imagine being Adam!

It must have been heaven on earth for him, but I wonder if he even knew he was experiencing such divinity as he harkened the rustle of God in the wind and His audible voice amongst the trees. Sometimes we don't realize what we have until it's gone. Did Adam comprehend the phenomenon that not only was he exchanging casual talk with God in the breeze of the day, but that his very personhood was enlightened by God's own image? He had it all: the authorization to rule over the entire Garden, the privilege of naming every creature that crawled on the dust of the ground, the honor of receiving a hand-crafted mate by God's own hands, and the responsibility of propagating the earth. But most spectacular of all, He alone, as the only human on earth, housed the awareness of God.

Yet in an instant, it all changed; Adam sinned! Because it's impossible for God to associate with unrighteousness, God kicked him out of the Garden, the place where He and Adam gathered for fellowship. I've often wondered: did Adam feel the removal of God's presence at that moment? Did he convulse with a cataclysmic faint when God pulled away from him? Did Adam's entire wiring as a human being encounter a ruinous shock when the core fuse of his existence switched from on to off, light to dark, joy to shame? Was he horrified upon experiencing for the very first time a sinister new consciousness: self-centeredness, self-promotion, and self-awareness? That's enough to make anybody sick! Amen?

The Bible continues the story, "And Adam lived 130 years, and begat a son in his own likeness, after his own image."[1] Ever since that birth, man has come into this world under God's vacancy indictment that reads: "I no longer reside in a connected relationship with man. There remains a division brought about by Adam's sin." Man now exists empty of spiritual life, born in the sinful image of Adam (not God), complete with an inner networking system void of any spiritual apparatus in receiving divine truth. Man, born dead to God in his spirit and labeled as a child of disobedience, remains that way until he yields himself to God's only pathway for a restored relationship: faith in His only Son, Jesus Christ. It was God who came to man's rescue, offering His Son as "The Connector," bridging the gap between God and man. Only through Christ could God's communion with mankind find reconciliation. If the moment God left Adam's presence in the Garden remains mankind's most catastrophic downfall, then certainly God's entry into men's hearts through Christ remains the grandest windfall.

Only through Christ could God's communion with mankind find reconciliation.

What happens at the moment when a person receives God's provision for a restored relationship with Him? God instantaneously replaces the old Adamic nature, the one in whom you were born, with a new birth from above made possible only through the Cross of Jesus Christ. The old Adam, the head of the old you, finds replacement with the Second Adam, Jesus Christ, the head of the new you.

Salvation's Miracle: The "Real Me" Comes to Life!

In our home we make a big deal about birthdays (at least, I do!). We buy the presents, hang the crepe paper, and blow the horns when another year rolls around. After all, it's the celebration of a unique and wonderful life. But *that* particular day pales in comparison to the significance of the "other" birthday we celebrate. It's the event when we commemorate someone's "second" birth, that day when one asked Christ into his heart. I imagine the holy horns of heaven and the angels' storehouse of celestial confetti flies high when we honor the origination of our spiritual awakening. It's a day to lift high the real you's glorious position before God and the inheritance you received upon uniting with Christ. My spiritual day is June 30, while others in my family celebrate September 19 and September 23. When's your spiritual birthday party, the day the heavenly hosts rally around you every year? (Like my husband, Rich, some don't remember the exact date. If you're a follower of Christ and you remember the experience but not the date, why not pick out a day of the year and let that date serve as a reminder of your "birth" day.)

I recall a wonderful event in my life over thirty years ago. I was eight years old. My family and I were in church worshiping God during a weekly revival service. I'm not sure why I was sitting in the balcony of the First Baptist Church in Pampa, Texas, all by myself, but I was.

Maybe mother and daddy were sitting a few rows away letting me be a big girl that night.

Then it happened, the most momentous event of my entire life! On June 30, 1960, approximately eight o'clock p.m., an arrow from heaven's throne was released to planet Earth with my name on it, Pamela Mae Martin. With precise accuracy and earthbound determination, it cut through the roof, penetrating to its assigned target, the heart of a little second grader sitting at the end of the first row overlooking the congregation. God placed an inward call in my heart to come to Him, and I responded. I certainly had no idea what a change was about to take place in my direction, demeanor, or destiny, but hardly without any sense of hesitation at all, I found myself descending the stairs and walking the longest aisle of a lifetime. All I remember was laying my brunette curls on the shoulder of Dr. Carver, my pastor, sobbing over the desire to live for Jesus. Indeed, the Spirit of Almighty God had radically performed an instantaneous miracle: He had placed a new heart in the life of this elementary West Texas girl. Who of us can begin to grasp the change that transpires the moment of conversion when our core beings unite with the life of Jesus Christ, the Light of the entire world?

I recall not long ago stumbling in the dark trying to turn on the lamp. I twisted its knob and nothing happened. Fumbling and probing, patting the walls for some signal of an outlet, I finally discovered one. Apparently, the cord had been unplugged while vacuuming. After making the connection, the sudden change in the room opened up a whole new world: *Light!* At conversion, when your darkened system plugs into Christ, imagine the inward revolution. Your very nature faces an immediate electrocution from darkness to light where it's very essence becomes infused with a new divine light, a new divine status, a new divine purpose, indeed, an inward awareness that "something" sensationally wonderful has just happened. I'm sure most of us at the time of conversion didn't have any idea what just happened to us when Christ came into our hearts. I know at eight years old, I certainly didn't! How was I supposed to comprehend the miracle that God's preordained plan for Pamela Mae Martin had just established its origin of spiritual birth?

My friend, it takes a lifetime to unfold the riches of God's grace! In fact, He's working right now in preparing you for yet another revelation of truth in grasping the wonder of your salvation experience. As you open your heart to *Will the Real Me Stand Up*, God will bring to light through the Holy Spirit a fresh awakening to the glories bestowed on you when He established your new personhood. You'll be amazed at your "100 I Am Blessings," all trophies of your glorious new design in Christ. Oh, the excitement and adventure of salvation's benefits!

The Bible uses a number of biblical terms describing the moment you united with Christ and received a new quality of life, one patterned after the likeness of God. In the following 100 entitlements, you'll notice references to many of these listed below, all of them virtually meaning the same thing:

- salvation (being saved)
- born again
- regeneration
- conversion
- the new creature
- the spiritual resurrection
- the new birth
- the new man
- the new life

Notice the unique and wonderful gift of God in each one:

Salvation-
The miracle of ongoing eternal life

No other word in the life of a believer releases more joyous emotion than the gift and concept of salvation. It's a word that discloses the fullest measure of God's love for His people where He rescues man from eternal ruin and grants him the riches of His marvelous grace, making him whole and complete. Salvation signifies the entire work of God.

When we are physically born, we enter this world apart from God, born by nature as children of wrath. When we reach the age of accountability, if we reject Christ, we become children of disobedience. Yet when we trust Christ by faith, we enter into God's plan of salvation and become children of God. Often people refer to the act of salvation as being "saved," a deliverance from sin and its consequences, an act that is only made possible through Jesus Christ's atonement for sin on the Cross. While that is true, salvation is more than a particular event in time.

While most people use the word "saved" to pinpoint a moment when they received Christ, salvation actually describes three aspects in the believer's experience. It's a process that encompasses the past, present, and future, all three describing what God has done, is doing, and will do. While studying the entitlements, much reference to salvation will refer to the *past* act in history when Jesus died for your sins, thereby beginning God's creative work in you. But another aspect of salvation will be seen in the light that your life with Christ continues in the *present*, whereby you moment-by-moment experience the saving power of God in your daily victory over sin. It includes a continual awareness for the need of confession of all wrongdoing, whereby you can be repositioned in unbroken fellowship with God. This present process, called "the working out of your salvation" or sanctification, continues a lifetime. And lastly, salvation reaches its final stretch in the *future* when Christ brings to a climatic consummation His plan for eternity where all His followers reign with Him in glory.

Born Again-
The miracle of being born from above

Here's a Bible story whose concept reaches even the unsaved world. How many times have men and women, void of the Light of Christ within them, labeled the Christian sect as being *born again* not knowing what in the world it meant? What does it mean to be born again?

John 3:1–10 comprises a dialogue between Jesus and Nicodemus, a man of the Pharisees, a moral and religious man who did not understand the concept of the new birth. And Nicodemus inquired, "Rabbi, we know that you have come from God as a teacher, for no one can do these signs that you do unless God is with Him." And Jesus answered and said to him, "Truly, truly, I say to you, unless one is *born again*, he cannot see the Kingdom of God." And Nicodemus confessed, "How can a man be born when he is old. He cannot enter a second time in His mother's womb, can he?" And Jesus instructed, "Unless one is born of water and spirit, He cannot enter the Kingdom of God...You must be born again."

Nicodemus was coming to Jesus for divine teaching and instruction, but Christ saw a deeper problem: a need for salvation. So He painted an analogy of the new birth: just like the wind is an unseen force that comes from an invisible source, so it is with the mystery of being born again. It comes from a heavenly source. And just as the first birth is necessary for physical life, so the second birth is necessary for eternal life. Jesus clearly made the point: physical birth was not enough. Unless there was a spiritual rebirth that occurred both outside the realm of the physical body, as well as a rebirth inside the physical body, we could not receive eternal salvation.

Why would God design man's restoration in this strange "new birth" fashion? Why did it have to come in the form of a supernatural spiritual rebirth? Here's the bottom line: because it is the genetics of reproduction to produce something of its own kind, God could only impart His righteous character into a nature born from above, apart from the flesh of man. Since Jesus Christ came from above, the new birth would have to come from above. It only makes sense that a supernatural birth from below would have to come from a supernatural birth from above. When you received Christ, you were born into Him, solely an act of God. It's "not a work of righteousness which we have done, but it's according to His mercy that He saved us."[2] Indeed, such a spiritual birth is only possible by an act produced by the Holy Spirit when a person believes on the Lord Jesus Christ, whereby his bondage to original sin is relieved forever. That's what Nicodemus needed to do. Simply hearing the truth wasn't enough. He would have to be brought to life spiritually by God's Holy Spirit through belief in Christ.

But belief, in and of itself, is not enough either. Belief means more than what you think. It does not mean simply acknowledging something as true. When Jesus walked the earth, many believed, or reckoned, Him as a true and honest man with great powers, but they did not believe in His personhood by receiving Him by faith. The Greek word for believe (*pisteuo*) means to place one's trust in another, to cling to, to rely upon.[3] A multitude of people in Jesus' day believed in Him only as a political defender of Israel, or a great leader, or a compassionate healer, but most didn't yield the control of their lives to Him. Nicodemus came so close to being born again. I wonder if he ever yielded his life to Christ before the two parted that night.

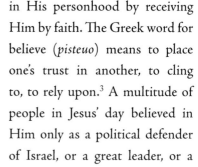

My friends, there are plenty of commandments Jesus says we ought to do, but only one we must do!

Perhaps the most unsympathetic remark of Christ concerning the prerequisite to obtaining all the spiritual blessings from God was stated in His four letter word that cannot be overlooked: *m-u-s-t*! You *must* be born again. With that being the case, the "100 I Am Blessings" belong only to those who belong to Christ. While the word *must* obviously means it's a moot point to argue otherwise, I find its opposite frightfully alarming.

Not to be born again is to miss the mark, to transgress from the way, to live out of the presence of God forever. I wonder how many people today teeter-totter in their belief that they still have time to make a decision for Christ, or they believe their human achievements and religious works for the church will be enough to get them into heaven. Perhaps some believe their intellect will be able to bend God's rule for them. My friends, there are plenty of commandments Jesus says we *ought* to do, but only one we *must* do!

Regeneration–
The miracle of a recreated life

I met Henry Becerra when he appeared as a guest on my TV show "Heroes of the Faith with Peter Pam." If ever I have seen the miraculous permanent impression of the life of Jesus that takes place in a person's heart at conversion, it is in my brother-in-Christ, Henry.

Born into a family where both his mother and father were evangelists, Henry knew all about Christ, having personally given his heart to Him at a young age. He attended church, youth camps, and performed all the duties of being a good little Christian boy. Yet at twelve years of age, someone in the church greatly wounded his spirit. What ensued was a dreadful journey down the low road of drugs and an upheaval of violence. He speaks of an incident of trying to kill his father with a knife and throwing his five-year-old sister against a wall, holding a cocked gun in her mouth, while the only words he could hear in his mind were his mother's: "Son, some day you're going to be in major trouble, and when it happens just remember, the blood of Jesus, the blood of Jesus, the blood of Jesus." Such a reminder spared his sister's life.

It was Valentine's Day when Henry's friends made the national news. His drug gang attempted to obliterate their opposing enemy whose members gathered one evening in an apartment complex. Busting into the room, the gang proceeded to murder eighteen people; however, much to their disbelief, they entered the wrong apartment. An elderly woman attending a fifteenth birthday party of a young girl answered the door, and she, along with seventeen others, including mothers, toddlers, and infants were shot. Henry commented, "Though I wasn't present at the shooting, those gang members were my best friends." In spite of Henry's brutal rebellion, no matter how hard he tried, he could not get away from the voice of his mother speaking to him the words of Jesus. That inborn seed of Christ that had been placed in his heart at conversion remained, where often Henry recalls the whispers of God's voice, an invitation to come back to Him.

On January 30, 2000, at ten o'clock p.m., Henry's mother's prediction came true. Henry fell two stories onto a concrete foundation breaking his spine in three places, fracturing every bone in his back, along with grave damage to his knees, arms, and shoulder. Upon waking up in the hospital, he saw gathered around him the face of his wife who had left him and his son, overhearing the announcement of the doctor, "Mrs. Becerra, your husband will never walk again!" She responded that she would forgive Henry for his wayward life and take him back, that she loved him and would never leave him. At that moment God quickened in Henry's heart that those words spoken by his wife were actually God's words to him, that God would receive Henry back into fellowship and through repentance, God would lovingly remain by his side. Henry lamented, "I remembered my mother's words that one day I would be in an accident and to remember the blood of Jesus."

What followed were eight surgeries, removing all the discs and placing a titanium rod down the center of his back. While being carried to church services in a wheelchair or on a stretcher, Henry would avow to the power of the blood of Jesus, singing shouts of adoration for God's loving-kindness in bringing him back into alignment with His will.

Henry testified time and time again, "Praise God! Praise God! By His blood I am healed."

I marvel today at Henry's story and the reality of what happens when the person of Jesus Christ spiritually enters a life. We may run from God, but we can't run long. While it's true that a believer can grieve the Holy Spirit to the point where he is turned over to the natural consequences of his sin (not losing his salvation but the privilege of ongoing fellowship with God), the newly implanted heart is a powerful voice in the spirit of man. Henry knew *the real Henry* lay inside, having been put there by the act of regeneration, that moment at salvation when God remade a new spiritual life. This new creation in Henry was not a matter of being rehabilitated but rather recreated. Believers have been regenerated into a condition unlike ever before, not merely remade into a nicer person but regenerated into a brand new kind. Henry remembered being taught about his new identity in Christ as a young boy, and though he strayed from practicing God's Word, God's reborn truth never left him.

Today Henry walks; he sprints; he jogs. He's a living miracle of the supernatural power of God to heal a body beyond the laws of science and medicine. He travels the world proclaiming the flamboyant power of Jesus Christ and His ability to restore a shattered life. He testifies to the most powerful agent in the world today: the blood of Jesus, the blood of Jesus, the blood of Jesus! He speaks passionately about the aggressive, unrelenting pursuit of the Holy Spirit in those who have gone astray. He bears witness to the authenticity of what happens in the human heart at regeneration. Paul, in his letter to Titus, voiced the same truth: "He saved us, not on the basis of deeds, which we have done in righteousness, but according to His mercy, by the washing of regeneration, and renewing of the Holy Spirit."[4] At salvation Henry was washed of all filth that was produced by his former spiritually dead life, given a thorough bath from head to toe, and cleansed by both the Word of God and the renewing work of the Holy Spirit. And when he strayed, the

Spirit, which became present at regeneration, fought to bring him back into fellowship with God. The act of regeneration when man receives his spirit life performs an irreversible change in the human heart. But it performs something else as well: an astounding miracle. Adrian Rogers explains the newly made person like this: "Rather than a tadpole who has finally turned into a frog, he is more like a frog who has been transformed into a prince by the kiss of God's grace."

A New Creature-
The miracle of a new nature

Every spiritual birthday party needs a favor! It's the highlight of the event, the part you take home with you as a reminder of the celebration! Don't you remember as a child your party souvenirs: a yo-yo or a paper bag with bubble gum, a spinning top, a Barbie ring, or the cardboard man's head with the shaving of hair attached with a magnet? I'm reminded every day when I look in the mirror of the party favor I received on my spiritual birthday at eight years of age: "I'm a new creature!" What a favor! When I received Christ, I brought home a new me! Yipppeeeeeee!

1 Corinthians 5:17 promises, "If any man be in Christ, He is a new creature, old things have passed away and new things have come!" Webster defines a creature as anything created, an animated person, owing a fortune to someone else, or a person subject to the will or influence of another."[5] As God's new animation, I replicate Him, representing His fortune, having been placed under His order, His design, and His influence.

So often when we think of something new, we remember TV commercials that entice us to buy their products: "Buy this *new and improved* shampoo today," but as a new person in Christ, I'm not *improved*, having been buffed and polished to shine all over again; rather, at regeneration I'm recreated *brand spankin' new*. C.S. Lewis said it well, "God became man to turn creatures into sons, not simply to produce a better man of the old kind, but to produce a new kind of man." The Greek word for new (*kainos anthropos*) does not mean something more recent in time, but something having been created in the likeness of God, a totally different quality, one with an uncontaminated nature, something never known before. Thus, the new me is a new humanity created in Christ with a nature unlike before.[6]

One of my favorite Bible stories in the Old Testament is Daniel in the lions' den. Do you remember when Daniel was thrown into the cage of the lions for his refusal to bow down to the god of Nebuchadnezzar? We marvel at the miracle of God changing the nature of the lions. They remain today the most powerful cat, weighing up to 500 pounds. They don't chew their victims; they swallow them in chunks! With one swipe, they tear their newfound lunch apart.

One of the most frightful images I have of the lion's violent nature is portrayed in the movie *King of the Night*. An evening atmosphere of death loomed over the villagers, hearts petrified that the lions might seductively crouch in the tall grass towards the village for an evening snack. Such a tragedy kept the community emotionally sedated in a continual ill-omened fear. And the Bible says that Daniel was thrown in a den with lions like *that*? Yet God sent His angel and shut the lions' mouths, and no harm was found on Daniel. In the next few verses those who accused Daniel were thrown in the same pit and crushed by the same lions before they even reached the dust of the den floor! God is in the business of changing natures!

Even more awe-striking than that is the fact that God changes the makeup of man, a specimen whose heart is evil *above* all else! Look at the depravity of man apart from Christ:

Adolf Hitler - a German dictator whose out-of-control ruthlessness resulted in the death of over 6,000,000 Jews and millions of others who didn't fit his perfect ideals

Elizabeth Bathory—a sixteenth century Hungarian Countess slaughtered an estimated 600 young girls for her beauty treatments, believing that regular blood baths would halt the aging process

Charles Manson—a psychotic who claimed to be the reincarnation of Jesus Christ, ordered his followers to commit multiple murders, the most famous being Sharon Tate Polanski, a woman eight months pregnant

Jeffrey Dahmer - a serial killer known by his bizarre experiments on his victims brutalized, mutilated, decapitated, and cannibalized the innocent [7]

And to think that God can change a nature like *that*!

Can a male become pregnant, or a human being fly like a bird, or giraffe perform the pledge of allegiance? Jeremiah continued the riddle, "Can the Ethiopian change his skin or the leopard his spots?"[8] No way! Yet, at regeneration, God changes the color of any man's nature if he will only come to Him through Christ. We should continually be stupefied over our new inborn beings. Forget the lions! Stand in amazement at the miracle of your own recreation!

The nature of a creature determines everything. It defines who he is and what he likes to do! For example, I don't share the nature of a dog or a pig. "The dog returns to its own vomit and the sow, after washing, returns to wallowing in the mire."[9] As for me, I prefer fresh food on the table and a clean bath every night. A penguin nestles with its honey at 94 degrees below zero and a rattlesnake thrives best in the dripping heat of 110 degrees of the desert, but as for me, I prefer snuggling with my honey at 68 degrees Fahrenheit. A turkey finds its nighttime rest in the trees and a crocodile under the water, but as for me, I prefer my Beauty Rest mattress. The point is this: a creature takes on the elements of its cravings and surroundings.[10] As a new person in Christ, I should take on the characteristic of the nature that indwells me. If Jesus is in me, I should replicate His nature by the Holy Spirit's enablement. For example, if Jesus talked to His Heavenly Father,

As a new person in Christ, I should take on the characteristic of the nature that indwells me.

then so should I. If Jesus lived a holy life, then so should I. If Jesus loved God's people, then so should I. It looks like this: person-to-person; heart-to-heart; therefore, nature-to-nature!

As believers we're amazed by the advancement in technology that allows individuals to change their gender. Some may say, "That's inconceivable!" Yet I wonder how many of us consider the even more inconceivable change that happened to us upon the moment of salvation. We've had a nature change! Considering that, how much more fully would we exploit our "100 I Am Blessings" if we approached our new identities as the miracle they are!

Chapter Three

My Arising

Little Susie walked seven or eight blocks to and from school every day. One Tuesday in particular, the morning clouds began to turn to darkness and by the middle of the afternoon her mother started wondering if it was good idea for her to walk home. By the time school was out, the weather began to display warning signs of an electrical storm, complete with howling winds and trickles of rain drops. Soon the sky turned an ominous gray, with occasional rips of thunder crackling through the sky, bending the backyard branches of the evergreen trees. Full of concern for Susie, her mother drove to the school in hopes of finding her before the children were dismissed. But by the time she got to the building, the boys and girls had already been released to scurry home, but where was Susie? With each shock of thunder, the mother became more and more anxious in finding her daughter. Finally she saw her fifty yards ahead! As she drove up beside her, she noticed with each flash of lightning Susie would stop, look up, and smile. This happened over and over and over. Finally the mother rolled down the car window and questioned, "What are you doing?" And Susie grinned, "God just keeps taking my picture!"

What does God think when He looks at you? Does He rejoice over His wondrous new creation, delighted in the reflection of Him that He sees, captivated by your loveliness while walking in the rain? Does He treat you like a Hollywood star, taking your picture with one procession of snapshots after another? Does He stand on His tip-toes just to find a delightful head shot, or bend low to capture a giggle, a facial expression, or a recommitment to Him? When someone asks Him about you, does He display His accordion billfold where 300 pictures zigzag to the floor, all portraits He's been collecting since your physical and spiritual birthday? Does He stop every angel flying by and ask them to join Him in His favorite pastime: gazing at you? You might feel such a response on God's part is not possible, especially concerning *you*!

Or maybe your reply would fall more along these lines: "God turns his head in disgust when He looks my way. I've failed Him miserably. How could He gaze at me in any manner but disappointment? I've sinned in so many shameful ways that I have another me internally tattooed, secured behind a secret vault whose door hanger reads: 'Herein lies a second rate creation of God.'"

Friends, why is it so difficult for most of us to see ourselves the way God does? Why do we struggle with the notion that He delights in us? What have we ever done to enchant His affections to such a degree that in His chain of love He would declare us next of kin? He loves and longs for us. Psalm 45:11 resounds, "The King *desires* your beauty." The Hebrew translation for desires (*awah*) means to crave, to be enthralled with, to covet with enflamed passion.[1] "Why would God yearn after me?" you ask.

I often consider my Heavenly Father's fanatical obsession for His children. As a mother I think about the love I possess for my precious children, Jason and Sara. I can't explain why it's there, it just is. Parents seem to have an innate love for their offspring. No one has to coach them to adore their little ones; they just do. You ask any new mother whose baby is the "fairest of them all" and she will wonder why you asked such a ridiculous question! Friends, we are God's sons and daughters bought by the blood of His own son at the Cross. Can you imagine your only child tying two 300 pound weights to each foot and jumping in the ocean just for the purpose of redeeming an entire race back into a right standing with you? How much would you adore those people for whom your son gave his life? Would you "crave after, be enthralled with, and possess an enflamed passion" for those for whom your son died? Make no mistake of your royal standing with God through Christ and His ardent love for you; you possess the invisible red mark of distinction on your heart of His Son's sacrifice and that alone makes you a candidate of God's affection.

But sadly enough, we have an enemy, Satan, who doesn't want you to discover your red mark's benefits. He wants you crippled, out of the fold, and unaware of your "100 I Am blessings!" He'd rather you never find out who you are in Christ, keeping you locked in your own chicken coop.

A Native American fable is told about a poor little creature who never discovered his true identity. It goes like this:

Created to Soar, but Soars Not!

A young brave happened upon a nest of golden eagle eggs. Wanting to raise one, he took it home and gently placed it in the nest of his prairie chickens. The eagle egg hatched and grew up with the brood of chickens. Believing himself to be like all the others, he tried scratching in the dirt. Not knowing what his wings were for, he never flew more than a few feet off the ground.

Years passed and one day the young eagle was clucking in the chicken pen when a fleeting shadow passed overhead. Seeing this strange flock gliding above in the breeze of the wind, the eagle gasped, "What a beautiful bird!"

"That's an eagle," his chicken friend informed him, staring upward. "He's the king of the air. No bird can compare to him." Then he lowered his head and commented, "But don't think another thing of it. You'll never be like him." So back to their mundane lives they returned, pecking and clawing in the coop. According to the fable, the eagle died as he had lived, never rising any higher than a prairie chicken's existence.

Beloved, every believer who has been born from above by God has received a radically new implanted nature generated and sustained by Christ. How wasteful to think that this new inside design might never mount up on God-given wings and catch the current of His created purpose, breathing in the air of knowing Him more intimately and releasing the beauty of His grace. Yet failing to appropriate God's inborn gifts and surrender his life to the pleasure of His God, he'll likely live below his means and die, having never discovered what he could have been. It's true: we can never find the fulfillment of our souls or be truly satisfied as long as we cackle in the world, continuing a lifestyle committed to ordinary spirituality. Such a life will never find the paramount of God's highest calling or the potential of the "real you" that resides inside.

Steppin' Up–
The Real You's Launching Pad

As a follower of Christ, how long have you been stuffing God's divine creation and settling for a foreign you that's not you at all? Where did this counterfeit person come from, and how long has the facade superimposed itself over the comfortableness of being you? In fact, you might not even be able to pinpoint when or why or how it happened. All you know is that you aren't enjoying your spiritual birthright benefits. "Surely there's more?" you ask. Yes, there is more! Much, much, much more!

Where do you start in unlatching the lock to the real you? How do you break away from the old establishment of seeing yourself on the basis of what your parents, peers, and past have declared to stepping into the new establishment of seeing yourself on the basis of what God's Word has

decreed? I suppose the first step is being willing to step out of the chicken coop and take the risk of leaving the old you behind, the one you've always known, and being willing to step into God's coop and take the risk of embracing the

We can never find the fulfillment of our souls or be truly satisfied as long as we cackle in the world, continuing a lifestyle committed to ordinary spirituality.

new you, the one you've never been. You might feel like it's a risk. But actually, it's not a risk at all because God is not a risky God. He's known before the day you were born this time would come. He's brought you to this very moment. Will the real you please stand up? It's launching time, my friend. I believe God is ready for you to fall in love with the real you, the one who's received a divine nature implant, a new internal essence that's whole, wholesome, and wholly devoted to Him.

Steppin' Out -
The Real You's Release

I love the word arise. It's the name of the ministry the Lord gave to me and yes, He gave me the name while I was turkey hunting with Rich, my husband (but that's another story!). To arise means to step above the mundane, to come into existence, to move to a higher place. In fact, our mission statement incorporates our ministry's purpose and commitment to lead others in knowing their identity in Christ. My license plate even spells out the passion of my heart: A-R-I-S-E. In grammatical terms, it's an onomatopoeia, that is, its sound suggests its meaning. Doesn't saying the word *arise* stimulate an upward movement in your spirit? Arise! It speaks into the soul of a believer, beckoning him to awaken to God's personality in his deepest part, allowing Him to bring to light the dawn of His very presence. Just like I purposefully place myself by my window early in the mornings anticipating the sun, my light of day, to arise over the hilltop, I must purposefully place myself on my knees every morning anticipating Jesus, my Bright Morning Star, to arise in my heart. Oh friend, you want the real you to stand up and come into the fullest blessings of your 100 entitlements? Then let the Holy Spirit release His power in you. And how does that happen? Let it unfold through the acronym of my favorite word, a word placed into your heart by God; He whispers; He beckons: *A-R-I-S-E!*

A= Acquiesce

To Arise is to acquiesce, which means to conform to, to yield, to place oneself under the authority of another. It's an inward invitation for you to place yourself under God's searchlight asking Him to daily examine your heart for any mark of sin that needs to be brought to the surface for confession. David pleaded in Psalm 139, "Search me, Oh God, and know my heart. Try me and know my anxious thoughts." When you ask God to investigate your soul, He dives into the depths with His search warrant and flashlight, detecting the musings of your heart for the purpose of refining and communicating through your spirit. To confess is to say the same thing about your sin that God says. It's to ask Him to move over your heart, find the dirt, and then be willing to extricate every particle.

I'm reminded of an interview with Ruth Graham and her family. She and Billy were scheduled to appear on national TV. She did what any housewife would do. She cleaned the room with a fine tooth comb. It was spotless, she thought. Yet when the room was placed under the television lights, suddenly you could see the dust and cobwebs that had gone undetected. When you acquiesce and put yourself under the light of God's holiness, He will reveal hidden dust and cobwebs. David pleaded, "How can I know all the sins lurking in my heart. Cleanse me from these hidden faults. Keep me from deliberate sins. Don't let them control me. Then I will be free."[2] To acquiesce is to agree with God about your sin and then turn from it.

In confession you replace your thoughts with God's thoughts, making new the attitude of your mind by taking off your former self, the Old Adam, and putting on your new self, Christ. God's grace has indeed "done a number on you!" Upon becoming a new creature in Christ, you are no longer the person you used to be. Your old way of living, thinking, and doing must be continually left behind. The Message Bible adds:

Everything connected with that old way of life has to go. It's rotten through and through. Get rid of it! And then take on an entirely new way of life, a God-fashioned life, a life renewed from the inside and working itself into your conduct as God accurately reproduces His character in you.[3]

To acquiesce is to yield to the command that the *real you* can't coexist with the *old you*. Your old way of thinking and doing must be laid aside so that your new way of life can perform its renewing work. Activating your renovated life comes from purposefully and intentionally launching God's thoughts rather than your own. Such a lift off only happens when you submit to God, acquiesce to His rule, and then actively replace any thought that doesn't line up with what God says about you.

R= Revere His Name

In chapter 9 of Nehemiah God speaks of a time when the people of God confessed their sins. He instructed his followers to move on beyond confession, "*Arise*, and bless the Lord your God, forever and ever." The pattern was set. Confession precedes praising and bringing homage to the name of the most high God.

They say practice makes perfect. So I practice early every morning by dressing my mind with spiritual workout clothes, pumping fresh blood and anticipation into an upcoming event. It's a moment I've tried to envision, and with each imagination, my amazement grows deeper and deeper. But I won't be alone when *this* happening occurs. You will be with me, accompanied by all your relatives who have died, along with my own mother and father. Others will share in the event: Billy Graham, Hugh Hefner, Saddam Hussein, the Apostle Paul, the leaders of the

Palestinian terrorist movement, along with Abraham, Satan, Jane Fonda, Moses, and Marilyn Monroe. Encircling this famed crowd will resound the swishing of angels' wings, Michael and Gabriel, and thousands of heavenly hosts. It will uncover the most bittersweet event in all creation, the moment that "at the name of Jesus, every knee shall bow of those who are in heaven, and on earth, and under the earth, and that every tongue shall confess that Jesus Christ is Lord, to the glory of God the Father."[4]

We will witness Christ's exalted position over the heights of heaven, that place where God bestowed upon Him a position of rank and authority, declaring His name, Jesus Christ, above every name. It will be a universal bending, where every category of beings imaginable will yield in solemn respect, either in willful joy or woeful sorrow. This event will fulfill God's preexistent decree that someday "all men would honor the Son as they honor the Father. For anyone who does not honor God's Son does not honor The Father."[5] Some will be obliged to bring honor and some will be forced! But one thing they will all do is bow and confess.

> *To be filled with the real you requires being filled with the real Him.*

Strangely enough, the Greek translation for confess (*exomologeo*) means to express agreement with, to assent with praise.[6] Now, won't that be interesting? *All* will kneel in acknowledgment that the Lord Jesus Christ is the True Messiah. As for me, I'm getting my knee pads ready. It'll be more than a mere curtsy; it'll be an inside transfiguration, a prostration bowed at the majesty, dignity, and lordship of Jesus Christ.

To arise is to revere the name of Jesus, to worship, to hallow, or to place a high regard upon not only His personhood, but also the spiritual sphere in which He reigns, the place where every prayer ascends. It accompanies an attitude of poverty, a humility that's poor in spirit in being able to accomplish any good eternal mark in one's own strength. It's an ingrained calling: "He must increase and I must decrease."[7]

Your "100 I Am Blessings" flow out of the water fountain of submission to Jesus Christ. When you subordinate your life to the authority of His name and identity, you find your own. To be filled with the real you requires being filled with the real Him. How can you enlarge the reverence due His name on a daily basis? Define Him.

Rehearse His Name

Begin making a list in your Bible of all the places God's Word speaks of His name. When bowing before Him every morning, recite His directory. Highlight these names of Christ in your own Bible by putting them to memory. Verbalize: "Lord you are the…"

Alpha and Omega	Revelation 1:8	*Sharp Sword*	Isaiah 49:2
Bread of Heaven	John 6:51	*Hope of Glory*	Colossians 1:27
Faithful and True Witness	Revelation 1:5	*Great I Am*	John 8:58
Friend of Sinners	Matthew 11:9	*Prince of Peace*	Isaiah 9:6
Anointed One	Acts 10:38	*Arm*	Isaiah 59:16; 63:12
Head over the Church	Ephesians 5:23	*Source of Life*	Acts 3:15
Consolation of Israel	Luke 2:25	*Wisdom of God*	Luke 11:49

Call on His name, acknowledge His name, rejoice in His name, trust in His name, and believe in His name! Lift high the wondrous name of Jesus.

Rehearse His Attributes

What happens when someone tells you all the reasons you are simply adorable? For me, it's not good enough for someone to tell me I'm wonderful; I want to know why! The same is true with God. Tell him His attributes and why He's so amazing. Celebrate His goodness! Verbalize these attributes from Psalm 119: "Lord, you are…"

- *Attentive* - You incline your ear to hear me.
- *Faithful* - I can call on You as long as I live.
- *Gracious* - When sorrow abounds, You save me.
- *Compassionate* - You take the side of the helpless.
- *Generous* - All your benefits are toward me.
- *Longsuffering* - You will accompany me until death.
- *Loving* - You have set me free for Your service.
- *Loyal* - When I'm at the end of my rope, You're there.

Add to the list from Psalm 27, 31, 33, and 48 and don't be bashful in throwing your arms open to His finest qualities in exorbitant praise. Doing so establishes His prominence in your heart and opens the pathway for you to believe the quality of His divine nature in you.

Rehearse His Deeds

David himself testified,

> Oh, give thanks to the Lord, call upon His name; Make known His deeds among the people. Sing praises to Him. Speak of all His wonders. Glory in His holy name. Let the heart of those who seek the Lord be glad. Seek the Lord and His strength. Seek His face continually. Remember His wonders which He

has done, His marvels, and the judgments, uttered by His mouth.[8]

To revere God through His Son Lord Jesus is to live in an attitude of retrospect, enumerating His mighty successes and feats, recalling His faithfulness in ages past. It is to esteem the Lord God by summoning all He's done. To recite His performances is to broadcast His praises among His people. God's blatant efforts in making Himself known are noteworthy of tribute. In today's society it's a popular fad among women to scrapbook pictures, words, and clever sayings of their children as a keepsake, a memorial worthy of remembrance. Shouldn't we scrapbook a keepsake enshrining the wondrous ways the Lord God Almighty has manifested Himself to His people? What past deeds of His greatness come to your mind?

- And David commemorated, "You are God. You made the heavens with all its heavenly hosts; you made the earth and the sea. You chose Abram and brought him out of the land of Ur of the Chaldees. And you found his heart faithful…You saw the afflictions of our fathers in Egypt."[9]
- And Stephen testified: "Hear me, brethren and fathers! The God of glory appeared to our Father Abraham…And He sent a famine in the land of Egypt…and later Moses was born, lovely in the sight of the God…"[10] And he continues to tell of God's mighty provisions.

Looking back to the ways of God reminds us of His power and girds up our confidence in Him. Why not recite the deeds He's performed in your own past! I have my list:

- Lord, you gave me wisdom in the years of being a single mother and strengthened me with Your comforting Word.

- You guided me to employment while raising the children, giving me a teaching job, not just *any* school, but the one closest to my house!

- You sustained me the twenty years I served as my parents' sole caretaker.

- You brought me an honorable husband in Rich and a wonderful new family.

- You turned my past failures into a greater cause of the gospel by birthing *Arise Ministries* with my amazing co-founder friend, Shelley Pulliam.

- You provided for a faithful prayer team that meets every Thursday afternoon to pray for the ministry.

- You gave me a community of Christian couple friends who meets every Monday night to pray and fellowship.

- And the praise report goes on and on!

My friends, nothing brings honor to the Lord more than performing a ceremony of thanksgiving. Reciting the deeds He's performed in your own past brings into focus the visible ways He has proven His faithfulness. To do so establishes His prominence in your own belief about who you are becoming in Him. It credits believability into your own entitlements. I can't help but testify with David: "I will tell everyone I meet what He has done. I will sing Him songs, belt out hymns, translate His wonders into music and honor His holy Name with hallelujahs."[11]

- Jesus, the One in whom your "100 I Am Blessings" flow

- Jesus, the One who replicates the perfect nature of God

- Jesus, the One in whom God Himself declared to be His firstborn, the preeminent One, the Highest of the Kings of the Earth.

- Jesus! How can you not revere His Name?

I = Immerse

How can you enjoy a delicious steak unless you consider your former position of being hungry? Or how can you appreciate a drink of water unless you consider your former position of being thirsty? Or how can you appreciate your new position in the Kingdom of Light unless you consider your former position in the kingdom of darkness? No other exercise enlarges one's appreciation of his new identity more than envisioning where he'd be without it. As believers, we're called to *remember*.

To arise is to recall, to immerse in what could have been, in other words, to go under, to peer at your previous circumstances, or to recollect the former you. When's the last time you took a dip with God in consideration of what "could have been"?

I wonder if ten years after Cinderella married the prince she ever thought what life would have been like had she remained a slave to her stepsisters? And I, too, wonder in my own story what life would have been like had I remained a slave in the domain of my enemy. Do you ever reflect what could have been if your Prince Jesus had not come your way? If not, then it's time to take a dip.

What's true about you when you lived under the bondage of the Old Adam? You were separated from God, a captive in Satan's camp, a child of wrath, destined for an eternity without God. Before Christ, people lived under the Old Covenant of God, an agreement He made with the children of Israel known as the Law. And though it brought those who believed under God's covering, it fell short. Look at the bondage it invoked:

+ It relied on self to fulfill its requirements, which led to continual failure and discouragement.

+ It listed impossible moral duties that generated a spirit of enslavement.

+ It served as a worthless tool in improving man's relationship toward God.

+ And it served one more purpose, as well, only this one for good: It exposed man's desperate need for the Messiah and prepped him for the New Covenant of Christ, a new set of promises enveloped in the canopy of His grace, bringing forth a lifestyle of usefulness and exhilarated power through the Holy Spirit. The Old Covenant showed what man could do *for* God, but the New Covenant showed what God could do *through* man.[12]

How often do you immerse yourself in the reality of what bondage you could have lived under apart from Christ, the One who gave Himself as the Mediator of the new and better covenant?[13]

But praise the Lord Jesus for "we have been crucified with Christ, buried with Him, and raised to walk in newness of life."[14] To arise is to take a plunge into the imagination of life apart from Him and then come forth into a new life you never knew existed. What does it look like to walk in newness of life? What noticeable differences can attest to the proof of Christ's life in you? Observe the astounding change in your new heart! Its transformation went from darkness to light; now look at it:

+ It's warmly aroused to the disciplines of Christ: prayer, alone time with Him, submission, and worship.

+ It's impregnated with the royal pedigree of God: holy, righteous, compassionate, long-suffering.

+ It's bent toward compliance in obeying His Word.

+ It's sparked with an indulgence to live a Spirit-filled life.

+ It's captivated by God's mighty deeds of the past.

+ It's animated to live Christ's life not only in you but *through* you.

+ It's hungry and thirsty for more and more of Him.

+ It's refurbished with a new set of desires in relating to others.

+ It's repugnant toward a continual practice of sin.

+ It's inclined to step out in faith and trust God.

+ It's a mirror of God's character: loving-kindness, faithfulness, goodness, and gentleness.

Friends, it's everything any human has ever longed to have in his soul, and never will a man be fully whole or content with anything less! Never! Never! So lift your hands high and praise the Lord for the exercise of remembrance!

S= Step into your cure

Not many people wandered by the northeast corner of the Old City of Jerusalem. And why would they? The stench of the pool permeated the air, for there lay a multitude of sick men and women, hazed in a state of stupor and bemusement, bodies crippled since birth, lounging on their mats, day after day after day waiting for someone to put them in the water. But for one man who had been an invalid for thirty-eight years, this was the day he would find new life. It was Jesus who braved the entrance into the area, and it was He who approached the diseased man.

"Sir," Christ inquired, "do you wish to be well? What? You have no one to put you in the water? Then arise, step into your cure!"

To arise is to believe, to take a risk, to be willing to embrace what Jesus says is true! Many believers know *about* their entitlements but won't step *into* their cure, launching their powers by speaking them out loud and believing them by faith. There's a breakdown between what they passively know to be true and what they actively prove to be true. They know, for example, that the Bible says, "I am a light in the world," but they don't envision themselves walking into a room, actively *putting on* the light bulb of Christ, letting His power generate through them.

To "will to be well" is not to just read about the truth but to speak it out loud by incarnation. It is to say verbally, "I am a light in the world" and then perform it through the Holy Spirit's enablement. Friends, you have the cure! You have the miracle! You have the abundant life! You have the tools in exercising your new identity, a fulfillment of wholeness and purpose. Jesus' finished work at the Cross established a new you granting its release into a resurrected life through the Holy Spirit.

But I'm afraid some choose to live under their resurrected life status. I wonder! If Jesus walked into your house today, would He see you on your mat of despair or helplessness or lack of hope? In what state would He find you: emotionally lame, spiritually lame, or prayerlessly lame? Would he find you unwilling to exert the faith required in order to be set free? Would He ask, "Do you *will* to be well? Do you *will* to arise?"

What keeps you from living the bounteous life? What excuses keep you on your mat? The invalid's excuse was that he had no one to help him. What reason would you give to Jesus why you won't allow Him to enforce your "100 I am benefits?" "Jesus, my life hasn't turned out the way I had planned," or "I've been mistreated," or "I believe I can live this life in my own strength."

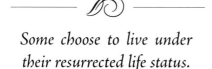

Some choose to live under their resurrected life status.

What keeps you from stepping into your cure of rejuvenated power? Notice the three things Jesus told the paralyzed man to do. I wonder if they speak to you, as well:

ARISE

+ Choose to exercise your mustard seed of faith and step out in confidence, claiming the fullness of your "100 I am Blessings."

+ Choose to let go of any besetting sins that keep you too weak to spring forth into the new you.

+ Choose to activate this revamped life by obeying His Word.

TAKE UP YOUR PALLET

+ Take a risk. Do something you've never done before, just like the invalid was asked to do. Christ invites you to the *coming out party* of the regenerated you.

+ Trace His light. Follow God with whatever amount of spiritual truth you've already received. Believe His truth asking the Holy Spirit to reveal more.

+ Trust God. Accept your circumstances as your mat. Take it up! Ask God to use your difficulties as the catalyst that makes you desperate for the execution of His strength and the revelation of the empowered you.

WALK

+ Leave your place of bondage and verbalize the realities of your "100 I Am blessings."

+ Leave the lies of the enemy behind. When he says, "You will never measure up to God's standards," say, "No. I am loved by God, fully forgiven, and complete in Him." To walk forward is to leave something behind.

+ Leave the results to God! Know when you yield yourself to Him, it is His responsibility to establish the fertile soil for your entitlements to take root.

So arise! Knowing who you are in Christ is the remedy to every man's struggle with his own self-image. When you know Jesus' worth, you know your own. Ask God to give you the courage to believe what He says to be true about you. God does not ask you to do what He will not accomplish, and He does not ask you to go where He will not lead. What's holding you back? What's God calling you to do? Go ahead. Step into your cure!

E= Expect

James, the brother of Jesus, encouraged, "You have not because you ask not." And he continued, "You have not because you *expect* not."

I'm certain you recall what it means to expect. Some say, "I expect to get a summer vacation," or "I expect I'll get a new camera for Christmas."

Knowing who you are in Christ is the remedy to every man's struggle with his own self-image. When you know Jesus' worth, you know your own.

You have proof to believe. Maybe you've heard your boss suggest summertime was a slow season, making it a great time for family vacations, or you heard your husband say he'd like a new camera in the family. To arise is to expect. It's a calculated belief backed by sufficient evidence. Many of us have proof of God's working in our lives but we fall short in receiving that extra measure of blessing because we fail to expect Him to perform it. Living in a spirit of confident expectation brings hope and a vibrancy of who we are in Christ. It serves as the reveille awakening the real you to step out and let Christ wield His life through you.

Not long ago I heard about a clock in Strasburg, Germany, whose dial inscribed these words: "One of these hours the Lord is coming." (Tick tock, tick tock.) How would you like a clock like that in your own heart? What would it do for your anticipation level of Christ's return? How would it instill a renewed perspective of what's important and what's not? How would such a reminder raise your eternity quotient? How would it hearken the real you to step out into God's higher calling? Would it arouse these identity truths: "I am an Ambassador for Christ," or "I am Eternity Bound," or "I am Assigned to the Age of Grace" for a God-ordained purpose? Friends, let the entitlements give birth to the higher you, the *real* you, the one God longs to fill with His Spirit. Let them stimulate any atmosphere in which you enter. Live in a spirit of divine expectation.

What constitutes a healthy hope in relation to your belief that God will perform His ultimate ascendance in you? I've discovered four contributors:

Personalization

To arise and let the real you surge is a reinstatement of the exorbitant value of *you*! You must take it personally that not only are the promises true, but they are true for *you*! 2 Peter 1 verifies the target. Verse 23 harkens that His precious and magnificent promises have been granted to *you* that *you* might become a partaker of His divine nature. Verse 8 reassures that these qualities of excellence such as self-control, perseverance, brotherly kindness, and love are for *you* and ever increasing. Verse 10 inspires that He chose *you* for these benefits. Verse 15 invokes that *you* are to call these truths to mind.

To expect is to embrace an aggressive mind-set that *you* are the recipient of these blessings, and God finds *you* worthy of your spiritual birthright benefits because *you* have been justified by Christ. Do you believe that? It is to invite God's faithfulness into your own situation. It is to expand your belief to the outer bounds of God's character, believing the words of the prophet Isaiah that "the Lord longs to be gracious to *you*, and therefore He waits on high to have compassion on *you*."[14] To arise is to take it personally.

Anticipation

In the process of arising you move beyond personalization into anticipation, that is, expecting to become someone beyond your own strength. I often consider the character of Superman. Who hasn't watched the cartoon episodes over and over? At given instances he would break through his own humanness and emerge as a super-power endowed with strength beyond His own capabilities, feats that enabled him to perform services for the betterment of humanity.

At conversion you were granted a superman costume with a capital "*S*" embossed on your chest: "*S*"avior power, "*S*"upercharged, "*S*"piritually endowed, "*S*"aved for the advancement of His Kingdom, "*S*"ervant of the most high God. God put His Holy Spirit in you to swell His power, wisdom, and revelation, in order to emerge as someone who expands beyond his own natural talents and capabilities, all for the glory of God. To anticipate God to perform His highest and best requires a spirit of insight, a Superman mentality, all executed by the Holy Spirit's timing and power.

When we built our new house in 2002, I knew the power I possessed as a believer in praying and speaking forth God's written Word into the lives of my family and all those who would enter our home. With great anticipation of how the Spirit would use the power of His written word, I inscribed with a black marker these scriptures on the concrete floors and wooden studs, all in an expectant vision that He would perform what I asked:

- In the living room for all the workmen I wrote:

"Whoever will call upon the name of the Lord will be saved."

Romans 10:13

- On the steps leading to Amber and Sara's bedrooms I inscribed:

"Oh, Lord that they would follow in Christ's steps."

1 Peter 2:21

- In my prayer closet for Jason I penned Hannah's prayer:

"'For this boy I prayed that He would walk after the Lord's righteousness."

1 Samuel 1:27

-In the living area for Ryan, my stepson, and Beth, my daughter-in-law and their children I wrote:

"For surely, O Lord, you bless the righteous; You surround them with your favor as with a shield."

Psalm 5:12

-In the newly cemented driveway I embossed Jess, my son-in-law's, favorite verse:

"For me to live is Christ, and to die is gain."

Philippians 1:21

-In my bedroom for my marriage to Rich I wrote:

"...that we might be knit together in love."

Colossians 2:2

To anticipate is to take action, to cast God's Word into others' lives believing that God will do what He has purposed to do.

And lastly, to anticipate brings into fruition all that has already been implanted. At conversion, God placed in you everything needed to live a holy life. And though God's promises in His Word might seem dormant at times because of lack of use, it's actually a living organism inside waiting for *someone* to generate its power by faith.

It reminds me of how my grandmother used to get water from a well by the pump's handle. As she primed its pump, the water began to trickle until it gushed into full blown power. That can be likened to the activation of God's Word. It's pure truth, stored in the well of your regenerated heart, waiting for activation. The more you allow the Holy Spirit to prime the pump, the greater the outflow of energized truth.

Do you sometimes feel like your well is dry? It is not! It's waiting for *someone* to set in motion its power. God placed in you at conversion your "100 I am Blessings," all dormant until you activate them by vocalizing God's Holy Scriptures by faith. So speak forth! Believe! Expect! Such an exercise brings to life what's already alive.

Appropriation

Perhaps we could learn this next principle by observing two year olds. They have no problem in saying, "Mine!" To arise is to take what's yours, to take possession of what's been legally assigned to you by God. It's to assert your rightful position, taking hold of your spiritual heritage of divine resources, such as prayer, faith, and the Word of God, that have been bequeathed to you.

God had a word for Joshua one day. Moses had died and Joshua was commissioned to take the people into the promised land:

> Moses, my servant is dead, now therefore, *Arise*, (go for it!) and cross the Jordan, you and all your people of the land which I am giving to them. Every place on which the sole of your foot treads, I have given it to you. No man will be able to stand before you all the days of your life. Just as I have been with Moses, I will be with you. I will not fail you or forsake you.
>
> Joshua 1:2

God had given them the land but their enjoyment of it depended upon their taking possession of it. That part of the land upon which they tread would belong to them.

In the Old Testament a faithful Jewish man was rewarded with physical blessings, such as long life and abundant crops. But in Christianity we are blessed with spiritual blessings, promises from God to supply all our needs "according to His riches in glory in Christ Jesus."[15] We have the blessing of the Spirit, everything in the spiritual realm we need for a satisfying Christian life, all these endowments by God originating from the heavenlies in Christ.

William MacDonald clarified,

> Our spiritual blessings are in Christ. It was He who procured them for us through His finished work at Calvary. Now they are available through Him. Everything that God has for the believer is in the Lord Jesus. In order to receive the blessings, we must be united with Christ by faith. The moment a man is in Christ he becomes the possessor of them all.[16]

I wonder. You are the possessor, but have you possessed? What has God deeded over in your spiritual entitlements but you haven't brought them to life by faith? What missiles or blessings of the Spirit of God wait for you to launch their effectiveness and power?

God gave Israel the land, but they actually possessed very little of it. They inherited over 300,000 miles of luscious terrain but only claimed approximately 30,000 square miles, about one tenth of what was rightfully theirs. What happened to the other 270,000 square miles? Wasted crops? Wasted wealth? Wasted potential?

Billy Graham reported that over ninety percent of all believers live defeated Christian lives. That means less than ten percent possess their rightful entitlement benefits! Look at the waste among believers of what could have been! What a shame to have squandered the spiritual blessings of God! There are approximately five billion people on planet Earth and few of them will ever maximize their God-given capabilities. Most will remain satisfied in living standard lives with the fullness of the "real you" left untapped. How disheartening to misuse what could have been a vast display of the Holy Spirit's release!

Possess your land; possess the real you; possess the riches of your divine inheritance and arise.

Some have the wrong idea about who should inherit these benefits. God does not operate like the world; the world chooses the rich and beautiful people to possess the land, but God chooses the common people like you and me, those incapable of doing great things for His Kingdom apart from Him because His power shows up best in weakness. When He chose a nation to pour out His affections, He didn't choose the stout Egyptians or their jewelry dripping queens in which to display His power, but rather a weak, unstable, and whiney Jewish nation of slaves. God chooses the weak so that His power can be made strong.

If you've received Christ as your Savior, He's chosen you to soar through these benefits becoming a man or woman of renown for Jesus, a person whose humble beginnings display the splendor of God. As Daniel Ericson said, "He's placed in you a greater yes," a yes in abandoning yourself to His extravagant purposes, a yes in yielding your past, present, and future to His calling, a yes to laying open your spirit that He might exploit His excellencies and greatness through you.

So take hold, friend. Possess your land; possess the real you; possess the riches of your divine inheritance and *arise:*

A - Acquiesce in submission. It induces brokenness.

R - Revere His name. It stimulates adoration.

I - Immerse in a consideration of what could have been.
   It generates thanksgiving.

S - Step into your cure. It liberates faith.

E - Expect. It launches full power.

I pray as you enter your arise journey through these entitlements, God will uncover an *arise* surprise as you discover the wondrous investment He's placed in you, one of stupendous value, one whose response bestows the glory due the name of Jesus!

Chapter Four

My Reservation

Can you imagine entering an exquisite place for lunch without securing a reservation? I tried that one time. While standing at the door's entrance, I gave reasons to the maitre d' why I should get into the tearoom. I was a faithful patron. I honored the dress code. I exhibited lovely manners. I even asked her to see if *maybe* my name was registered on the guest list. Yet nothing worked! The facts remained: I did not have a reservation. There would be no seat for me inside the brunch facility.

Friend, these entitlements serve as gifts bestowed to those who have received Jesus Christ as their Lord and Savior. At some point in time, they gave over the control of their lives to Christ, repented of their sin, and asked Him to come into their hearts. At that moment Christ came into them, securing a heavenly reservation where their name was sealed in God's reservation book, the Lamb's Book of Life. If your name is not registered in *this book* as having invited Christ into your heart, you will not enter heaven's glory. Only those who have made reservations find entrance into eternal life with God.

The message of God abounds with His love to all mankind. He desires that every man and woman and child on this earth come to Him through Jesus Christ. The heart of the gospel is this: sinners are forgiven by God and set free from the bondage of sin, death, and hell by the atonement of Jesus on the Cross. God made Christ your substitute, allowing Him to die so that the penalty of separation from God might be paid. God's justice was satisfied and now repentant sinners can come to Him through Christ alone and be made right with God forever.

How is that possible?

- God has a plan for your life.

> "For God so loved the world that He gave His only begotten Son, that whosoever would believe in Him would not perish but have everlasting life."
>
> John 3:16

- Man is sinful and separated from God; thus, He cannot know and experience God's love.

> "For all have sinned and fall short of the glory of God."
>
> Romans 3:23

- Jesus Christ is God's only provision for man's sin.

> "For there is one God and one Mediator between God and man, Christ Jesus."
>
> 1Timothy 2:5

> "And Jesus said, 'I am the Way, the Truth, and the Life. No one comes to the Father except through Me.'"
>
> John 14:6

- Man must repent and individually receive Christ as Savior. [1]

> "If we confess our sins He is faithful and just to forgive us of all sin and cleanse us from all unrighteousness."
>
> 1 John 1:9

> "If we confess our sins and believe in our heart that Jesus is Lord, then we will be saved."
>
> Romans 10:9

What a disheartening thought that anyone would proceed past this point in reading *Will the Real Me Please Stand Up* and not make their eternal reservation with God. Perhaps you know for a fact that you have never had a personal encounter with Christ. Is there any reason why you wouldn't settle that issue right now? You can ask Jesus to be your Savior and receive the assurance of eternal life.

I invite you to secure your eternal position with God right now by saying this prayer of faith. The Bible says, "Whoever will call on the Name of the Lord will be saved."[3]

Pray this prayer:

Dear Lord Jesus,

I know that I'm a sinner. I turn the control of my life over to you. Forgive me for all my sins and receive me into your Kingdom. Will you come into my heart? I give myself to you. Thank you for residing in my heart. Amen.

Congratulations, friend! It's your spiritual birthday! If you prayed that prayer for the first time, then you passed from spiritual death and separation from God to spiritual life, union with Him. Welcome to the family of God! May God's peace be with you, and may these "100 I am Blessings" enrich the *new you!*

Part Two

My Divine
Inheritance

THE 100
I AM BLESSINGS

I Am Chosen to Bear His Fruit

I Am the Salt of the Earth

I Am Renewed

I Am an Expression of Christ's Love

I Am Complete

I Am an Expression of Christ's Love

I Am an Ambassador

I Am Valued

I Am Blessed with Spiritual Blessings

I Am Afflicted but Not Crushed

I Am a Sanctified Saint

I Am a Branch

I
AM

I am crucified with Christ, nevertheless I live;
yet not I, but Christ liveth in me...

Galatians 2:20 (21st Century King James Version)

DEATH TO LIIFE

The Fountain of the "100 I Am Blessings"

The Miracle of Passing from
Spiritual Death to Spiritual Life

D= Delivered   L= Legalized by Adoption

E= Elected   I= Indwelt by the Holy Spirit

A= Accepted   TO   F= Forgiven

T= Transferred   E= Eternally Glorified

H= Holy

Chapter Five

My Foundation

What primary doctrines summarize the Christian faith?

1. I am Grounded

Welcome to the debut of your entitlements from God. Every structure secures its strength from its foundation. In your "100 I Am Blessings," this one, "I am Grounded," states briefly the base of your salvation fountain that serves as the first nine entitlements listed in the book, all nine construct the platform from which the other ninety-one blessings will emerge.

The benefits of salvation and the blessings of walking in newness of life as His redeemed creatures resemble a water fountain. The basis of the *real you* finds its core identity in the positional change that occurred when you received Christ. You passed from a state of being spiritually separated from God to being spiritually united to Him through Jesus.

Today in the country of Mexico lies a unique church. Located in the heart of Mexico City stands a 400-year-old structure, The Metropolitan Cathedral. Government architects warn that if urgent measures are not taken, it will topple over some day. The entire city is sinking as a result of the draining of underground water, but the cathedral is submerging faster, having already sunk several feet below the surrounding streets. Unlike the cathedral that's losing its footing, the base on which you stand as a believer will never sink, sway, or shake. Your foundation,

Jesus Christ, remains a stalwart understructure, one impenetrable from the forces of evil and fully fortified by God's preexistent will.

Do you ever feel uncertain about the solidarity of your earthly existence or eternal home? You ask, "How can I be certain I'm heaven bound? Am I going to have what it takes to face tomorrow?" You need *not* question or feel unsettled. You remain well-grounded and unmistakably anchored on the anointed ground of God's sovereign plan.

Growing in the fullness of who you are in Christ comes out of an understanding of your new creature foundation: *death to life*. Its acronym contains core truths granting a firm footing for not only now but throughout all eternity.

D = *Delivered/Redeemed* - God instantly rescued you out of Satan's jurisdiction or authority and brought you to Himself, delivering you from the dominion of sin. Christ's death and resurrection redeemed you from the enemy's kingdom.

E = *Elected* - You did not choose Christ, He chose you. God is loving and merciful, and in His grace He chose you for His purposes. This sovereign act of God is called election. You are the chosen, His elect.

A = *Accepted/Appeased* - To appease means to bring into a state of reconciliation. Christ met God's righteous standard by paying sin's penalty. God brought you from a state of hostility to a state of peace, declaring you not guilty, justified.

T = *Transferred/Secure* - Upon deliverance from Satan's domain, God placed you in the Kingdom of Light, forever protecting your relationship with God. As a subject of God's sphere ruled by Christ the King, you possess eternal security.

H = *Holy* - Because you are in Christ, you've been pronounced holy and blameless. Your position is marked by God's separation and purity, fully clean and without blemish.

TO

L = *Legalized by adoption* - God officially brought you into His family, having inherited a divine status as an adopted child. Such a position granted you legal rights to all the inheritance benefits of His only Son. You are joint heirs with Christ.

I = *Indwelt by the Holy Spirit* - God's installment of power resides in you through the person of the Holy Spirit. He enables you as an image bearer of Christ in becoming more and more like Him.

F = *Forgiven* - All sin past, present, and future found clemency at the Cross granting you a new status: holy, free from condemnation, adequate, complete, and fully forgiven.

E = *Eternally glorified* - God works in you for His ultimate destination: an existence of being outwardly and inwardly unstained, thereby, giving perfect glory to God forever.

You stand on Sacred Ground: secure, stable, and suitable for the outpouring of God's most benevolent gifts of grace!

"God's solid foundation stands firm."

2 Timothy 2:19

2. I am Delivered/Redeemed

Seven-year-old April labored for months making a doll out of her grandmother's old clothes and used-up dish rags. Finally it was finished.

Stunning! An exquisite masterpiece of her own hands! Taking her new-found companion to the park to play, she happened upon a friend, leaving her doll on the picnic bench as she ran off to swing. Upon returning, the doll was missing. She traveled home sobbing over the loss of her most prized possession. Six months later she was strolling down the street with her uncle and noticed her doll in the window of the pawn shop. "There's my doll, Uncle Gordy! I'll buy it back." But the cost was far more than what she had in her piggy bank. So she raked leaves in order to earn enough coins to return to the shop. Finally, the day came. As April walked out of the shop, she clasped her dolly to her chest, "I made you, and I bought you back. I had you, and then I lost you. I've paid the price. Now you're mine!"

That is the story of redemption, a loving God whose crazed love for you has no bounds, the One who lost you to sin but bought you back into a love relationship with Him through Jesus. You once belonged to God, then sin placed you in Satan's grip. You have been redeemed by the ransom of Christ's blood, purchasing your soul out of Satan's domain, forever releasing you from the consequences of God's holy wrath. God placed His only Son on the Cross! Christ redeemed you from the slave market of sin. It's as if God said, "Ahhhhh, I made you, and I bought you back. I had you, and then I lost you. Now you are mine." How zealous and deliberate is His affection for you! Christ's blood, the ultimate sacrifice, satisfied the requirements of God for a restored relationship with Him. Can you imagine His possessive love toward His dolls, the masterpieces of His own hands? It was Christ, His only Son, who yielded Himself at the Cross to perform the most successful rescue mission of all time, an undertaking that forever gave back to His Father His most prized possession, you!

Consider the process of entering into the realm of the redeemed. Because of Adam's sin, you were placed in Satan's market place, his slave among other unregenerate souls destined for an eternity of hell and tortuous separation from God. Incarcerated in the enemy's dungeon and restricted from God's light, you were confined to perpetual chastisement. Yet having been thrown into the slaughter market of eternal death, your acceptance of Christ brought you out. For God so loved you, that He sent His only Son to unshackle your chains of damnation, rescuing you from Satan's province of darkness. To be redeemed (*exagorazo*) means to buy out of the market place.[1] No longer are you a prisoner for sale, incarcerated as Satan's bond-slave, but you are set free, acquitted from your guilty sentence, unbound from the chains of sin's penalty. Now you stand liberated to your fitting and rightful sentence of timeless freedom, forever forgiven of your sins past, present, and future. Christ's blood compensated for the ransom required, releasing you from the just condemnation you deserved.

We don't like to think about the doctrine of hell, but not doing so causes us to grow dull and unappreciative of our new identities and what Christ did for us at the Cross. Hell was originally prepared for the devil and his angels, not for man. But man made his choice. Someone once said, "Hell's a real place and no murderous nightmare racing across a fevered mind could ever dream of a picture to match the mildest level of hell." It's a place of never-ending torment where caverns of groaning souls who neglected the message of Christ call out for help, without the slightest hope of release. Can you envision a created place encapsulating God's grandest fury? No wonder the heavens rejoice when one lost sinner repents!

Beloved friend, rejoice for you are redeemed, absolved of all unrighteousness and rescued from Satan's dominion. It's indeed your supreme gift from God! May you enjoy your freedom as you celebrate Jesus, the Blessed Emancipator. And may you never, never forget *what could have been!*

> "Christ has redeemed us from the curse of the law having
> become a curse for us."
>
> Galatians 3:13

3. I am Elected

Did you choose God or did He choose you? No other doctrine of Scripture is more difficult to understand than this one. The most knowledgeable students of theology have sought to explain in human terms the doctrine of election. Warren Wiersbe commented, "Try to explain divine election and you may lose your mind, but explain it away, and you will lose your soul."[1] I liken studying it to eating an artichoke. With each peeling there's another layer of unanswered questions. Some doctrines must be laid to rest in the bosom of God, and this is one of them. For me, it all comes down to these ten words: God is God, and He alone does what He chooses.

The Holman Bible describes divine election "as the gracious purpose of God—the incredible love and wisdom that He exercises in drawing sinners to Himself. This is not inconsistent with the fact that He has given us the responsibility of free choice, but is rather a display of His immeasurable grace. None of us deserves or can claim the right to be saved. God alone in His goodness has extended salvation to us. He draws all men to Himself but not all respond."[2] 2 Peter 3:19 affirms God's heart "not wishing for any to perish but for all to come to repentance."

The fact that God first chose you by the gracious act of His sovereign will labels you as "the called"[3] or chosen one of God. As an eight-year-old at Stephen F. Austin Elementary in Pampa, Texas, I remember what it felt like to be called out. At recess we'd play the game "Red rover, red rover, let Pam come over!" Just to hear them call out my name was a great thrill. Upon the selection of the other team, I exercised my will, "Would I respond to the call?" As a child of God you've been summoned, and it's your turn to take joy in God's calling of you. In Colossians 3:12 He substantiates His affection for His own that you are chosen and dearly loved. To be the elect of God is not a volunteered enlistment, an earned reward for good works, or an inherited privilege; rather, it's a divine position uniquely appointed by an Almighty God who cannot execute a decision that is not solely pure, perfect, and principled.

Matthew 22 paints a picture of a wedding celebration where invitations were sent out to many, portraying everyone who would hear the gospel message through Jesus Christ. However, upon receiving the invitation, few responded choosing not to join the ranks of the elect. The outcome remains quite clear: if you want to know if one is chosen of God inheriting eternal life, examine what he has done concerning his relationship with God's Son.

As a follower of Christ, you've been predestined to spiritual blessings, 100 of them listed in these pages. Are you making good use of His blessed favor? Such kindnesses from God come from having been reconciled to Him through Christ's blood. The Lord predetermined the destiny of those who would respond to Him; they would be made right with God. For God knew His people in advance, having chosen them to become like His son, granting them forgiveness where their sins would no longer be counted against them. As the chosen of God, having submitted your life to Christ, you have obtained an acceptable position before God. You've been justified, or declared "just right," in His eyes. Hallelujah! Hallelujah!

As the elect, God has a purpose encompassing preplanned works in order to strengthen your faith and bring honor to His reputation. Christ died to bring to Himself a people "zealous for good works,"⁴ workman ready to bring into fulfillment God's methods of bringing Him glory and equipping the church. Sometimes these deeds seem out of our comfort zone. For example, when God called me to write this book, I commented, "God, I can't." Then He reminded me *Will the Real Me Please Stand Up* was already written before the foundations of the earth as one of His good works to be delivered through me to the body of Christ. What a humbling privilege the saints of God possess in having been selected by Him to invest their acts of service in the advancement of His Kingdom. Friends, if He calls you to an assignment, He'll enable you to perform it. He desires to exhibit mighty deeds if you'll thaw out your unbelief! After all, you're the chosen, not the frozen chosen!

"You did not choose me, but I chose you."

John 15:16

4. I am Accepted/Appeased

Watching a hamster in his cage paints a tiring picture of the way many believers see themselves in gaining God's approval. They go round and round from one guilt trip to another, trying harder and harder with more good deeds and more self-promoted efforts in seeking that inner peace where they finally *feel* right with God. I had one woman in my Bible class tell me her measure of whether she felt like God smiled upon her was solely based on whether she read her Bible every day. As a result, her ability to find contentment felt more like a roller coaster than a hamster wheel.

Perhaps no other positional truth of who you are in Christ serves as a more critical nucleus in experiencing the joy of all the other entitlements than this one: it's key; it's first base on God's baseball field of the divine life; it's fundamental to the thermostat of the enjoyment of your relationship with God. Here it is: you are justified or placed in a right standing before God, appeased by having been brought into a state of harmony with Him through Christ. It's too good to be true! Most of us are used to the idea of earning our merits with God; we've been programmed to believe the principle of effort and reward. "I do good, and then God accepts me." I took a survey at a conference where 92% of the women believed God was in the sticker chart business ready to deck their charts with gold stickers if they pleased Him by their behavior. Nothing could be more untrue. God's unwavering love for us is based on Christ's sacrifice on the Cross, not on the resume' of our works. His acceptance of His children remains secure. There is nothing we can do to fall out of God's eternal graces. We've been placed in a permanent position of favor by receiving Jesus Christ by faith.

Justification. What is it? At the Cross a legal edict was pronounced creating a new covenant with God's children, a declaration of permanently reestablishing a relationship with God. On the Cross God acted as if Jesus had lived our lives of sinfulness, so that God could see us like we had lived Christ's perfect life of holiness. "God made Him who had no sin to be sin for us, so that in Him we might become the righteousness of God."[1] God removed from our account the sin of our old life, thereby, depositing in its place a blank check of Christ's uprightness and virtue, declaring us forever on God's side. To be justified is *not* to "make righteous" but to "declare righteous."[2] God *declared* it so, thereby, settling the matter whether we feel it or not. It's a legal transaction establishing an acquittal of all former and future offenses, changing our judicial standing before God from a state of condemnation to a state of reconciliation. Such a gift of restoration unites the sinner to God as if he had never sinned!

As a follower of Christ, what is it that keeps you from believing that you have been made right with God? An abortion? A season of blatant rebellion? Can you say, "I have been justified *'just as if I'd'* never performed that sin?" You have been reconciled with God through faith in Christ. There is nothing you can do by your good works to improve or add to this work of grace. Any efforts on your part to win God's favor must certainly be a slap in Christ's face who gave His life to set you free from the treadmill of trying to win His Father's approval. Galatians 2:21 confirms, "If righteousness comes through some human fulfillment of God's divine standard, then Christ died needlessly."

Consider this repulsive story. A teenage boy was rock climbing in the Himalayas and began yelling for help. Upon seeing the danger, a lady with two children on a nearby cliff hurried herself to give the boy the added rope he needed, only in doing so, she fell to her death. After the incident, the father of the teenager made a sincere visit to the house of the children who lost their mother. In honest gratitude and trying to express his thanks, he said, "I want to give you all the change in the glove compartment of my Corvette. Here's $9.43 as an expression of my appreciation."

What? How could he think he could add to the work of the woman who gave her life in freeing the teenager? And how do we think by our good deeds we can add to the gift of the Cross? Jesus Christ paid it all! All means all! So step off of the hamster wheel of trying to earn God's acceptance. You already have it, and you have it all!

and you are "justified as a gift by His grace."

Romans 3:24

5. I am Transferred/Secure

Can a saved person lose his salvation? Can he be found and then lost again? If one is hidden with Christ in God one day, can one be unhidden with Christ in God the next?[1] Is it possible to behave in such a way that God kicks one out of His graces? Is salvation a work of God or man? When Jesus said, "No one can snatch my children out of my hand,"[1] did He mean no one except Satan? Do you think if Satan could snatch your salvation out of Jesus' hand he would? These questions find Christians standing on differing sides of the fence in defending what they believe about the assurance of salvation and the security or insecurity of the believer. You can know beyond a doubt that you are transferred to God's Kingdom, saved forever. You need to know what and why you believe. I know what I believe and here's why.

One of the greatest anchors in my walk with Christ is the peace of mind I enjoy knowing no matter how ungodly I act or how ungodly I think, I can do nothing to fall out of His graces. To believe that I could lose my salvation by the way I act would do one of two things to me. It would make me subconsciously prideful that *I* was doing a good job, or it would make me terribly fearful. What if I was praising God one month and the next month living my life the way *I* wanted, totally irreverent of God's Word? I would live in a perpetual state of anxiety, "hoping upon hope" that I wouldn't die on an off month. Is that God's grace? Does His grace have conditions on it? Was Jesus' blood on the Cross incomplete? Was it His blood plus your good works that satisfied the wrath of God? Or was it His blood plus your promises to never overeat, drink alcohol, or use His name in vain? Yes, doing good works and making promises are vital for spiritual growth and following His commandments, but are they conditional clauses strapped to the t-bar of the Cross? Do I not remember Jesus' final words on the Cross concerning the sin debt that was accomplished and brought to God's perfection once and for all: "*It is finished*,"[2] or did Christ mean, "It is almost finished?"

The Father, Son, and Holy Spirit all testify to the security of the believer. The righteousness of God assures eternal security because His son alone fulfilled the requirement of God's plan of redemption by "becoming the substitute or propitiation for our sin."[3] Lewis Chafer confers,

> The eternal security of the believer cannot be challenged without challenging the righteousness of God. Thus His faithfulness to His promises, His infinite power, His infinite love, and His infinite righteousness combine to give the believer absolute security in his salvation.[4]

Jesus' substitutionary death on the Cross seals the believer's security. Because His death paid for *all* sins, past, present, and future, how is it that anyone's sin can undo the seal if Christ already died for that sin? Isn't it true that some think a Christian can lose his salvation because of a sin? Wait! I thought Christ already paid for that sin. And the Holy Spirit assures us of eternal security. When you became a Christian, the

Holy Spirit, the Sealing Agent and the Spirit of Promise,[5] came inside of you permanently establishing a new birth, whereby you inherited the divine nature of God. And just like a newborn baby can't reverse the act of life once it comes out of its mother's tummy, a new creature in Christ cannot reverse the act of regeneration once it comes out of the old life into the new. If God's divine nature was placed in you by Him at conversion, how could *you* take it out? Eternal security is solely an act of God with no ties to your human merit.

I suppose the bottom line question is this: was the person ever saved to begin with? If he was, then he can rest in the eternal security of God knowing that for the rest of his days, the Lord will keep him safe. But take note: for the Christian that strays, letting opportunities for spiritual effectiveness and growth drift away, consequences will follow: loss of earthly blessing and eternal reward. 1 Corinthians 3:15 teaches that fire will test the quality of every believer's conduct and motives. If it survives the fire, he will receive a reward. If not, he will "suffer loss but he himself shall remain saved."

So rejoice! If you've received Christ, your reservation in heaven is deadbolted in the vault of God, and for that I say, "Thank you, Jesus!"

"We are kept safe and sound by a faithful God."

1 Thessalonians 5:23

6. I am Holy

Some of these concepts of our identity in Christ seem so foreign and strange to us. It's because our spiritual eyes have not been fully opened to the spiritual reality of what happens when we pass from spiritual death to spiritual life at conversion. We read that we are holy and immediately think, "I'm not holy. I sin every day! I'm not blameless. I find evidence to condemn myself over and over." So we recoil at such a description because it makes us feel guilty that we should do better. But here's the truth. You can try all day long by your conduct to "be holy and blameless" but you will never attain perfection because while you're on earth, you're wrapped in the curse of the flesh. But praise God; through Christ, you're granted an alternate plan to live above the lure of sin through the Spirit's power. So what does it mean that "I am holy and blameless"?

By position you were declared holy before the foundations of the earth when you were chosen by God, yet by daily practice during this brief earthly visit called life, you exercise various spiritual disciplines—like obedience to His Word, prayer, and godly fellowship—which move you towards that final perfection of holiness when you see Him. So who are you by God's preordained placement? Are you defiled, common, and unclean? Are you condemned, marred, and blameworthy? No! You are holy and blameless:

holy–(hagios) a state of being or a position marked by separation, purity, morally clean, devoted to the service of deity;[1] therefore, upright, sharing in God's purity

blameless- (amomos)–spotless, the absence of internal blemish or an external spot, having no deficiency;[2] therefore, guiltless, uncondemned, unblamable.

I often picture my holy and blameless position like this: do you remember the former Miss America pageants how the contestants would enter a soundproof booth, set apart and secluded from the atmosphere of the rest of the contestants? In like manner, at salvation you are sanctified, set apart, placed in Christ, God's soundproof booth, and in Him you are "in the world, but not of the world,"[3] protected from the contamination of sin and the destructive pull of evil forces in which Satan, for a short time, reigns. Upon booth entrance, you pass from inadequacy to completeness, unworthiness to worthiness, contamination to spotlessness, unrighteousness to holiness. You become what Christ is by nature solely by your new location. In the booth, you are crowned king or queen of the pageant, with ownership entitlements to all the spiritual bouquet of roses that Jesus holds: a *new* position of identity, a *new* catalogue of privileges, a *new* promise of destiny, and a *new* fulfillment of transformation assuring a progressive growth and revelation of Christ's likeness. And for what reason were you granted such favor? Because Jesus Christ gave Himself for you as "a lamb unblemished and spotless."[4] You have been given throughout eternity His unblemished nature that "He might present to Himself the church, in all her glory, having no spot or wrinkle or any such thing: but that she should be holy and blameless."[5] The ultimate purpose of Christ's death was to eternally present to Himself a wedding present: you, His bride, exquisitely adorned in all her splendor having no mark of spiritual decay. When He takes you to glory, you will reflect the perfection process (glorification), having been made radiantly perfect and superbly complete. Astounding! It's Cinderella's fantasy and the prince's headpiece of glory!

So what difference should this make in your practical life? Your ability to live like who you *really* are, holy and blameless, comes from the practice of yielding to the Spirit who leads you into the holiness and character of Christ.

H - Have the awareness that you are set apart from sin for the purpose of making His perfections visible in you.

O - Obsess over God's standard for righteous living by remaining blameless in heart and life.

L - Live with intentional purpose in viewing yourself *in* Christ, *in* your soundproof booth, separated from the common, everyday world of ungodliness.

Y -Yield to Christ in continual humility and repentance by keeping your spirit in agreement with His.

"Just as He chose us in Him before the foundation of the world, that we should be holy and blameless before Him."

Ephesians 1:4

7. I am Legalized by Adoption

If anyone has ever doubted God's love, then doubt no more. If anyone has ever lived in the bondage of loneliness, then feel alone no more, for you have been adopted by God, brought into His family by faith in Christ Jesus!

Most of us did not grow up living apart from *both* parents, so we may not fully connect with the glorious celebration of what it means to be adopted, that is welcomed into someone else's family. Upon receiving Christ, we were rescued from the orphanage of Satan's domain and royalized into God's family as His very own son or daughter. Such a privilege of sonship finds great meaning when revisiting the process of adoption in the Roman world.

Adoption was a procedure intertwined with the complex rules of the Roman magistrates. Permanent consequences accompanied the process. When adopted, an adoptee lost all rights to the former family and no contact was permitted. With all of his debts cancelled, he entered the new family with a clean slate, a "free" agent with no baggage, totally released from all former sums unpaid. He joined his new kin as a full-fledged heir, co-equal with all other siblings in regards to inheritance. In the eyes of the Roman courts, he was an official natural son of his new father. What a change! Great benefit awaited the son or daughter of adoption.

Can you imagine having all your debts erased? Today you owe $10,000 on your Visa bill, and tomorrow you don't. Today you live with a guilty conscience, and tomorrow you don't? What would we give to have an opportunity to receive a clean slate, be adopted and receive benefits like that?

We don't have to give anything except receive Christ through faith. For "God predestined us to adoption as sons through Jesus Christ."[1] Indeed, "For you have not received a spirit of slavery, leading to fear again, but you have received a spirit of adoption as sons by which we cry out 'Abba Father.'"[2] As sinners we became sons of God with legal privileges of drawing on His divine wealth. As adopted children, we lost all rights to the grip of guilt and shame concerning our past. No longer do we owe the debt of making things right with God by our performance. All bondage has been cut off, forever wiped clean at the Cross. As an adopted child of God, we've been placed in a new family given a loving Heavenly Father and a fresh new start.

In the Roman culture, it was forbidden for a newly adopted person to visit their former family. Can you imagine an adopted child trying to live simultaneously in two families? Then why should we live in the past life replaying mistakes and regrets? We're in a new family now, having been granted an exalted position sharing in His rule, not as a foster child but as an heir to all God's riches.

J.I. Packer commented that in the Greco-Roman culture

... adoption was a practice ordinarily confined to the childless well-to-do. Its subjects were normally not infants, as today, but young adults who had shown themselves fit to carry on a family name in a worthy way. In our case, however, God adopts us out of free love, not because of our character showing us worthy to bear His name, but....just the very opposite. We are not fit for a place in God's family; the idea of Him exalting us sinners just as He loves and has exalted the Lord Jesus sounds ludicrous and wild—yet that, and nothing less than that, is what adoption means.[3]

Can you imagine going to an adoption agency and requesting, "I want the most deformed and neglected baby available in order to bestow my multi-trillion dollar inheritance?" Yet while we were sinners, wanton and unlovely, God brought us into His fortune as privileged sons and daughters. There is nothing about us that deserved a place in His family as an heir. Yet as adopted children, we share the same inheritance that God's only Son shares. You and I partake in the same favor that Jesus Christ enjoys. And that's not all! Because we are joint heirs with Christ, our spiritual blessings will extend into the Father's limitless treasures and resources throughout all eternity. Our Father's indulgence over the "adopted ones" is inconceivable! Amen?

> "He predestined us to adoption as sons through Jesus Christ
> to Himself, according to the kind intention of His will."
>
> Ephesians 1:5

8. I am An Heir Calling God 'Papa'

Some of the most precious stories in the Bible evolve around the theme of adoption: the Pharaoh's daughter finding Moses floating in a basket in the Nile and bringing him into the Palace as her own child; Mordecai adopting his cousin, Esther; and, of course, my favorite, the endearing story of King David bringing Jonathan's crippled young son, Mephilbosheth, into his royal palace as an heir. I love the story of Jonathan's castaway son! An insignificant crippled outcast, a "nobody" becoming a "somebody," not on the basis of anything he had done, but on the goodness of heart of someone else. Little Mephilbosheth who stood as the only heir of Saul, living in accordance to what his name implied "the shameful one," living in the town of Lo-debar: "the place of no pasture."[1] Yet this unworthy subject found himself eating at King David's table and given an inheritance of which he was not legally entitled. Who doesn't love the exploitation of unmerited benevolence and lavish grace, especially to such a pitiful subject?

What a graphic picture of God's adoption of believers! Is that not what we have received? We, the shameful, pitiful ones formerly living in the barren pasture of sin, were sought out by God to indulge at the King's salvation table? If that was the end of the story for us as banquet children, that would be enough, just to be crowned as an honored guest at His feast! But that's not all; there's more!

I imagine the Jews in Galatia could hardly believe what Paul was teaching when he introduced God's new way of life for them through grace. They had been told David and Mephilbosheth's story for centuries, but never could they grasp this new truth Paul was presenting by declaring the Old Covenant, the Law under Moses, obsolete, and asking them to enter into this New Covenant of Grace through faith in Christ alone. They had only known God as Jehovah, a God to be respected and held at a distance, but now Paul was debuting a foreign concept about their relationship with God. God didn't want to be their distant Heavenly Father, or even their gracious neighbor or friend; He inaugurated through Christ a new relational position for them. He wanted to be their Abba! Abba is the Aramaic word for papa, our daddy in English language, a term of personal intimacy rarely, if ever, used in Judaism when addressing God.[2] The Galatians were likely feeling it was rather sacrilegious of Paul to announce that God had sent the Spirit of God's Son into their own hearts calling out "Abba, Father."[3]

How could they relate to such a new revelation of God? The New Testament word for adoption meant to place as an adult son. The term implied endearment, to be placed into God's care or lap while reaping the benefits of sonship, an adult privilege between father and son. Such an image would mean that Mephilbosheth was not just to sit at the king's table, but sit in the king's lap. Amazing!

How about you? Do you ever sit in your Papa-God's lap? Your rightful position finds itself most comfortable on your Papa's knee. How often do you address God in prayer: "Dear Daddy." Or will God ever hear you say, "I just don't know what to do about this situation. I'll ask Papa." Yet *that* kind of intimacy awaits every adopted child who relates to God as He truly is: Papa—a daddy up close and personal!

Why is it that most people have a difficult time relating to God in that way? For many it's a proven fact that however you see your earthly father, you will see your Heavenly Father. If your earthly father was distant, then God will appear far off. If your father was harsh, then you will see God as "the Big Man upstairs with a short fuse." What was your earthly father like? Be truthful; do you see God in like manner? Many miss out in experiencing Papa-God's love because of an incorrect view of Him. Maybe it's time to reassess the way you connect to your Heavenly Father. Is it possible to establish a Papa-God connection?

My friend, God put the Spirit of Adoption in your heart, the Holy Spirit, whose urgings beckon you to your Papa's lap. It is not only possible but easily accessible. You can share an intimate relationship with God on a deeper level. Crawl up in His lap through prayer; Papa-God's waiting!

> "You have received a spirit of adoption as sons by which we cry out, 'Abba, Father!'"
>
> Romans 8:15

9. I am Indwelt with the Holy Spirit—(Part 1)

Nothing thrills me more than the reality of the workings of the Holy Spirit! Of all the topics I love to teach in the Christian faith, the Holy Spirit ranks in the top three. I just love Him! Yet how amazing it is that many believers know next to nothing about Him! For example, if you were asked to write a paragraph on each of the following, which would you know least about: the Father, the Son, or the Holy Spirit? No doubt most people would choose the Holy Spirit. Or what if you were asked to choose: would you rather have Jesus in your life or The Spirit? I suppose you would pick Jesus. Yet Jesus Himself testified, "It is to your advantage that I go away so I might send the Holy Spirit."[1] Jesus announced the Holy Spirit was your greatest life benefit.

Who is the Holy Spirit? The Holy Spirit is the third part of the Trinity, co-equal with the Father and the Son, and the author of God's Word having inspired men to write it. He's the inner testimony of God who continually transforms you into Christlikeness, and He is your witness before God that you belong to Him. And most obviously, He is holy and an invisible spirit. But in His invisibleness, He has attributes of not only God and Jesus, but that of a real person. As an invisible person, He acts and can be treated as a person. He possesses a personality and a vocabulary, which means He talks! Do you recognize when His gentle voice prompts an awakening to a spiritual truth? Have you ever heard Him talk to you? Acts 13:2 relays a time when a group of men were ministering to the Lord, *"and the Holy Spirit spoke to them."* He speaks! Why? He communicates to make the Father real to you and connect your will to His. Because He is the One who searches "the deep things of God,"[2] He works that you might fall in love with Him and yield yourself to His training and filling. He wants you to experientially know Him and the blessings of His unfathomable grace.

And the Holy Spirit owns another unique quality; He possesses a mind, a will, and emotions. He feels! Like you and me, He experiences insults, resistance, grief, and joy, and *unlike* Satan, He is eternal, all-knowing, and all-powerful. But the most astounding reality is this: He seeks a body to indwell, and at conversion, He takes up residence in you, thereby securing your ownership to God. The person of the Holy Spirit dwells *in* you. When you're alone, entering a restaurant to grab a quick snack at noon, do you tell the hostess there are two of you for lunch? What difference would it make in what you read, drank, said, or did if you envisioned the image that the Holy Spirit is your Siamese companion?

What does the Holy Spirit do? Here's the place where getting to know Him becomes wonderfully adventurous! He activates the gospel's power in you when you yield to Him. The Greek word for power, *dunamis*, suggests a *continual* source of energy.[3] He never loses His heartiness or get-up-and-go in leading you to Jesus. Just like Christ pointed people to God, the Holy Spirit points you to Jesus with one ultimate goal: to glorify the person of Christ while speaking in harmony with the nature of God. God has assigned His power unto the Holy Spirit to be let loose in you. What if the Spirit was unconfined and free to be on the rampage in you? What would His drive and unleashed energy look like if you gave Him permission to liberate God's greatest gusto?

An American with an English gentleman was viewing the Niagara whirlpool rapids, when he said to his friend: "Come. I'll show you the greatest unused power in the world." Taking him to the foot of Niagara Falls he said, "There is the greatest unused power in the world!" "Ah, no my brother, not so!" said the Englishman. "The greatest unused power in the world is the Holy Spirit of the living God."[4]

Fathom such a reality! *This* torrent, the Holy Spirit of God, dwells in you waiting for permission to gush forth His Father's good pleasure. And for what reason has God granted such potential dynamism? Is it to be overlooked? Ignored? Harnessed? Silenced? No! The Holy Spirit of Almighty God resides in your radical new nature for one stupendous purpose: *release*!

"Do you not know....that the Spirit of God dwells in you?"

1 Corinthians 3:16

10. I am A Conduit of
the Holy Spirit's Release—(Part 2)

Like a baby chick seeks release from the confinement of its shell, the Holy Spirit seeks release from the incarceration of being trapped in your flesh. His release is simple. It's spelled out in nine letters: s-u-r-r-e-n-d-e-r! When you yield your full concentration on the affections of Christ and continually look to Him for grace, the Holy Spirit finds an outlet in discharging His power. For me, becoming familiar with His activity and looking for His fingerprints in my day has become my favorite pastime, an amusing hobby in which I take great delight! It's not bird watching I love, but Holy Spirit watching. Getting to know the Spirit as my greatest life advantage has awakened a new thrill in observing His tangible hand-prints in my day. Notice the ways the Holy Spirit releases His energy through His various roles. I love His creativity! He's a blast to know!

The Holy Spirit is a Bodyguard-

"But the comforter will be sent to you."

John 14:26

Who of us wouldn't like our very own protector who continually stood close by our side with a first aid kit? The Holy Spirit never leaves your presence, and He's always on duty. In fact, the Greek word for com-forter, *paraclete,* suggests the idea of a helper, one who comes alongside.[1] I'll never forget the father/son image in the summer Olympics of 1966. Remember? A runner trained his whole life for 440 meter race. Upon turning the corner, he pulled a hamstring and fell. Onto the field came a man, his father, to come alongside him and assist in finishing the race. It portrayed a gripping comparison: that's what the Holy Spirit does for you. He keeps your feet on the ground exerting His energy in your race of life until you cross the finish line.

The Holy Spirit is a Navigator-

"When the Spirit of Truth comes, He will guide you into all truth."

John 16:13

Isn't it enlightening how the Spirit uses daily occurrences to relay His truth? Because we are sons of God, we are led by His Spirit. Not long ago I was in the airport and felt this *tap tap tap* on my foot. I was blocking the path of a blind lady and her bold Labrador! As they walked off, I observed the helplessness of the youth without the aid of her dog, and the Spirit whispered, "That's the way I want to guide you, a manner in which you totally trust Me when you can't see ahead!" In fact, the original word for guide suggests one who leads into uncharted territory.[2] Anyone entering a new season in life? Anyone need reassurance that God knows the way? Anyone need the *Holy Spirit Guide Dog* to lead the way?

The Holy Spirit is a Teacher-

"But the Helper the Holy Spirit will teach you all things."

John 14:26

How does the Holy Spirit release His power? He dives into the depths of God and brings to light all that God wants you to know. He's God's walkie-talkie. His teaching results in a personal transformation, a life whose purpose is wrought in the heart of God. He works to bring into alignment your choices with His Father's will. How does He do that? Have you ever been reading the Bible and an arrow of truth jabs your heart? Who do you think awakened that truth? You? No! You are incapable of stirring up true spiritual awareness. That piercing revealed what God wanted you to know. So beware, and the next time you feel that inside quickening while reading His Word, stop! Verbally recognize the Holy Spirit's activity. He's your personalized tutor!

The Holy Spirit is a Policeman-

> "When the Holy Spirit comes, He will convict the world of sin."
>
> John 16:8

It's the policeman's job to see to it that no one's breaking the law. Because God is holy, the Holy Spirit leads you to repentance when you break the laws of His Word. I remember a day in December when 'The Heavenly Policemen' pulled me over by the badge of His impelling spirit. Years ago I bought a velvet dress for a Christmas party and ruined it with the iron; so with the tag still on it, I drove back to the store to exchange it. As I arrived at the store, I heard this inner voice, "And what about the person who buys your dress?" Horribly ashamed, I realized I was grieving the Spirit who was blowing the whistle on my sin. That's His job, to uncover unrighteousness and handcuff any offense toward God! It's painfully true: He's not only the comforter, but He is the *uncomfortable* comforter,[3] and most of the time it's not pleasant when our defiance comes under His arrest. Of course, I took the black dress home and arrived at the party with an iron imprint tattooed on its sleeve. Simply lovely!

The Holy Spirit is an Alarm Clock-

> "...and He will bring to remembrance all that I have spoken to you."
>
> John 14:26

Often when I am studying during the day, I set the alarm clock to remind me of an afternoon appointment. The Holy Spirit works in the same way. Have you ever been driving down the road and *out of nowhere* an inside buzz reminds you of the second point to the pastor's Sunday sermon? Why does that truth come to your mind? Is it by accident or is it by a calculated arrow from God? It is the Holy Spirit's function to affirm the specific will of God concerning you, and it happens through the networking of the Trinity. "For the Holy Spirit will not speak on His own initiative, but whatever He hears from the Father."[4] So pay close attention to those out of nowhere moments! They are not out of *nowhere*. Those divine promptings and messages are out of *somewhere*, yes, that *somewhere* originating from the throne of God! After orchestrating your circumstances, God knows the exact time in signaling the Spirit to bring to remembrance what lies in accordance with His will. Isn't it a staggering reality that the Spirit incessantly labors to conform you to the image of Christ?

The Holy Spirit is a Secret Agent-

"And He will disclose to you what is to come."

John 16:13

Who needs horoscopes and palm reading? You have the omniscient Holy Spirit who discloses future events as the Father initiates Him to tell. I've witnessed the power of the Holy Spirit in various ways, but the times I've experienced *this* particular function of His, my faith has deepened in subservient devotion to the reality of the Spirit's generous love for me! Forever etched in my mind, echoes a depressing day in 1986 when I sat slumped in my study. I cried uncontrollably, distraught that my first husband of ten years had left me. I faced a new role: single motherhood, and the Holy Spirit so gently revealed my future: "Pam, start writing journals, keeping track of this difficult journey, and someday I will utilize your sorrow and raise you up to testify of My delivering power to do the impossible!" And that's exactly what has happened. I'm humbled! I'm honored! I'm reverently speechless over the divine encounter of that day more than twenty years ago. Does God still come to our aid revealing His plan like He did with the shepherds who were abiding in the field when Jesus was born? Does He still unfold His blueprint for His loved ones who are abiding in their living room with a broken heart? He does! His inner voice came to me bringing to light my future, and for that I graciously attest, "I love Him! I love Him."

There remains today a mysterious interdependence between the Trinity and you. It is God, the Father who searches your heart and knows what the Holy Spirit desires, and it is God who grants the request of the Spirit by assigning Him permission to awaken a truth in you. Then when you respond in obedience to His quickening, the Spirit completes the cycle by releasing fresh power and vision.

How superlatively amazing! It's the Holy Spirit, the One who transcends all human limitations and expectations, who inflates God's resolve in you. He's your significant life companion, comforter, and consolation. The Holy Spirit: He's a miracle! He's a phenomenon! He's a wonder! And He's waiting for release! What's keeping you from setting Him free?

> "Yet He lives because the power of God....has been directed towards you."
>
> 2 Corinthians 13:4

11. I am Filled with the Holy Spirit (Part 3)

Picture this. Twelve-year-old Lisa Lester won her fame by entering a smiling marathon placing her in the *Guinness Book of World Records.* For ten hours and five minutes, Little Lisa stood before a panel and literally smiled her heart out! How it must have tickled the judges!

No other grace gift more gloriously blesses the life of the believer than Christ's joy. And what is His joy that He bestows? It's that inside smile of the Holy Spirit standing before God, a quality of undisturbed peace and satisfaction that enables you to rejoice even amidst life's greatest sorrows. It's that divine attitude of pleasure that arises from a personal, ongoing communion with Christ, whose source of ecstasy remains totally unrelated to earthly circumstances or emotions. While happiness is an emotion that comes from outside circumstances, joy is a state of mind that depends on the inward filling of the Holy Spirit, and indeed, it lasts much longer than ten hours and five minutes!

It was an intense tug-of-war afternoon in Jesus' heart when He voiced His last prayer to His Father before He crossed the ravine of the Kidron Valley approaching His crucifixion. Indeed, no other prayer of Christ expressed more dramatically the Shepherd's farewell address to His disciples and all future believers than His conversation with God in John 17. Perhaps Jesus pondered, "How will they rise above life's most treacherous challenges? What will serve as the bedrock of their strength? What will keep their oneness of fellowship with Me intact once I'm gone?" So He asked His Father to give them the ingredient that had sustained His earthly life and kept the oneness between Him and His Father strong; He asked that "His joy be made full in them."[1]

He wanted them to be filled and running over with "an inexpressible joy, full of glory,"[2] a state of being that expressed a transcendent gladness of heart. Jesus would connect them to Him through the Holy Spirit and grant them the capability of experiencing His delight.

Isn't it true, to be full means something has to be poured into something else in order to make it so? Jesus prayed a Christ-filled life for His followers, a life where His joy would infiltrate every cubby hole of their heart. But so often as recipients of His prayer for fullness, we find ourselves running on empty. What generates fullness? The answer: the filling of the Holy Spirit. I often compare the Spirit's filling with my passenger ride experience in a hot air balloon. In order for the balloon to be useful, every inch of the inside cavity had to be permeated with hot air. Once it was filled, it automatically lifted, gliding care-free above the disturbing traffic and pollution below, and when the balloon began to faint, a blast of hot air quickly restored its soaring capacity.

Likewise, at salvation you received the balloon, your new identity. But without the filling of the Holy Spirit, your Christian life will lack vitality and power for greater service and usefulness. The balloon rises only as the operator allows the hot air to fill it. Your joy level suffers great degrees of deceleration when you live by self-will instead of God's will. No other commandment from God is more vital for joyous living than this one. No wonder Jesus prayed that His people would exercise the avenue that afforded them soaring power! The Spirit-infectious life is a choice. How often do you ask Him to infuse your balloon with hot air?

- Surrender everything to the Lordship of Christ: your body, your abilities, your past, and your regrets. Your filling is in direct proportion to your submitting.

- Understand that being filled with the Spirit is not an option but an order from God. Joy! It's a commandment.

- Live consciously in Christ's presence as if He's standing beside you. Practicing His company fosters the filling.

- Activate the filling by asking Him to do so. His promises and enablement go hand-in-hand!

In Bible days when olive oil was applied to one's hair, it oozed down the face, soothing, comforting, restoring the human spirit. Won't you let the oil of Christ's joy do the same in you through the filling of the Holy Spirit?

"Be filled with the Spirit."

Ephesians 5:18

12. I am Forgiven

My friend, please open up this gift from God and receive it for yourself; you are forgiven! Would you let the truth of God's Word break loose that lie that says God is disappointed in you and finds you unworthy of His endowment of grace? Satan knows that if he can keep you trapped in condemnation and shame, then you will be incapable of walking in newness of life, feeling disqualified to receive God's forgiveness. If he can trip you up *here*, then you will be crippled in experiencing all the other spiritual blessings of your rightful inheritance as a child of God. No other gift is harder for us to believe than this one. Why do we feel we deserve punishment more than forgiveness? Oh, the torture many have induced on themselves by believing Satan's lie. Karl Menninger, the famed psychiatrist, once said if he could convince the patients in psychiatric hospitals that their sins were forgiven, seventy-five percent of them could walk out the next day.[1] Oh, the tragedy of attaching the tentacles of guilt over the truth of grace! Jesus knew man's deepest need: forgiveness of sin.

It was likely a sunny afternoon the morning Jesus visited his friend's house on the northwestern shore of the Sea of Galilee. In every city crowds flocked to Jesus, and Capernaum was no different. Jesus sat in Peter's house teaching the Word among many. But it was the four friends who lowered their palsied man on a cot through the thatched roof that captured Jesus' attention that day. Who wouldn't want their friend cured when The Healer was only a few houses away? I'm sure they focused all their hopes on Jesus' first words in anticipation of hearing, "Arise, run, and leap!" But rather they heard the Savior of the world pronounce, "My son, your sins are forgiven."[2] What? Did Christ miss the point completely? Who cares about forgiveness of sin when all they wanted was freedom of feet? Yet, Jesus knew the heart of man! More than anything the paralytic needed to know of God's forgiveness of sin and that freedom on the outside comes from freedom on the inside.

What's your inside spiritual thermometer? Does your conscience bear witness with God's spirit that you are truly forgiven for all your wrongdoings? Or is your testimony this: "I believe in my head that Jesus forgave me, but I still feel guilty." Somewhere between the head and the heart there's a breakdown. The Greek word for forgiveness, *aphesis*, means to release or to send away,[3] yet the effect extends a step deeper. It implies not only a sending away of the offense committed but a sending away of the guilt associated with that offense! So God's forgiveness essentially means that He removes the guilt from the wrongdoing. You've been granted amnesty against the charges. Did you hear that? You are guilt-free, discharged from condemnation. Though it is obviously impossible for God to blot out the event of the sin, it's not impossible for Him to alleviate the shame that follows. If He has pardoned your guilt, then why do you hang on to it?

Perhaps you've failed to appropriate the greatest commodity in your life. Do you know what that is? It's what makes it possible to obtain God's pardon. For God chose the means of reconciliation between your sin and His gift of forgiveness: Christ's blood, for "without the shedding of blood there is no remission of sin."[4] No blood, no forgiveness! So let the remedy of God's acquittal of blame and shame melt from your head to your heart with this truth: Christ's death took away the penalty of sin, and His blood covered your guilt, removing it as far as the east is from the west. So if you continue to feel guilty again for a sin you've already confessed, then visualize Christ's red blanket laying over your shame. No guilt, past, present, or future can keep you from a deep friendship with God.

Your sin has been "cast into the depths of the sea."[5] Leave it there; learn from its lesson; liberate yourself from Satan's lie; and live, love, laugh in your newfound freedom.

"And when you were dead in your transgressions.......He made you alive together with Him, having forgiven us all our transgressions."

Colossians 2:13

13. I am Eternally Glorified

Hollywood Memorial Park is the cemetery behind Paramount Studios. It contains the remains of many well-known people from the entertainment industry. Among the buried is Mel Blanc. Mel was the actor who gave creative voices and sounds to many cartoon characters like Daffy Duck, Tasmanian Devil, Bugs Bunny, the laughter of Woody Woodpecker, and the most memorable stuttering of Porky Pig. His grave marker has one simple epitaph, "That's all folks."[1] While it makes one snicker just for a moment, the alarming truth according to God's Holy Word is this: that's *not* all folks! For those who treasured Christ as their Savior, their physical body of death and decay will resurrect into a glorious new body forever; indeed, the climax of their earthly journey. Paul says it like this, "It was for *this* that He called you from slavery's corruption into the freedom of the glory of the children of God."[2]

What is it about the story of Cinderella that all young girls love? My granddaughter, Karsen, gravitates to the fairytale of the girl who turned from rags to riches. It's a simple tale about a scruffy ordinary woman who is suddenly dazzled into a princess who waltzes the night away with her lovely Prince Charming. Ahhhh! Fascination! Glitz! Romance! Indeed, the "belle of the ball!" In every creature whether it is a five-year-old or sixty-five year-old, there dwells a craving for the radiance of all that is exquisite, a place where one dances with the prince all night long. That yearning was placed there by God as a mechanism causing us to seek Jesus, the one True Prince Charming. Once we find Him, the Holy Spirit begins the process of transforming our inner person into Christlikeness, for the Prince's ball that lasts not for a night but for eternity.

When you received your new identity, a process called sanctification began. It's a development that takes a lifetime whereby God sets you apart for the purpose of making you holy in your actions. The perfection occurs with one spiritual experience built upon another. You've often heard, "God's not finished with me yet." No, He is not. You are being made into the likeness of His image step by step. The last step in this progression occurs when you see Jesus, that day when your body transfigures from a mortal body of flesh into an immortal body of God's glory, a transformation called glorification. It's the consummation of sanctification where your body of humiliation or decay[3] translates into your body of glory, which is identical to that of Jesus Christ. Not only is your body like His, but the new nature you received on earth will reach its final perfection, too. You receive the ultimate makeover that defies your own human imagination!

In 1 Corinthians 15, Paul contrasts the two bodies: the *old body* with which you were born, the one whose image is tainted by the sin of Adam, and the *new body*, the one that bears the image of the immortal Son of God. He characterized the qualities of each by envisioning your body as a seed that, when it dies, is sown to the earth. In due season, it is resurrected into a different shape, yet still carries the personality of the old. Paul differentiates between the two bodies: the body is sown a perishable body, made to deteriorate; but it will be raised imperishable, never to corrupt again. The body is sown in dishonor, one whose potential for pleasing God has been marred by sin; but it will be raised to glory, one perfected for praising its Creator. The body is sown in weakness, feeble and prone to disease and growing old; but it will be raised in power, agile, having the capacity to go beyond the universe, from one galaxy to another without limitations. And the body is natural, only suited for the physical realm on planet earth; but it will be raised to a spiritual realm adaptable to the lifestyle of the grandiose heavenlies.[4]

I'm unfathomably awestruck with childlike wonder over the supernatural realm awaiting my glorified entrance. What will it be like stepping into His glory? I'm sure I'll behold starry hosts, infinite paradise constellations, heavenly kingdoms, and "that's not all folks!"

"And whom He justified, He also glorified."

Romans 8:30

Chapter Six

My Position

In what capacity is my new identity in Christ experienced?

14. I am In Christ

Apart from the divine inspiration of the Holy Spirit and accepting Scripture by faith, one remains incapable of understanding the infinite mysteries of the Word of God. One of the vast phenomenons of the Bible is this: you are *in* Christ. I liken it to holding an apple. You're not just holding the apple, but the seeds inside; you are the seed of His likeness in union with Him. Upon salvation, you were baptized *into* Christ Jesus and *into* His death and raised *into* His resurrected life.[1] Your new position placed you *inside* all that He is: changeless, holy, and all-powerful, so that you could enjoy all that He owns—the eternal riches of grace!

The life of faith is spoken of as life *in Christ*. To be in Christ expresses the nature of the Christian experience where individual new creatures are placed in His body, or church, where there are no isolated members, for "all are one in Christ Jesus."[2] To be in Christ is to be in a community with other Christians where human barriers no longer exist, for they all share in the body life adventure together. And though they are one assembly of believers, they are uniquely gifted and "individual members of it."[3]

Having this new identity with Jesus is not just an outward connection, like you know *about* Him; rather, you are *part* of Him, united *with* Him and in Him in a bond of effectual care. I am gratefully overcome

PAM KANALY

with appreciation that I have a God who unites with His own in a permanent union, whereby, His followers can enjoy an active relationship
with Him through Christ. I applaud God's comment about His own
generosity: "There is no other; there is no one like Me."[4] Amen! Amen!
As Christians, we share a relationship with our Creator that no other
religions in the world partake, since their members do not have the
privilege of being one with their religion's creator; they merely yield to
his rules of conduct relating to the now and hereafter. How cold and
impersonal! Yet in Christianity, our Creator did more than just give us
a set of regulations; He left the glories of heaven and became a part of
His own creation that we might be *in* Him and receive the riches of our
inheritance.[5] Hallelujah! We're beyond being mere spectators of His
infinite blessings; we're participants and owners of them.

Like a baby finds nourishment and advantage while being in its
mother's body, you possess advantages while being in Christ's body; so
celebrate! Make merry and rejoice!

In Christ you:

partake in the radiance of God's glory. Hebrews 1:3

transmit the light of God in your heart. 2 Corinthians 4:6

possess the hope of glory. Colossians 1:27

have an abundance for every good thing. 2 Corinthians 9:8

enter God's rest. Hebrews 3:18

inherit a clear conscience. Hebrews 10:22

embrace an intercessor at the throne of God. Hebrews 7:25

harvest the fullness of God's love. Romans 8:35–39

discover grace and mercy in times of need. Hebrew 4:16

seize victory over the evil one. 1 John 5:18

perceive songs of deliverance. Psalm 32:7

find a refuge from troubles. Psalm 34:19

garner companionship. Isaiah 30:18

secure rewards for perseverance.   Hebrews 10:36

acknowledge peace and confidence.   Isaiah 32:17

gain access to God through prayer.   Job 22:27

become a vessel useful to the Master.   2 Timothy 2:21

prevail over all wounds.   Jeremiah 30:17

acquire counsel and instruction.   Psalm 32:8

comprehend God's love.   John 3:16

grow in power and strength.   Isaiah 40:29

share in His sufferings.   2 Corinthians 1:5

ask and receive from Him.   1 John 3:22

achieve His favor as with a shield.   Psalm 5:12

increase in wisdom.   Psalm 32:8

approach the grave in full vigor.   Job 5:26

reap eternal life.   John 3:16

It's a blessed union: you in Christ and Christ in you, a consummation serving as a timeless anchor for not only this age, but throughout all eternity.

"God willed to make known what is the riches of the glory of this mystery: Christ in you, the hope of glory."

Colossians 1:27

15. I am Hidden with Christ in God

When I was young, my mother would on occasion let me have a slumber party. One of our favorite games in the house was Hide 'n' Seek. I didn't want to be the person who was it. I preferred to be the one who hid. Maybe it was because I knew all the secret places in the house. I especially loved the spot in my parent's bedroom behind the turquoise chair. It was there that I would hunker down next to the heating vent on the floor and receive the warmth and safety that secured my position to win the game.

The Bible says that I am still engaged in this childhood game for I am *hidden with Christ in God*. How can I be tucked away with Christ in God? I find that a difficult concept to grasp, much less explain. In order to get the picture, I have to peek into the spiritual realm recalling that my *real* citizenship, or spiritual livelihood, no longer resides in the earth's sphere but in the heavenly sanctuary of the risen Christ where "I am raised up with Him seated in heavenly places in Christ Jesus."[1]

To be *hidden with Christ in God* means my affections for the things of this world have been declared dead. Paul states, "I have died and my life is hidden with Christ in God."[2] It's as if the apostle's argument was this: "When you sank under baptismal waters, you disappeared forever from this earth. The world knows nothing henceforth of your new life, and your new life knows nothing of this world."[3] The early Christians regarded baptism as dying and rising again. When a man was dead and buried, the Greeks spoke of him as being *hidden in the earth*, but the Christian has died a spiritual death and he is not *hidden in the earth* but *hidden in Christ*, buried out of sight.[4] In other words, in baptism the Christian dies and rises again where his affections belong to Christ, hidden in God. I wonder, when I get too attached to the riches of this world, have I forgotten that my earthly ambitions are nothing more than cotton candy, sweet for a moment then melted quickly with nothing eternally to show for it?

To be *hidden with Christ in God* means I am eternally secure. While the Greek word for hidden (*krupto*) means to conceal, the root word means to be placed in a sheltered sanctuary.[5] When I received Christ, my eternal destiny was locked in the vault of "that place," *hidden with Christ in God*. Jesus promised to those whom He had given eternal life that they would "never perish and no one would snatch them out of His hand."[6]

To be *hidden with Christ in God* is not only a concept affecting my eternity but a truth I can enjoy now. To see myself concealed in His rest is to exchange my unsettledness for His peace. It is to abide in Him.

Francis Schaffer suggests, "To abide in Christ is to practice active passivity." It is to work hard at doing nothing, to let go, to rehearse a life of serenity and trust in the One in whom you are hidden. It is to say, "I'm swinging in His hammock of peace, cushioned in His palm. I'm fortified by His love. Nothing will get to me without passing through His fingers. I can release my personal pain because God sees the outcome for good and watches without interruption what shakes my sense of stability. If He is *in* me, and He's at peace, then I can be, too." To abide above is to loosen up below.

Like the game of Hide 'n' Seek, one has to hide and one has to seek. Why don't you do both? You can hide. You can find in Him an undisturbed asylum of rest, where no disheartening circumstance in life will ever destroy you. As a refugee, you can nestle in His *calm*. Or you can seek. You can hunt behind every bush for opportunities to let Him be your fortress of safekeeping. He wants you to find Him. He watches you peeking behind every hedge plant but His. He listens for your footsteps to come His way. He longs to hear, "You're it, God!" Why would God beckon you to a deeper relationship with Him and never come out from hiding? For He Himself said, "For those who seek me, shall find Me."[7]

> "For you have died, and your life is hidden with Christ in God."
>
> Colossians 3:3

16. I am A Sanctified Saint

What does it mean to be sanctified? Its meaning covers a broad range of spiritual experiences. Sanctification is what I call the living out of your Christian life between the time you came to Christ and the time you see Christ. It's solely a work of God where He progressively makes righteous those He has brought to Himself through Jesus. Primarily, sanctification refers to the practice of godliness in a believer who's been set apart for the accomplishment of God's goal in conforming His followers into the image of Jesus Christ. We were made in His likeness, given the nature of spiritual-mindedness, and it's the Holy Spirit's job to prune, purify, and perfect us to look more and more like Christ. At conversion we enter the beauty shop of the Holy Spirit.

When you received Christ as your savior, two truths were set into motion concerning this process of transformation. First, you were instantaneously placed in a position or permanent classification for the purposes of God. *Hagi*, the root word, suggests a separation from one thing to another: from Satan to God, from sin to holiness.[1] You were washed, sanctified, and justified in the name of the Lord Jesus by His Holy Spirit. God tattooed on your forehead for eternity these words, *righteous, set apart, holy*, because of the offering of His Son's blood once and for all. No sin of yours will ever take away that position. That place of being set apart is as true for the most sinful believer as it is for the most holy believer. Your good works did nothing to gain that position so your bad behavior can do nothing to lose it.

Secondly, your sanctification is a progressive experience. With each yielded opportunity, you become more and more like Christ. You are a continual work in progress. Progressive sanctification reminds me of a Polaroid picture. At the time of salvation God takes a snapshot of you, visualizing your completed picture of glorification when you see Him. The time in between conversion and when you receive your glorified body is sanctification, the lab where the chemical of the Spirit begins transforming the image.

As a youngster at Kanakomo Camp, I participated in the camp format. The entire group was divided into two tribes for the purpose of whole-hearted competition and fun. Each tribe was distinctly set apart. You were either a Kiowa or a Kickapoo. With immense pride we wore our tribal name stamped on the front of our t-shirts. The Bible says God has two distinct "tribes" on this earth, not Indian tribes, but classifications of people based upon their acceptance or rejection of His Son, Jesus Christ. If you've trusted Christ as your Savior, your new title is saint. As a follower of Christ, you wear an invisible "SS" on your t-shirt, *Sanctified Saint*. It's not an imprint given on the basis of your performance or the daily quality of your everyday life, but solely on the basis of what Christ did for you at the Cross. As a born again believer, you might see yourself more like a sinner, and though you might not act saintly at times, you've been confirmed by God with this title: saint. When Princess Diana was alive, we all knew her as *The Princess* by title. I'm sure she didn't always act like a princess, but nevertheless, she was a member of the royal court of England, a princess by name, having accepted the ways of the palace. Likewise, you are a member of the royal priesthood of Christ, a saint by name, having rejected the ways of the world. So who is a saint? Some believe the title pertains solely to a dead person who has been honored because of his holy life, and though that might be true, Jesus extends the title to all born again believers.

Do you see yourself as a saint, a holy brethren set apart in the symphony of God's cantata? You are indescribably precious to Him with opportunities and privileges to serve King Jesus, not only now, but later when Christ returns. As a sanctified saint, you will be the people in the coming age who will "be the priests of God and of Christ reigning with Him for a thousand years."[2] What an honor to be royalized and adorned with His favor! May you walk in a manner worthy of your high and holy calling!

"Now may the God of peace Himself sanctify you completely…"

1 Thessalonians 5:23

17. I am A Worshiper

How much more could they take? Did the Roman magistrates know whose clothes they were ripping apart as they beat them in the market place? And just how many more blows to the head would it take to kill these two men? Soon, the provincial governor would hear the charges against them and pronounce an even stricter punishment. These weren't ordinary criminals: one possessed the much prized Roman citizenship badge, having earned an indelible reputation as a brilliant scholar with a noteworthy social calendar. His name was Silas. And his partner in crime, Paul, flagged an even more prestigious résumé: a 'Hebrew of Hebrews,' a Roman-born citizen himself, having established a fanatical repute as a Jesus freak. And these two zealots for Christ found their feet chained to wooden stocks in a prison cell.

When we hale the enormity of God, His voice that speaks out of a whirlwind, His hand that commands the dawn of the morning, His very essence that adorns "Himself with eminence and dignity,"[1] we envision a God who remains satisfied apart from any response on our part. But nothing could be more untrue. It is God, the passionate One, who extends to you a new heart, one that's pliable and made ready for life's most exotic experience: worship!

Worship: it's that outward expression of an inward homage that comes out of a genuine transparency before God. Worship: it's more than an act; it's an attitude that continuously celebrates being in fellowship with Him. Worship: it's the activity of the soul, demonstrated not only by a Sunday morning experience but a lifestyle of expressing the 'worthship' of deity. Worship: it's the atmosphere in which God can speak. Worship: it's practiced when life soars high and put to the test when life drops low.

It was approaching the midnight hour when God thumped the prison cell in Philippi causing an earthquake. Surely Paul and Silas must have lain on the dusty floor discouraged, suffering from the open wounds and bruises from their earlier afternoon beatings. Surely the sudden jolt found them squandering in fear over life's next misfortune. Yet when the clock struck twelve, their fellow inmates marveled not at their crisis and pain, but their celebrated posture of worship. They were praying and singing hymns to the most high God, allowing the spirit to rise up above the prevailing doom that awaited their early morning indictment. Oh, glory to God! Can you imagine their own shock when their chains broke loose? And imagine the trembling of the jailer who had been roused out of his cell to find his prisoners set free!

My friends, when you're trapped in what looks like an impossible situation, worship by singing, thanking, and idolizing the immortal God. Doing so breaks the barriers of the heavenlies, inviting a catastrophic change! In an instant of worship, your trials can turn to triumph and your woes to winning's victory. Your praise is simply irresistible to God. In fact, if you want Him to show up in your need, praise Him. Just the smallest peep of yielded devotion sends His feet running to your cause. He waits for your praise! He dwells in your praise! He moves mountains in your praise! Just take inventory of Paul and Silas' prison layover and observe the possibilities of extravagant worship:

- *True worship with a fellow believer releases explosive faith.*
  "And Paul and Silas were praying and singing hymns to God."

- *True worship invades hell and implores God's power.*
  "And the chains were unfastened."

- *True worship demands notice of curious onlookers.*
  "And the prisoners next to them were listening."

- *True worship invites salvation.*
  "And that very hour the jailor was baptized and all his household."

- *True worship swells with unstoppable courage and defends the cause of Christ.*

  After Paul left the prison to go to the jailer's house, he returned to the cell that night in order to exert his legal rights in protecting the reputation of the newfound church. How hilariously amazing!

  "And the magistrates were afraid of Paul and Silas and begged them to leave town."[2] I love it! You go, God! Just look at the thunderous power of praise!

  "Oh come, let us worship and bow down. Let us kneel before the Lord our Maker."

  Psalm 95:6

18. I am A Glory Giver

In Hosea 7:16 God calls the nation of Israel a deceitful bow, for they had committed spiritual adultery and formed political alliances with foreign nations. When's the last time you perfected your skills as an archer? One thing is for certain: if your bow is bent, your aim will miss the target. What use is a broken bow? God was saying to Israel, "You've missed the mark! You've failed to partake in the reason I brought you to Myself." I wonder at times if I'm a deceitful bow. Would God ever say to me, "You've missed the mark in daily practicing the very purpose for which you were saved?" And what is that purpose? As new creations in Christ, we became bows for one use: to give God *glory*!

Jerry Chaffer points out that since the Bible is God's message to man, its supreme purpose is His supreme purpose, which is that He may be glorified. Look at the ways he records the Bible speaking of God's manifested glory:

•Angels and men, the material universe and every creature are all created for His *glory*. Colossians 1:16

•The nation of Israel is for the *glory* of God. Isaiah 43:7

•Salvation is unto the *glory* of God. Romans 9:23

•All service should be unto the *glory* of God. Matthew 5:16

•The believers' new identity is for the *glory* of God. Romans 5:2

•Even the believer's death is said to be to this one end: to bring *glory* to God.[1]

Friends, there's no getting around it. Whatever we do, from start to finish, from head to toe, from morning to night, we're to become skilled at giving God *glory*. We live to subordinate ourselves to the majesty of His glory.

What is God's glory? His glory is His manifested presence, stunning radiance, immeasurable perfections, and the illustriousness of His beauty. His glory speaks of His reputation and authority. The Hebrew word for glory, *kadob*, means importance or weight.[2] To give God glory is to speak of His magnitude and to be personally filled with the heaviness of all His attributes: filled with compassion, filled with faithfulness, filled with a gracious spirit, filled with His spectacular nature. To give Him the praise due His name is to allow every thought and action to aggrandize the splendor of God. The defining purpose for which we exist is not to minister to others, go to church, or read the Bible, although those are wonderful, but it is to bring honor to God, to further His glorious reputation, to model His character, to serve as a shrine whose new nature shows the world what God looks like. God calls His people special in order to "proclaim the excellencies of Him who called us out of darkness into His marvelous light."[3] John Calvin wrote, "The first duty of the Christian is to make the invisible kingdom visible."[4] This happens when the world sees His Glory in you. Jesus

Himself testified, "The same glory You gave Me, Father, I give to them."[5] Astounding! You inherited His glory!

Ezekiel 36:20 speaks of the deceitful bow, Israel, and how they turned their back on God by failing to give glory to His name. God pronounced, "They profaned My holy name." The Hebrew word translated as profane means to 'treat as common or ordinary' or 'to wound.' Dwight Edwards commented, "Their lives made God ordinary. They neutered God's reputation on earth. There was nothing in their conduct that elevated God's name. Israel had wounded God's prestige. His name now limped among the nations."[6]

What an alarming statement! How conscious are you of bringing credit to the reputation of God? In what ways do you give this godless world evidence of God's glory? Does what you say or do cripple or elevate God's image to others? Does your coming and going make God look ordinary or does your life expose the splendor due His name? 1 Corinthians 10:31 exhorts: "Whatever you do, do all for the *glory* of God." What is it that you do? Christian behavior should be for the glory of God. Does your life at home enhance God's repute? In your workplace, do your words advertise His name? Does your lifestyle showcase a God whose promises never fail? Does the way you live give convicting proof that Jesus Christ is alive and well in you? Is what you're doing bringing notoriety and dignity to God?

I was told a story of Reverend Billy Bray, a nineteenth-century preacher, who with every breath understood his purpose in life and continually heard the voice of the Holy Spirit within him. While reading a book of John Bunyan's, he was brought to Christ and delivered from a life of excessive alcoholism. He said, "I can't help praising the Lord. As I go along the street, I lift up one foot, and it seems to say, 'Glory,' and I lift up the other, and it seems to say, 'Amen,' and so it goes all day long."

Friends, we're told to walk in the Spirit. Doesn't walking require two steps? Maybe that's our new nature's condensed celebration song: Glory-Amen, Glory-Amen, Glory-Amen! Such a melody in our spirit hits one bulls-eye after another!

"Ascribe to the Lord the glory due His name."

Psalm 29:2

19. I am A Living Stone Being Built Up in Him

I love the second chapter of 1 Peter. No other section in the Bible kaleidoscopes more vividly the portrait of your new creation in Christ. As a new creature you are "a chosen race, a royal priesthood, a holy nation, a people for God's own possession,"[1] but most uniquely, a living stone! In the Old Testament Israel built a temple of fine laden gold, but in the New Testament God is building a temple of fine laden living stones whose radiance inhabits Jesus Christ, the Tested Stone.[2] He's the One anointed by God as choice (*eklektos*) the best of its kind or class.[3] In you resides the excellence of God's prized stone, the One unequalled in value.

When I was seven our family would drive by the bank in Lubbock, Texas, on Christmas Eve and view the forty-foot Christmas tree dazzling in the glassed corner of the building. I still recall its magnificence! Each light displayed its own shape, color, and personality, enhancing the tree's brilliance. As living stones, we serve as miniature Christmas lights in God's tree individually beautifying the universal body of Christ, collectively mortaring a spiritual dwelling place called the household of God. What an astounding thought! You are a living organism of God, interdependent with other believers forming a tower that reflects the splendor of God, a celestial Babel reaching into the heavens. Who are you in Christ? Imagine you and a group of friends standing in a circle holding a strand of tree lights that reach to the sky. You are the ornate and uniquely designed red one!

As a member of the strand of lights, you stand on a solid foundation. You are a member of God's family, His house, built on the foundation of the apostles and the prophets with Christ as the cornerstone. You've been carefully joined together with other saints becoming a holy temple for the Lord. All of God's children represent a role in the building of this house: the apostles and prophets of yesteryear proclaimed the message of Christ as pilgrims, the believers of today bring glory to the message of Christ as living stones, and Christ, who is The Message, laid the foundation. In ancient structures the head capstone gave strength to the structure. Jesus became the hewn out cornerstone, becoming the stabilizing support of the entire building. Indeed, Christ holds the monument together, and someday He will complete this temple of living stones and take them to glory.

As a living stone you function as a holy priesthood. In the Old Testament, priests offered animal sacrifices for the atonement of sin, but now because the treasure of God's grace poured out by the blood of Christ, you function as a holy habitation of God, a priest who daily offers spiritual offerings, such as adoration, to His Son, Jesus, the eternal High Priest. Remember the stone that was rolled away at Christ's resurrection leaving the tomb empty? Now you are that stone representing the empty tomb because Christ now resides in you! He's entered your living stone, your temple! His glory no longer resides in the temporal tabernacle of the Old Testament, but in your body, this new spiritual temple being built up in God through the Holy Spirit. It's a sanctuary that will last forever, having superseded the tabernacle of the Old Covenant. You, along with others, inhabit "the household of God, which is the church of the living God."[4] Who is the *real you*? You're a sacred temple, a living stone, whose radiance reflects the glory of Jesus!

As a living stone your heart is an altar unto Him. Peter exhorts, "to *offer up* sacrifices acceptable to God through Jesus Christ."[5] To offer up means to bring up on the altar of your heart all unconfessed sins, sorrows, heartaches, and competing passions as a pleasing and acceptable aroma to God. How precious to bring the inner you to God, laying it down as a surrendered stone that He might consecrate you as a living stone.

Often, when gazing into a shallow lake bottom, I'm reminded of who I am in Christ. The sun catches the crystals of one stone in particular dazzling with sparkling beauty. That's me when God sees the reflection of His Son.

> "And now God is building you, as living stones, into His spiritual temple."
>
> 1 Peter 2:5

20. I am The Temple of the Living God

Hollywood just might be on track with something. For years filmmakers have mastered the art of producing high-impact movies about robbers capturing jewels that lay enthroned in a case of glass. Such movies like *Indiana Jones and the Temple of Doom* awaken our senses to a most astounding theme: an inconceivable treasure sealed within the walls of glass.

When's the last time someone came up to you totally stupefied, throwing their hands over their mouth in astonishment because they saw *in* you an unimaginable fortune? And why shouldn't they be awestruck? You enshrine the living Holy Spirit of God, the One who serves as God's secret agent performing His work in the world. Since He's a spirit, wouldn't you think He'd need a physical body to indwell? Amazing! At salvation, you became that body, a sanctuary, a temple, His address.

When I think of myself as the house of God, I can't help but compare my temple with the temple that Solomon built in the Old Testament. It served as a visible palace where God would make His presence known. Every detail of its structure pointed the Israelites to an act of purification and an opportunity to be made right with God.

Today we don't have to go through those ceremonial rituals. Jesus' blood on the Cross took the place of those requirements. However, I find it enlightening to look back at my spiritual heritage, Solomon's temple, and trace the fingerprints of Christ along the way. And what was God's mission? Through the death, burial, and resurrection of Christ, I would have direct access to my Heavenly Father.

When I see myself as a temple approaching God's throne through prayer, I enjoy strolling through memory lane and envisioning Solomon's Temple, an ostentatious structure taking seven years to complete. I'm enamored by the extravagance of people and material King David amassed to build it: 24,000 foremen, 6,000 officers, 4,000 musicians, 4,000 gatekeepers, 1,000,000 talents of silver, 70,000 woodsmen in moving the Cedar from Lebanon, and 80,000 stonecutters. Can you imagine? But even more fascinating than that is to open your eyes to the silhouette of Jesus Christ behind every nail and every angel hovering nearby. To see our Savior enthroned within that temple fortress only enriches my pilgrim's prayer of thanksgiving and humble devotion.

> Father, within these walls of mine resounds a sacred portrait of the temple. I see the *Bronze Altar*, that place where the Levites offered up a perfect lamb as atonement for their sin. Thank you for Jesus, the perfect lamb, whose blood restored our broken fellowship. Make me a living sacrifice, one that's poised for worship. Thank you for the *Bronze Basin*, the place where the priests cleansed themselves. Jesus, my Bronze Basin, cleanses me when I confess my sin. What a joy to enter your palace of strong support! Thank you for the *Two Bronze Pillars* holding up the entrance roof. Those beams serve as a reminder to be strong in trials, for Jesus promised, "Those who are faithful in trials will be made a pillar in the Temple of God."[1] Thank you for the *Golden Incense Altar*, that burning altar where the prayers of the priests ascended into Your presence. May my

prayers arise as pleasing incense. Father, unlike the Israelites who only had a priest, I have the Holy Spirit, the Interpreter of God, providing continual access into your presence. Thank you that the *Holy of Holies*, your most sacred place, abides in me.

It's an astonishing reality to behold. I embody Solomon's Temple, made perfect and complete with the coming of Christ. As a child of God, I am one glorious Holy Place!

> "Do you not know that you are the temple of God and that the Spirit of God dwells in you?"
>
> 1 Corinthians 3:16

21. I am A Child of Light

The miracle of our new birth in Christ finds one of its greatest images in the word light. What is it about light that fascinates even a two-year-old? And why is "Twinkle Twinkle Little Star" one of the first songs we teach our toddlers? God placed in us an inborn fascination with light because we are made in His image. 1 John 1:5 declares that "God is Light" and those placed in the light of His presence will walk as children of light because He is their source. How often do you see yourself as His reflector, an instrument illuminating the sheen of His light within you? When you walk into a room at work or at home, do you consciously think, "I am the light of God twinkling or emitting little winks of His glory!" Ephesians 5:8 instructs believers, "You who were formerly in darkness are now light in the Lord so *walk* as children of light." What does it look like to walk in your new identity as light? Ephesians 4–6 beams a path generating your light.

Ten Commandments for Sustaining a Bright Light

1. *Be renewed in your mind.* The transformed mind comes from reading the Word of God. Your outward light shines only as bright as your mind submits to your inward redeemed nature.

2. *Be careful with your words.* An unharnessed tongue squelches your glow. God places the tongue inside the cage with your wisdom teeth for a reason. If you want to know what's in a man's heart, listen to the spiritual thermometer of his tongue. It's the real you, the tattletale of your heart. If you can control your tongue, you can control anything!

3. *Be forgiving and tenderhearted.* Nothing serves as a more destructive filter of dimming God's light than bitterness; it's that inward settled hostility that poisons the whole inner man. But God provides a healer that removes the filter: forgiveness! Either forgive or relive.

4. *Be an imitator of God.* As a child at birth has the nature of his parents capable of imitating their behavior, we have at our rebirth the nature of God capable of reproducing His behavior. The character that you embody as God's child obliges you to not just resemble, but mimic Him.

5. *Be pure in speech.* Paul lists three 'light crushers' concerning your conversations: 1. obscene stories: avoid filthy or disgraceful words; 2. *silly talk*: stay far away from dull, stupid, or gutter mouth language, whose root meaning, *morologia*, addresses the word moron;[1] 3. *coarse jesting*: refuse to turn what was said in innocence into crass humor.

6. *Be a God pleaser.* Seek to know what honors the Lord. Practice the spiritual disciplines that bring Him glory: praise Him, pray, seek righteousness, hunger for knowledge, live by faith and above reproach, and walk blamelessly.

7. *Be an opportunity seeker.* Make the most of your seasons in life. Colossians 1:10 "Walk in a manner *worthy* of the Lord." *Worthy-* to live in a manner equal to the Lord's standard.[2] Each season is purposeful and brief. Seize it.

8. *Be Spirit Intoxicated.* Live an intentional life of joy under the sway of the Holy Spirit. The Spirit-filled life is one inebriated by the effects of letting the Word of God and the Holy Spirit richly foster its influence within you.

9. *Be strong in the Lord's power.* Satan seeks to annihilate your brightness. 1 Peter 5:8 suggests, "Be collected and vigilant; your enemy makes due use of opportunities to take you under." Claim your position; claim your power; claim your wardrobe. Dress yourself in the potent armor of God.

10. *Be prayerful.* Prayer realigns your will to God's. It changes you, others, and your circumstances. Prayer propels the distance your light will project. It's the only force that travels faster than the speed of light.

As a child of light, live with such visibility that you carry your Family name well!

"And He has made His light transfer to you."

Psalm 118:27

22. I am In the Eternal Plan of God

I don't think any of us would question the fact that God knows more than we do or that His love for us reaches as high as heaven's glories! He loves us! Us! I don't think anyone would disagree that God's ways are higher than ours. His plan for us is more exotic than what we could ever hope or dream! "For indeed it hasn't even entered our hearts"[1] what delicacies the

Lord has planned for those who love Him! It's beyond our realm of even fantasizing. I don't think any of us would have the nerve to assume the role of a critic before the throne of *The Almighty* and have the audacity to say, "I want to challenge you, Creator of all things, about your correctness in what You said in Your Word." Are you kidding? I don't think any of us would argue the fact that God is God, and we are not. Did He not put Job in his place reminding Him of His superiority over humans' finite minds that even at their genius best, their understanding resembles a pea in a haystack? Remember His brazen words to Job: "Where were you when I laid the foundations of the earth? Tell me if you know so much. Who supports its foundations, and who laid its cornerstone as the morning stars sang together and all the angels shouted for joy?"[2]...and on and on God spews for another *102* verses of His magnificent transcendence. Whew! God makes it quite clear! He is the Supreme Being of all creation who by His own sovereign will created a blueprint of how to sustain and maintain His creation, and even who would play a role in it.

Some doctrines in Scripture lay far outside our human capacity in explaining them. This entitlement, "I am in the Eternal Plan of God," serves as one of those complex doctrines to comprehend, yet because it's clearly a foundational truth taught in the Word, it can't be left out in our entitlements just because we might question it. As it is true with the entire Bible, we accept it by faith. By so doing, we release the magnanimous wonderland of just how deep and far and wide and high is our Father's love for us.[3]

We sometimes marvel at man's plans. He can come up with spectacular ideas, can't he? Fifty years ago, who would have ever imagined our technological world? In your wildest inventiveness, can you imagine what a plan of God would resemble? It would look like an alien from another world, too sumptuously beautiful to be true! That's God's plan: so far out there we can't begin to stretch our arms around it, but let's try.

What does it mean to be in the eternal plan of God? God's divine program revolves around His unquenchable love for His Son and His choice to let those who love Him share in His destiny. You, as a reborn saint, have been selected to be a part of God's eternal, magnificent plan! How often do you think, *By His stupendous design, I'm in His bubble, His itinerary, His course!* Just look in amazement at the depth of His love in choosing you, all of it for the praise of His own glory:

Election- You are chosen as the elect, one picked out by God before eternity's past for salvation, not on the basis of your good works, but solely on the merit of God's will. God's love called you out to be a people unto Himself. It's a work of His grace. Jesus declared, "You did not choose me, but I chose you."[4]

Foreknowledge- Related to the concept of election is God's consent before eternity's past that you would have a distinct role in His Kingdom having received His inward call. His plan included all He purposed to do before human history, a plan appointing you into His salvation blessing. You were considered in times past, foreordained by His merit and received by His recognition to play a part in His rule.

Predestination- From God's foreknowledge of you, God's aspiration defined a purpose for those whom He would call. They ultimately would be conformed into the image of His begotten Son, Christ. You, His elect, would gradually be brought into a change until it resembled the likeness of Jesus, the result being a transformation of the inner heart by the Holy Spirit.

Astounding! You have been in God's mind, His eternal array of glory since before eternity's past! He chose *you*, foreknew the value of *you*, and predestined *you* to an expansive life whose inner nature would be transformed into a replica of Jesus Christ, His Beloved, to live with Him forever. I'm totally stupefied!

Oh friend, let me humbly drive home the point: your identity in Christ was remarkably fashioned in God thousands and thousands of years ago. God's eternal plan for you is no small matter! Reckon its amazing love! Reckon its dramatic power! Reckon its elaborate joy! Reckon its inconceivable splendor! Bow low in sheer amazement and let His plan bless, possess, and caress you as it unfolds its stunning design in *you*!

> "And whom He foreknew, He also predestined to become conformed to the image of His Son...and whom He predestined, these He also called."
>
> Romans 8:29-30

23. I am Dead to Sin

A startling reality takes place when someone you love dies. Things on earth abruptly change. The life you once knew when they were in your presence remains no more and life's future memories unfold anew! Death's effects bring an abrupt realism: a new position in your living, a new alteration in your thinking, and a new lifestyle in your doing.

I took care of my mother and father in nursing homes for over twenty years. My father, Moon Martin, who called me Pamicita, passed away while the fireworks welcomed him into God's Kingdom on July 4, 1995; and my mother, Melba Martin, celebrated her passing into Heaven's glory in January 2004. When someone dies in Christ, his life transcends into the most dramatic change known to man: death to life, a cessation from the mortal body wrapped in limitations to the immortal body, unwrapped in liberation. There is no change more catastrophic to man's experience on earth than that, except one.

Even more dramatic than one's change of address from earth to heaven or hell is the spiritual transaction of the new human nature at conversion, a life delivered from our unredeemed natures we received from Adam, to the redeemed natures we received from Christ. Its change brings to light three truths concerning our new relationship to sin. *A new position in our living*—we are now in a new environment, in Christ, a new location that alters sin's ability of controlling us like it did in our former position. *A new alteration in our thinking*—we now have the capacity of pursuing Christ's thoughts concerning our ability to resist sin's temptations. *A new lifestyle in our doing*—we now possess the power through the Holy Spirit to resist sin's compulsions in our actions. While it's true that sin is that driving force, that ongoing struggle of evil that continually works to enslave all of us, we have the capacity of shutting down its domination over us because of the Cross. Christ's resurrection afforded the finished work of sin in that it removed permanent physical death, bringing into fruition an eternal state of spiritual life. The believer has already died to sin but now must put its control into action by faith. Just as Moon and Melba are dead to the physical power of life in their human bodies on earth, we are equally as dead to the operating control and lordship of sin in our lives.

Do you carry a besetting sin that holds a firm grip on your life, paralyzing your ability to break its chain? At the Cross of Christ, sin's power was dethroned as master, declared inoperative in being your leader, bringing freedom from its tyranny; however, it still remains active in bringing temptation just like it did before you received your new identity. Sin now can't rule in your spirit, but it can dominate your body if you let it. That's why Paul said, "Do not let sin reign in your mortal body that you should obey its lust...For sin shall not be master over you, for you are not under the law, but under grace."[1] God's canopy of grace grants power in reckoning sin's appeal as dead. Just as you are buried in Christ and raised to walk in newness of life, your sin's power is put to death in Christ, as well.

So consider yourself dead to sin's power. The Greek word for *consider* means to occupy oneself with calculations.[2] Calculate that you are out of commission to sin's lures by adopting a lifestyle that is unresponsive to sin. Stay away from areas of temptation where you're most vulnerable and respond to them as a dead person would respond. Resist the devil, and he will flee. Use your weapons of resistance: faith, prayer, and the spoken Word of God. Find the strength through the Spirit to withstand the enemy's enticements to sin by following Christ's example. The Bible exerts: "And Jesus, full of the Holy Spirit, said to Satan, 'It is written,'" then He quoted out loud Scripture.[3] Exercise your God-given power. Rely on God for a way of escape, which actually means "a way out of the sea," implying that God can supply a deliverance outlet while enduring the trial. And take heart: Remember that God will never let you down; He'll never let you be pushed past your limit; and He'll always be there to help you come through any trial.

"Consider yourself dead to sin."

Romans 6:11

24. I am Alive to God

According to "It Happened in Canada," during the early days of northern Ontario's gold rush (1909), Mr. Sandy McIntyre discovered what is now the famous mine bearing his name. He sold out for $25 in order to buy liquor. Years later, he still passed his time crying in beverage rooms, while the mine produced gold worth $230 million![1]

Oh my! What a disheartening waste and pitiful picture of what could have been! I wonder as we study these entitlements together, how many Jesus followers are experiencing only $25 worth of their new identities, while their net worth in Christ exceeds well over $230,000,000? What keeps us from entering into the inexhaustible fortune of our wealth in the King of Glory? Is it merely lack of knowledge of what we own, or could it be we choose to live on less than what we possess?

Perhaps no other book in the New Testament more profoundly encapsulates the net worth of these benefits from God than the book of Romans. Martin Luther confessed, "Upon reading it, I thereupon *felt myself to be reborn* and have once again gone through an open door to paradise."[2] How many times as a believer have I felt discouragement roll in, but when I opened the Bible, God's Holy Witness, *I felt myself to be reborn* and immediately was ushered into the paradise of His abiding presence once again. Such an encounter testifies to the reality of our wondrous new personhood. When we acquiesce our wills to God and reckon our minds and ungodly choices as dead to sin, then we experience the foundational nature of our new identities: Life! Life! Life! "I have been crucified with Christ and it is no longer I who live but Christ lives in me and the life which I now live in the flesh, I live by faith in the Son of God who loved me, and delivered Himself up for me."[3] It's amazing!

Have you ever known a person to be dead and alive at the same time? You are! You are dead to sin and alive to God. In fact, the life others see you living is really not your life at all; it's God's life made alive in you! How often do you consider the reality and function of "The Other Nature" living in you?

♦ *His 'aliveness' in you comes from Himself.* Unlike other false gods who are dead, your God is called the Living Father, the One who possesses life in Himself. It's not that He gives life from another source, but He is life and from Him your blessings originate. Peter testified to the nature of God, "You are Christ, the Son of the Living God."[4]

♦ *His 'aliveness' in you seeks fellowship parallel to His own personhood.* 2 Corinthians 6:15–16 presents a question, "Of what harmony has Christ with the devil? Or what agreement has the temple of God with idols? For we are a temple of the living God." W. Weirsbe commented, "It is a nature that determines association. Because a pig has a pig's nature it will associate with pigs in a mud hole. Because a sheep has a sheep's nature, it will munch grass in the pasture. But you have a divine nature."[5] With whom will you choose to associate? Nature to nature: Christ in you seeks fellowship with others who match His makeup.

+ *His 'aliveness' in you will never run out.* Your source of union with Christ will never exhaust its energy, but continue on without end. The Greek word for alive means to spend one's existence.[6] You will spend the rest of your existence exerting what comes out of your union with Christ: fundamental power!

+ *His 'aliveness' in you gives birth to a living hope.* "And God has caused us to be born again to a living hope through the resurrection of Christ."[7] You will never be in a circumstance without Christ's life-blood of hope. When your strength falters, hope in God will come to the rescue. David relied on that delivering power. Psalm 71:20 states, "Though you have made me see troubles, many and bitter, you will restore my life again; from the depths of the earth; you will again bring me up."

You are *not* at the end of your rope, perishing in your troubles, and without access to heavenly help; you *are* animated with His strength, efficient, and armed with His power!

"Consider yourself...alive to God."

Romans 6:11

25. I am A Member of a Kingdom of Priests

My sister, Vicki, tells of a time when she entered Carnegie Hall to see Mary Jane, her famous friend from high school, sing and perform. Before the concert, she exercised her VIP backstage badge to gain entrance behind the curtain. Vicki recounts the fun of serving Mary Jane, treating her like a queen, filling her water glass, and polishing her jewelry. Oh, the joy for her to have direct access to the master performer.

In the Old Testament priesthood, God called forth a man who was granted an exclusive backstage badge with Him, the High Priest. Once a year this chosen minister was given an admission ticket to go behind the veil in the temple into the place where God's presence was on display, the Holy of Holies. It was there in the tabernacle that the high priest offered sacrifices of worship, mediated on behalf of the people, and performed services that pleased the Lord.

In the New Testament God inaugurated a better way of coming into His presence. When Jesus Christ shed His blood on the Cross, rose from the dead, and entered the heavens as your High Priest, the veil that separated God from man was torn in two and those who trusted in Christ were given free unlimited access to God. You need no other person to take you behind the veil to God except Christ, the Mediator. Upon Jesus taking His position at the right hand of God, you were enlisted as His follower priest on this earth given divine privileges. As a follower priest, God declared you holy, giving you an exalted position to live outside the realm of the ordinary. You were awarded an updated VIP badge, as well as a badge that pulled back the curtains of the mundane, thrusting you into the realm of the divine. You were hand-picked by Him, to live as a priest for a holy purpose, to offer priestly acts of sacrifices to Him. Imagine! You are the priesthood of God ordained and placed in a position to minister to the Almighty!

Many have a false idea of the word sacrifice, feeling it's something you must give up for a season, an act of doing without. But to sacrifice is to willingly give over permanently for the purpose of bringing delight to another. As a follower priest, your aim is to bring pleasure to your High Priest. You can delight the heart of God! What priestly duties or sacrifices can you perform that would please Him?

• *The sacrifice of self* - To offer yourself is to "present your body as a living and holy sacrifice, acceptable to God which is your spiritual service of worship."[1] It's to yield all your human faculties as an instrument of righteousness, a vehicle of God's glory.

• *The sacrifice of good works* - To carry out acts of charity is to "be careful not to neglect doing good."[2] Such deeds of benevolence performed for His glory is a service to God that communicates your commitment.

• *The sacrifice of winning souls* - To convert sinners to God is to share the good news of Christ with those who have never received Him. It's to extend the gospel as a priest whose service becomes suitable and sanctified by the Holy Spirit.

• *The sacrifice of worship* - To pay homage to God is surrounding all of you to His all-encompassing goodness. It is to recognize God's worthiness and desire Him above all else. Worship is a proper response to an encounter with God.

You are a follower priest, but you are not alone in performing these priestly acts. You've been placed in the sphere of God's community among other priests who collectively maintain devoted worship to God. Together you function as a divine kingdom, a dominion of saints working in unity forming a community called the body of Christ.

When's the last time you saw yourself in a missionary role of a priesthood of believers, a saint dressed in a sacred robe dipped in the blood of Christ? You are eternally privileged and granted unlimited access into His blessings of grace. He's your Master Performer awaiting your presence. It's time to enforce your valued position and use your backstage pass.

> "And He has made us to be a kingdom of priests to God. To Him be the glory and dominion forever."
>
> Revelation 1:6

26. I am Abraham's Seed

Have you ever wanted to be famous? Maybe star in the Olympics, wear the crown of Miss America, or land a front page story in the *Guinness Book of World Records*? I thought that would be really fun, until I ran across a lady by the name of Feo Vassilyev, a peasant from Shuya, Russia. Her fame doesn't appeal to me at all. She holds the world's record for the woman who gave birth to the most children. Are you ready for this: sixty-nine! Wow! Yes, my friend! Can you imagine what her Mother's Day was like?

But I know of a person who should replace her in the book of records! The Bible speaks of a man who had so many descendants that they couldn't even be counted. Other than Jesus Christ, no other name remains more of a status symbol than *this* man's. Christians and Arabs alike vigorously salute the heritage that *this* man brings into their own religions. *This* man is presented to mankind as an important forefather to whom God would entrust a covenant, a pledge that would bind God's heart to *this* man's seed throughout all eternity. And most astounding, God would make you an embryo in *this* man's family tree. *This* man was Abraham.

It all began back in the days of Adam and Eve. After they sinned, God gave them a prophecy concerning their future deliverance. The foretelling prophesied two seeds: the seed of the serpent, and the seed of the woman. The seed of the serpent, Satan, would be destroyed by the seed of the woman, Jesus Christ. Abraham's lineage would be impregnated with the seed, and this seed, Jesus Christ, would restore a relationship between God and man. It's true; the covenant of grace and redemption that governs the Bible came through Abraham, and all who by faith would embrace the promise brought through the Spirit would be defined as spiritual descendants, Abraham's seed.

If Christ was the seed of Abraham, and you are in Christ, then you are a seed of Abraham, an heir of His promise. When God inaugurated the covenant with Abraham saying, "and I will bless you, and make your name great, and so you shall be a blessing,"[1] then that promise of favor was prorated into your own life, fulfilling the promise to Abraham of universal blessing. And how would you, as Abraham's seed, activate that blessing? It'd come by faith and obedience in Christ alone. You'd plant yourself in the soil of His Holy Word and sprout shoots that resemble His character. You would simply fulfill your role as a seed.

A seed is meant to multiply itself, to transfer pollen. How diligent are you in pollinating your world with your boss at work or the clerk behind the counter at Walmart? Do you approach people with the purpose of spreading the seeds of God's redemptive story into their soil? You are a sower cross-pollinating the Word of truth into the fields around you. But so often as seed tossers, we get discouraged because the seeds we cast seem to lie dormant. For days, maybe years, there appears to be no sprouting. But take heart; here's the truth: no seed planted dies without eventually accomplishing God's purpose. So, be a patient seed sower and learn to wait on God to water the seed.

In 1539, King Henry VIII demanded the closing of a local monastery. The monks abandoned, leaving their luscious gardens to ruin. Some 400 years later, an archaeologist began excavating the entrance of the courtyard finding seeds that had been inactive for hundreds and hundreds of years. Without cause these seeds began to grow! How could this be? Yet an amazing miracle occurred! After the archaeologist began disturbing the *earth*, they sprouted. So learn the lesson: you sow the seed and let God *disturb the earth*.

The world's tallest tree towers in the coastal area of California, the cone-bearing redwood reaching heights of over 369 feet. How could such a wonder of nature come to life from a seed smaller than a thumbnail?

In eternity, the seeds of Abraham will gather for a family reunion. What a celebration that will be: the cone-bearing redwoods, the whispering pines, the diminutive cedars, and even the miniature shrubs. How will you fare in the Father's forest?

> "And if you are Christ's, then you are Abraham's seed, and heirs according to the promise."
>
> Galatians 3:29

27. I am Hated by the World

There lay in His heart a bittersweet fellowship with the ones He loved most passionately. It was an evening before the Feast of the Passover that Jesus reclined at the table, gazing into the hearts gathered around him, men whose wide-eyed devotion resembled eager little puppies; yet Jesus remorsefully knew their earthly fate that would take them through the slaughterhouse, segregating them into a class all their own. Their choice concerning their relationship with the world's system would collide with their core belief about the validity of all The Messiah had taught them. Jesus knew something the disciples had yet to learn: to follow Him meant vicious rejection, fierce opposition, and brutal hatred. The gospel message of which He had called them to carry ran counter to the society's commitments and idols. And though Jesus ordained the wondrous inheritance that awaited their eternal state, he also fatally envisioned in living color their earthly martyrdom: Nathanael would be flayed alive in Armenia; Peter would endure crucifixion upside down during Nero's reign; Andrew would be crucified on an x-shaped cross. And it was Jesus, in that final evening, who alerted His disciples to their upcoming dangerous position hoping to disarm their disappointment: "If the world hates you, you know that it has hated Me before it hated you."[1] In other words, "In this world you will be an object of ridicule. There's a price to pay."

Nothing has changed! Turn on the news. Is that not true? The same world that hated Jesus when he was born still hates those who claim to be His image bearers. The world, a system estranged from God comprising organizations, philosophies, and cultural varieties, displays a mind-set that lies grotesquely outside God's will and hates those who claim to lie inside it. Why would I list *this* one, 'I am hated by the world,' as an entitlement? Coming to Christ delivers you from a position (in darkness) to another position (in Christ.) To ask for the real me to please stand up is to embrace a stern reminder that there's position in which to stand: a posture whose backbone of steel sides aggressively with Christ whose prophetic words have yet to unfold: "Vengeance is mine," says the Lord, "I will repay."[2]

Why does the world hate Christians? To know who you are in Christ is to know why you're hated. Maybe you have someone in your own sphere that raises an eyebrow at your unyielding beliefs. I recall a suspicious eyebrow turned my way from a football player in college who refused to take me to a party: "Oh, isn't she's the one who wears a Bible around her neck?" Why was that offensive to him? Better yet, why did I want to meet him in the first place? What about you? Who recoils at the thought of your witness for Christ?

The world hates Christians because they identify with Jesus, the One who modeled the standard of God. While Christ was on earth, those who opposed the Savior mocked and laughed at Him, and today those who deny His teachings will do the same to His followers. We've been transferred to the Kingdom of Light where our lifestyles of exhibiting the nature of Christ expose the deeds of their darkness by the Holy Spirit's power. Often a believer's very existence in a room can make the unsaved uncomfortable. Indeed, your very presence preaches. Because Christians maintain a set of principles that fall under the dynasty of Christ, it's understandable how His life in His people can agitate the opposing system in those who reject Him.

And the world hates Christians because they choose not to live like the rest of the world. Jesus conceded, "The world would love you if you belonged to the world, but you don't. I chose you to come out of the world, and so it hates you."[3] My friend, if the world hates you, expect rejection! Welcome the fact that others notice you're different because you are! Don't reside in the shadows of your faith for fear of being shunned. Live in contradiction by returning love for hatred, joy for rejection, and self-control for opposition. It's rather comical: while the world repels the Christian witness, it's simultaneously compelled by its voluptuous mystery. How stunning of God! He even uses hatred for good!

"You will be hated by all nations on account of My name."

Matthew 24:9

28. I am An Enemy of the Devil (Part 1)

I recently contacted one of our government agencies inquiring about a six month program called "Train Up," an intense series of classes concerning military employment taught by their commanding officer in charge. The sessions address such topics as chemical warfare, topography, land navigation, and rules for engagement, just to mention a few. Basically the program's intent is one: *know your enemy*! Can you imagine the secretary of defense engaging in a foreign war without tediously educating the soldiers about explosive devices or how to administer first aid? No soldier would go into battle without education as to why there's a war, who the enemy is, what his schemes are, or how he can be defeated; Yet, I find it alarming that numerous believers know little about their enemy, Satan, and his strategies. No wonder many saints live under the canopy of ongoing oppression! My friend, Satan is real! I shall never forget the demonic experience I witnessed in 1997 while sponsoring a youth mission trip in Matamoras, Mexico. After an hour of observing our Mexican pastor perform an exorcism on an unbelieving woman, she finally stood on her feet, pale and limp, and professed to the crowd, "Jesus Christ is Lord, and I surrender to Him alone!"

It's a fact: Satan cannot possess a born again believer because the Holy Spirit resides within, but the enemy can harass and vehemently come against those who belong to Christ. Certainly, you've felt his attacks! You have an all-encompassing foe who seeks to destroy, and he's good at it! And why shouldn't he be? He's been practicing for thousands of years! No wonder his lies feel so real. Wouldn't you be an expert if you'd been practicing on something that long? Nothing will bring more deception to the believer than living outside the reality of the present danger his enemy poses. And though Satan's power over sin in a believer was defeated at the Cross, he has been granted for a short while rulership over earth's affairs, launching attacks against God's beloved: you! Why? It's *not* primarily that Satan hates you, but he hates God, and because you are His, you remain his primary target because the only way he can attack God is through you. Know this: your success as a new creature in Christ lies paramount in activating your role as a soldier in this supernatural revolution in which you've enlisted, a war zone fighting against the demonic strategies and forces of darkness in an attempt to usurp God's authority! Are you engaged and ready, "girding up the loins of your mind"[1] for battle?

How can you appropriate an ongoing victory? Let's examine in the next few entitlements your own "Train Up" questions: How did I get into this battle? Who is the enemy? What strategies does He use? How can I assure perpetual victory?

How did you get in this battle anyway? When the war in the heavens began between God and His holy cherub Lucifer, (Satan), he turned against the Creator declaring, "I will make myself like the Most High."[2] "And war broke out in heaven; Michael and his angels fought against the dragon. The dragon and his angels fought back, but they were defeated, and there was no longer any place for them in heaven. The great dragon was thrown down, that ancient serpent, who is called the devil and Satan, the deceiver of the whole world. He was thrown down to the earth, and his angels were thrown down with him."[3] His rebellion against God's dominion cast him out of that realm into the human sphere on earth, all a part of God's crusade between the forces of evil and light. A spiritual battle rages in the heavenlies, a war that indirectly affects you. Such a feud that began long ago will continue until Christ returns to earth establishing His earthly kingdom, annihilating Satan's regime, sin, and the world system. It's for *this* ultimate victory that you persevere until the end!

Who is this enemy that attacks? He is Satan, the fallen archangel of God, a living being and abhorrent hater of God's children. Can you imagine hating someone so vigorously that you scheme to destroy their baby, yet that's what Satan did? "The dragon (Satan) stood before the woman (Israel) who was about to give birth (to the Messiah) so that when she gave birth, he might devour her child."[4] Satan's decisive goal since the day he was thrust out of heaven was this: exterminate everything and everyone concerning God's redemptive plan. And how would he do that? He'd employ his network of organized helpers, called demons, and he'd enter human beings to carry out his bidding; he moved in Herod the Great to slaughter all the male children; he persuaded the Jewish leaders to shut down Christ's mission, and one day he will enter the Antichrist in one last effort to overthrow God's rule. Satan: he's the dragon, the old serpent, and though he's fallen from God having already been judged by the Cross, he still possesses through God's permission a vast influence over the world. Listen here! Make no mistake: he is real, and despite a recent survey that cited half of all *born again* Christians view Satan as only a symbol of evil, he is not![5] He is a living being! So follow Paul's advice: "Don't be ignorant of his schemes."[6]

"Your adversary, the devil...seeks to devour."

1 Peter 5:8

29. I am Alert to the Enemy's Schemes (Part 2)

Who better to write a letter to fellow Christians in the northern parts of Asia Minor on resisting Satan's attacks and knowing his schemes than Peter? It was he who wrote to his beloved brothers and sisters encouraging them against the alluring entrapments of the evil one, the one whose schemes he personally knew so well: "Be on the alert. Your enemy, the devil, prowls around like a roaring lion, seeking someone to devour."[1] He was saying, "Come to your senses, people! Avoid the intoxicating entrapments of the world. Wake up; be cautious to the possible calamity you face. I'm begging you, open your eyes or you're going to 'be swallowed up' in one gulp!"

How intentional are you in identifying his schemes that seek to engulf you? Do you know the areas in your life most vulnerable to his attacks? I certainly do. I have two significant ways the enemy can shut me down, and isn't it just like him to attempt putting one of them right in front of me at a most opportune time? He's cunning, crafty, and immensely powerful, but "greater is He who is in you than he who is in the world."[2] You already have the victory, but you need to be wise in detecting where he prowls in your family and secret life. Do you carry in your wallet the "Believer's Guide of his Schemes?" You need to!

Paul exhorts in Ephesians 6:10: "Stand firm against the schemes of the devil." The word for schemes, *methodia*, suggests a deliberate, intentional method to be employed against you.[3] It's the idea of a killer animal stalking an innocent prey for just the right time to pounce. In junior high school a friend and I toilet papered a house after dark. We schemed with a premeditated plan to shower the house with our onslaught of destruction. Satan schemes in the same way, not to toilet paper your house but to obliterate it! How can you avoid his destruction if you're not cognizant of his plans? Let's address the next question in our "Train Up" session: What strategies does the enemy employ? Beware!

Satan rules. He's "the prince and power of the air"[4] wielding feverishly a demonic spiritual empire. "For we struggle against rulers, powers, against the world forces of darkness against the spiritual forces of wickedness…"[5] His network of associates or demons operates through organized rankings, infiltrating the world's political systems, affecting both national and international policies that destroy the plan of God. His schemes affect global peace! Dear soldier, open your eyes. Consider the bigger picture!

Satan blinds. "In the case of the 'god of this world' he blinds the minds of the unbelieving that they may not see the light of the gospel of the glory of Christ."[6] No wonder your unbelieving friends think your walk with Christ is a little weird! He opposes the work of God, hardening the concepts of their minds, hindering their insight. Pray God will open the eyes of their hearts.

Satan sifts. With the sieve of his lies, he shakes deep with perforated craftiness in order to remove all confidence in God, leaving you stripped in weakness, intimidation, helplessness, shame, and fear. Jesus warned Simon Peter, "Behold, Satan has demanded permission to sift you like wheat." But remember Jesus' words, "I have prayed for you, that your faith may not fail."[7]

Satan hinders. The Greek word for hindered means to cut a trench between one's self and an advancing foe, to prevent progress.[8] Paul commented, "We wanted to come to you, but Satan thwarted us."[9] How many fruitful deeds of well-intended acts of service have been frustrated by Satan's stratagems of confusion, laziness, prayerlessness, preoccupation with self, or moral failure? Stay vigilant in meditating on God and His Word.

Satan sows tares. In the parable of Matthew 13:38, Satan plants in the midst of true Christians counterfeit imposters or tares, those who bear the image of Satan but appear as noble agents of God. Be watchful of those among you that teach false doctrine in the 'name of the Lord.' Avoid partnerships with the ungodly.

Satan tempts. Satan schemes in order to break down your spiritual power through the lusts of the flesh. He tempted Jesus for forty days in the wilderness distorting the Word of Truth. He will suggest God can't be trusted, He doesn't care, He isn't real, and He doesn't uphold His promises. If he can get you to doubt God's character, he's won the battle for your mind.

Satan deceives. Just how far will he go in deluding the truth? One night in an Oklahoma town in August of 2005, three siblings were asleep when their father shot them. He said he wanted to give them back to God. Where does such a deranged thought come from? Or what about a child of yours who was raised in a Christian home but doubts the solidarity of the Bible or doubts the truth that Jesus is God's only way to heaven?

So be alert! Be noble-minded! Be smart, but don't be afraid. The enemy only has schemes, but guess what? You have *weapons*!

"Be on the alert....resist him."

1 Peter 5:8–9

30. I am Armed Against the Enemy (Part 3)

An old deacon who used to pray every Wednesday night at prayer meeting always concluded his prayer the same say: "And, Lord, clean all the cobwebs out of my life." The cobwebs were those things that ought not to have been there, but had gathered during the week. One fellow in the prayer meeting, getting tired of the same 'ol prayer, jumped to his feet and shouted: "Lord, Lord, don't do it! Kill the spider."[1] And that's exactly what Jesus did at the Cross concerning Satan, the spider. He set the date of his final execution day. For now, his cobwebs of permanent despair have been rendered inoperative by use of the believer's combat kit: his divine weapons. Through Jesus Christ, you've been granted Kingdom authority with Kingdom weapons in enforcing daily victories over Satan's weavings of destruction. A *spiritual* God, fighting a *spiritual* enemy, in a *spiritual* war, will demand *spiritual* weapons, and God invites *spiritual* human beings, like you, to use them.

Unlike Satan who has limited knowledge, you have the all-knowing God inside you fortifying a continuous triumph as you put to use His resources. Words fail to express the demonstrative ways God has proven to me the reality and reliability of these divinely bestowed weapons! I know from hundreds of personal experiences that they dismantle discouragement, assassinate helplessness, halt-crippling despair, and the best part, they are *yours* for the using! So utilize them. They are mighty for the demolishing of lustful thoughts, worldly values, and disbelief. Yes! You need *not* fall prey as a prisoner of war to Satan's wiles! God's given you all you need in laying siege to your opponent and enforcing your rightful place of triumph as a new creature in Christ. How can you assure a perpetual victory? Use God's weaponry. Lack of use is abuse! Notice your weapons:

> *The Lamb's Blood.* You don't fight Satan's regime solely with an emotional outburst of fiery words, but you fight him ultimately with the blood of Christ. The blood of Jesus did one thing concerning your position with Satan: it placed you on God's side, so now you can face Satan with authority and without fear. God forgives your sins on the basis of His Son's blood, so what accusation can Satan charge against you? When the enemy asserts condemnation, ask God to point him to the blood of Jesus. Against Christ's blood, Satan has no appeal. Activate your bloodline.

God's Armor. God grants every soldier an invisible wardrobe emitting divine protection. Wear it. *The Belt of Truth:* Wrap God's principles around your waist, standing ready to obey in truth. *The Breastplate of Righteousness:* Cover your heart with the imparted righteousness and virtue of the Holy Spirit in securing confidence in the battle. *Sandals of Preparation:* Walk in a steady pace of reliance on the gospel message in your pursuit of peace. *Shield of Faith:* Hold high your unwavering trust against the darts of unbelief. *Helmet of Salvation:* Protect your mind against Satan's lies knowing your life source in Christ remains secure throughout all eternity. *Sword of the Spirit:* Exert the Word of God as an offensive tool in resisting the devil.[2] Dress for success.

Believing Prayer. Communicating with God puts Satan and his henchmen on notice to give back the ground you gave to them through unbelief and negligence in standing firm. In prayer you knock down spiritual strongholds that have entrenched themselves on 'the spiritual property' (that's you) that belongs to your Heavenly Father. "Pray at all times in the Spirit."[3] Pray to your Father, through the Son, and in the Holy Spirit. Activate the Trinity.

Holy Behavior. See your lifestyle, or the way you live, as a weapon, indeed a channel of God's power. Whether or not you yield to the Spirit's control allowing Him to fill you with His strength and power will determine the degree of your impact against the kingdom of darkness. Caution: conduct godly conduct.

God's Strength. Can you think of any greater force in repelling Satan's aggression than colliding with the muscle power of Almighty God? Just how strong is He? Paul encourages the Saints in Ephesus to be strong in the Lord's might. It's not the quantity of strength but the source of the strength that matters.

Weakness. Weakness? How can that be a weapon? Any limitation that's either inherited or can't be changed constitutes a weakness. I always thought such flaws were a bad thing, but not so. Your imperfections yielded to God serve as a medium for His power to reveal itself. The Lord noted, "For power is perfected in weakness."[4] Jesus affirmed, "My strength comes into its own in your defects." Didn't Paul say to boast in your weaknesses? If Christ can appear strong against Satan through your blemishes, then shouldn't your shortcomings be celebrated as a weapon?

Simply stated, you're packed with a punch against the enemy; so go ahead, employ your instruments!

> "For the weapons of our warfare are not of the flesh, but divinely powerful for the destruction of fortresses."
>
> 2 Corinthians 10:4

31. I am A Dangerous Threat to the Enemy's Domain (Part 4)

Friend! Friend! Friend! Listen here! You have *no idea* what privileges your new identity in Christ has afforded you. You have *no idea* what power came upon you when you received Christ. You have *no idea* what possessions in the Spirit you inherited when the Holy Spirit invaded your old nature replacing it with the new. You have *no idea* what a Holy Presence encapsulated you when you became an enlisted soldier in the army of The Most High. You have *no idea* what a prodigy of the Almighty you are in this world! Simply said, you have *no idea* who you *really* are: you're not who you think. Then who are you? You are a dangerous threat to Satan's counterfeit empire and his company of minions. Indeed, one of Satan's greatest and most clever schemes, his blindfold trick, might be covering your eyes right now in recognizing the supreme dominance you possess, an obliterating force that can reduce Satan to a mouse. While I'm not minimizing his formidable power, (I *greatly* respect it, actually), I am lifting up my position in Christ and exercising my God-given authority to flip the switch on who Christ says I am: I am a child of Light! I operate in the light of Jesus, The Light Everlasting, and in the sovereign authority of His holy Word.

And, by the way, in contrast to the light, may I draw your attention to this fact: Satan works in the dark. Any household person knows when the light switches to the on position, the mouse scurries under the cabinet. You are the light of Jesus Christ and your verbal commands spoken through the commissioned authority of Jesus Christ summon Satan's demons to find refuge under the kitchen sink. Therein lies the fact that the devil, as powerful as he is, can be defeated; how? By your choice not to remain neutral in your position. You are a terrifying foe, an immensely dangerous dismantler to the enemy's province. He rules a doomed dominion, for he knows his time on earth is short; so he slinks about for every opportunity to rape the hearts of men in violating them from knowing who they *really* are in Christ. The last thing he wants is for the "real me to please stand up!"

Satan knows by personal experience that Jesus Christ and His hierarchy are real, that indeed, He is the Sharp Sword, the One called The Lord, strong and mighty. He knows the power of God. It reverberated through Satan's very soul like an electrical shock when he was excommunicated from heaven. In Luke Jesus reminds his seventy followers, "And I was watching Satan fall from heaven like lightning."[1] It's not that Satan *felt* like lightning, but rather in his falling he was lightning, feeling the horrific electromagnetism of heaven's limitless electrical fields. Can you imagine experiencing the entire wrath that God's power could muster-up? Satan knows the shocking reality of Christ's kingdom, probably even more so than you. James 2:19 alarmingly states, "For even the demons shudder." Have you ever trembled at the reality of God's power? Satan has. It's a fact: it's an all out war and Satan is feverishly, violently, ravenously plotting to disembody your eyesight from seeing the truth. He knows something perhaps you don't even know, and something he hopes you never find out: you have the resurrected power of the Almighty One actually jolted in you just waiting to come out! You are one potent creation, filled with God's nature giving you the authority to burn a fuse in Satan's revolt against the Kingdom of The King of Glory!

Listen! Wake up! Wipe the sleep out of your eyes and put on your rightful authorization to perform mighty feats in this battle. You are not without help or hope! No! You're inoculated with the Holy insulin of The Leader and Commander of Chiefs, Jesus, in walking in the victory that's already yours. How?

- By choosing to believe by faith
- By voluntarily falling under the leadership of God
- By speaking out loud to God through the blood of Christ
- By commissioning the devil to flee
- By taking leadership over the areas of your life you've given the enemy permission to taunt (Hey! If you give him an inch, he won't take a mile; he'll take your life!)
- By absorbing and obeying the Word of God as the sole authority in which you live, breathe, and address life

Is it true that you have two feet? Then it's also true that they *will* stand *on* something: either your own opinions and calculations, or His holy divine inspired Word, which was authored by The Maker of heaven, hell, and earth, which, by the way, is The Source that will permit your very next breath! Defeating Satan on a moment-by-moment basis is a decisive choice of your will made in your mind, the enemy's beachhead. He sits on it wondering if you're going to give him permission to:

- rob your joy
- molest your peace
- infest your faith
- adulterate your values
- contaminate your priorities
- compromise your affections
- assault your self-worth

Listen up! You have a Power of Attorney, the magnanimous name of Jesus! Just like kryptonite melted and rendered powerless the might of Superman, when you hold up the name of Jesus Christ of Nazareth, it breaks down and storms the gates of hell, ambushing Satan's master plan in blockading your realization and activation of who you are in Christ. No wonder believers crater under opposition, confusion, irritation, humiliation, disgrace, and doom and gloom. Their kryptonite sits on the shelf collecting dust!

You have Kingdom Authority! Will the real me please stand up and enthrone your royal position? Will the real me please stand up and command Satan to sit down? Will the real me please stand up and usurp Satan's annoyance in your life by the commanding name of Jesus Christ? Will the real me please stand up and take Jesus at His word?

One day Christ addressed seventy followers who took Him at His Word. They came to Him ecstatically alarmed over their ability to cast out demons. And Jesus commissioned, "Behold, I have given you authority to tread upon serpents and scorpions, and over all the power of the enemy, and nothing shall injure you."[2] Christ had enlarged their territory as His missionaries that day. He had granted them His power over the forces of evil whereby nothing could come against them that didn't first come through the permission of God. Jesus saw in the exorcisms a higher miracle. Indeed, Satan's citadel of power had taken a demoralizing blow, and now Satan would be subject to the followers of Christ. It was as if Jesus kicked up His feet in adulation: "Satan's power is broken. I've invested in you divine potency from on high. Look! It worked! I've disarmed and conquered the seat of your enemy's control. Now the souls of men will be released from bondage. It's only a matter of time before Satan's fortress on earth will fall to destruction for all eternity." And perhaps Jesus knew that after He went to the Cross, the gospel message would reach the ends of the earth, which would in turn usher in Satan's final extermination, escorting into play His earthly glorious reign.

What about you? Do you have that kind of authority like the seventy followers? Can you come against the spirits that harass you or your family? When you are troubled for yourself or others, is it possible to pray against the spirit of sickness and infirmity, against the spirit of jealousy, or the spirit of timidity, fear, despair, distortion, or even divination? What kind of authority do you have? It was Jesus who refuted the accusations from His enemies who claimed that He was in a league with Satan. He challenged them, "But I cast out demons by the finger of God."[3] Do you possess the finger of God? The finger Jesus referred to was God's Spirit. In the beginning the Spirit of God only resided in the heavenlies, but God sent His Spirit, or finger, to the planet through the person of Jesus Christ. Jesus is gone from earth now, but God's finger has now been moved into you as a believer. And Jesus concluded His discussion to His enemies saying, "Now the Kingdom of God has come upon you."[4] God's Kingdom lies in you and you will cast out demons, set captives free, heal the sick, and proclaim the Kingdom of God, and that's not all. For Jesus added, "And greater works will you do because I go to my Father in heaven."[5] Yes, you have been granted Kingdom authority! Reservoirs of divine power reside within you, for you belong to Jesus Christ, the "Blessed and Only Sovereign of God."

So what will you do with your authority? How will you view yourself from this day forward as one of His soldiers in this raging battle between these two kingdoms? Will you pray for God's enablement as you resist the enemy in your daily affairs? Will you rest in the power of Jesus Christ to fight your battles for you? Will you once and for all believe who you are in Christ? Will you let the real you please stand up?

One day while discussing the supernatural world, a professor, not knowing his position in Christ, admitted, "I'm afraid of the devil." One of his students responded, "But sir, it's not a matter of whether you're afraid of the devil, is the devil afraid of you?" When the enemy sees you coming all dressed in the armor of The Almighty, the One who expelled his presence from the heavens, does he know he's facing an excruciating encounter? May I comment on the thought of the young student; is the devil afraid of you? No, he's not afraid; he's *terrified*!

> "Behold, I give unto you power to tread on serpents and scorpions, and over all the power of the enemy; and nothing shall by any means hurt you."
>
> Luke 10:1,17–19

32. I am Led in Christ's Triumph

What is it about waking up on a snowy January morning and observing the snowflakes fall, or shaking a glass snow globe that enlightens our souls with a spirit of delight? Or how invigorating it is to witness a 'ticker-tape' parade! Don't you recall those urban settings where jettisons of large amounts of shredded paper were showered down on the champion being honored by the community as a hero? Indeed, such an atmosphere created the effect of a snowstorm-like flurry of gaiety. It was in *that* setting that Paul compared the triumphal victory of Jesus Christ to one of the grandest spectacles of ancient times: a triumph.

To any general in the Roman Empire, the most prestigious honor obtained was the celebration of a triumph, a parade-type pageant consisting of captives taken in war, state officials, and trumpeters who marched to the temple of Jupiter through the streets of Rome. Such pomp and ceremony only exalted their crowned general, draped in robes of embroidery gold while riding on his chariot. Such merriment ensued after a monstrous victory of colossal proportions: extensive territory gained, exquisite plunder acquired, and at least 5,000 enemies slain in battle. The Romans understood the concept of extolling a hero, and it was in this light that Paul boasted of Christ as being the Commander in Chief in the victorious parade over death, hell, and sin. It was *He* who would lead both the victors and captives to their destinies. Picturing such an event makes me want to shout: "So let us one and all exalt God's King of Glory and resound in one accord: 'Hail! Hail! Hail the Victorious Warrior, Jesus Christ, the One who through the Cross triumphed over the devil and disarmed His power.'"[1] Praise and glory to our King who has granted us the trophies in His royal procession, a place of honor where we share in His victory, becoming co-conquerors with Him.

What does it mean that you are being led in His triumph? How often during the day do you catch a glimpse of your Commander in Chief's victory sign before you? One of the names of God is Jehovah Nissi, the Lord is my Banner, who goes before you waving His ensign or standard, guiding you through the difficult obstacles you encounter. In ancient times a banner was a type of flag or a pole placed at the front of a military grouping. When the soldiers were fighting, they would look to see the king's sign held high. Such a glimpse would give them the confidence to continue in battle. How often in the day do you stretch your neck looking for His pole? To be led by Christ is to know that He alone is your strength, the One in whom you place your confidence when you can't see ahead. Following His lead is to rely wholly on Him and not your circumstances. When you look to Him, you're granted confidence that carries you onward.

When you see His banner, you're granted influence that carries you outward. In the Roman triumph, garlands of sweet-smelling flowers were scattered in the streets and placed on the temple doors, while fragrant odors of burning incense filled the air with a perfumed scent. As one of the recipients in Christ's procession, God works to manifest through you the sweet smelling aroma of His gospel, goodness, and the grace. How potent is your scent of Christ to God? How poignant is it to your friends and family? Perhaps the greatest challenge in being led in Christ's triumph is allowing yourself to be filled with His Spirit, thereby diffusing the fragrance of the knowledge of Christ. It was Paul who asked us to be odor conscious. Oh, that we would follow his example for "wherever he went, men knew Jesus better, and the loveliness of the Master's character became more apparent. Men became aware of a subtle fragrance, poured upon the air, which attracted them to the Man of Nazareth."[2]

> "But thanks be to God, who always leads us in His triumph in Christ, and manifests through us the sweet aroma of the knowledge of Him in every place. For we are a fragrance of Christ to God among those who are being saved and among those who are perishing."
>
> 2 Corinthians 2:14–15

33. I am Spiritually Circumcised

Maybe you're thinking what I'm thinking. "Lord, I'm grateful for all these entitlements this book says that I am: I am loved by God, I am a temple of the Holy Spirit, I am forgiven, I am enabled, I am favored, but spiritually circumcised? I'm not sure I want to be *that!*"

Circumcision was a symbolic act in the Old Testament initiated among the Jews before the establishment of an actual sanctuary. It functioned as a powerful image in the Old Testament. It was performed as a sign and seal of the covenant between God and Israel whereby God had selected His chosen people. He had given them a promise saying, "I will be God to you and to your descendants after you."[1] To circumcise meant to cut, and Jewish babies were cut on the eighth day after birth whereby they removed the male foreskin on the reproductive organ as a way to demonstrate their membership in the covenant community. It symbolized a need for cleansing if a holy God was to have His way in an unholy body. To be circumcised was an expression of purity and a statement of faith that God's promises given to Abraham would be practiced. Why the reproductive organ? Perhaps it served as a symbol of man's deepest need for cleansing. After all, it was *that part* that would reproduce another sinful life and propagate the Jewish race.

Generally speaking, people have come to understand that to circumcise means to cut back what's impure, to make clean. When you became a new creature in Christ, Paul says you were "circumcised with a circumcision made without hands, in the removal of the body of the flesh, by the circumcision on Christ."[2] Your sinful nature was cleansed, cut off, not by human hands but by the Cross of Christ. You've been spiritually circumcised from all unrighteousness. Your old self was crucified with Him with the bondage to sin and its penalty cut away. You emerged into new life. Now you are "the true circumcision, who worships in the Spirit of God and glory in Christ Jesus where you put no confidence in the flesh."[3] In the Old Testament, circumcision was a symbol of obedience and purifying oneself before God. In the New Testament, baptism serves the same ritual, an outward sign of the inward cleansing that took place at conversion. It's an outer testimony to 'cut away' from the old life, a picture of leaving behind in the baptismal waters all sinful affections and past sins, emerging into a new resurrected life of faithful obedience in Christ Jesus. Have you followed the Lord in believer's baptism? Those who desire to follow His commandments will be baptized.

Is that all God requires of us? He draws us to Him for spiritual circumcision, and then we become a member of a community called The Body of Christ. Is that all there is? You and I have both known people who say they are followers of Christ but exhibit no spiritual fruit; you certainly can't tell Christ lives in them by their speech. Their new redeemed nature still follows the flesh of their old ways. Could it be they need a circumcision of the tongue? God sees the problem, and He rushes straight for the heart.

Is your heart living in unity with your soul and mind? Do all three of them serve the Lord in union testifying of your abandoned promise to Him? "And you shall love the Lord with all your heart, soul, and mind."[4] Sin nullifies the benefits of circumcision. Moses scolded the people of Israel, "Circumcise then your heart, you stiff necked people."[5] And Jeremiah did the same, "Circumcise yourselves to the Lord and remove the foreskins of your heart."[6]

What excess skin needs to be cut away from your heart? The foreskin of a critical spirit or legalism, busyness or preoccupation with self? In the Bible, circumcision was often a test of loyalty or an expression to recommitment. God says those who turn to Him and humble themselves shall stand in the pathway of His blessings. Are you in His pathway?

> "The Lord your God will circumcise your heart and the heart
> of your descendents, to love the Lord your God with all your
> heart and soul in order that you may live."
>
> Deuteronomy 30:6

34. I am Crucified with Christ

My precious sister, Vicki, had breast cancer, and praise the Lord she survived. Another dear friend of mine, Gay Cunningham, my high school Sunday school teacher, called last week, "Can you add a prayer request to your prayer wall? I have breast cancer!" For me it was devastating news, but for Gay it was an opportunity to see God at work.

Cancer! For those who initially hear the news, it's an aggressive race to arrest its hostile take over by taking chemo or radiation, or whatever it requires to stop the disease. I've never known anyone with the announcement of cancer to ignore this inside fire. We know the statistics! We know its danger! We know the final chapter if we do nothing about it! It's real! It's alive! It promises to spread, and it promises to do one thing: kill! Yet how many of us realize we're infected with a disease much like cancer. Sin! If we ignore it, it, too, will infiltrate itself into every cell of our bodies. It's a cancer we all wrestle with on an ongoing basis; it guarantees a bleak destiny: destruction and murder to God's greater plan. The penalty for our sin (eternal damnation) and its power to overtake us was broken at the Cross, granting sin's power no longer preeminence in the believer's life. But it still has an open door to taint and terrorize with its relentless cravings. What lies beneath God's provision as we reckon ourselves nailed to the Cross with Christ?

Do you see yourself as a potentially very ill person? You should! If you saw yourself as a bedridden patient to the effects of sin's cancer, you'd more aggressively apply the chemo of sin's spread, which is to activate this principle: I am crucified with Christ. To identify with Christ on the Cross is to declare yourself dead to all the avenues you pursue in getting your needs met apart from God. It's to pronounce your lusts inactive to all the competing passions that fight for first place in your heart. To be *crucified* with Christ acknowledges its perfect verb tense in Scripture, a previous action that took place at the Cross, but also a current action that continues displaying effects. It's to say, "I have been crucified with Christ at the Cross and am now being crucified with Him over and over." Crucifixion is death to the sin of self, and to keep it dead requires 'keeping it crucified,' day by day, hour by hour, second by second.

Do you see yourself crucified to the lure of sin: gossip, lust, or the self-centered life? How does selfishness play out in your life? What does crucifixion to the self-life look like? It's first and foremost a will decision, a choice to surrender. It's to become one with Christ, to let go and trust God by delivering up all pride and pretense of impressing others. It's relinquishing all claims of what you think you deserve by yielding any disillusionment, crisis, or the need to control to Jesus. It's to sign your own death certificate! Notice your signature agreement:

- I am bought with a price. I'm not my own. "I have been crucified with Christ."[1] I have no claims to personal rights. They serve as a judgment against me.

- I choose to identify with Christ's death. Like Paul proclaimed, "Always carrying about in the body the dying Jesus that His life might be manifested in my body."[2] I usually think of Christ as *the living Jesus*. But how often do I consider *the dying Jesus*? To carry His dying is to willingly endure through suffering. "It is no longer I who lives, but Christ who lives within me."[3] It is to allow hardships the avenue of displaying the power of the living Christ. To carry suffering is to carry a badge of nobility.

- I let go of my intellectual reasoning and choose to believe by faith. "And the life I now live in the flesh, I live by faith in the Son of God, who loved me and delivered Himself up for me."[4] Faith is not a mustered up formula of beliefs put there by my efforts, but a faith put there by the Son of God, a faith that transcends inconceivable limits. You are crucified with Christ. How often do you consider yourself a walking dead person?

> "I have been crucified with Christ…"
>
> Galatians 2:20

35. I am A Citizen of Heaven

Immigration issues have become a hot topic all over the world. In 2006, America fought its own battle in the lawsuit of Duarnis Perez vs. U.S. Government.

In 1994, Mr. Perez was deported from the United States to the Dominican Republic. In 2000, he was captured trying to re-enter the U.S. from Canada. Perez served three and a half years in prison before it was discovered he was already a U.S. citizen. During preparation for his second deportation hearing, Perez found out his citizenship was secured at the age of fifteen when his mother was naturalized in 1988. Although he filed suit against the government, Assistant U.S. Attorney Sara Lord argued that Perez was at fault for *not knowing his status.*

Not knowing his status? This bizarre turn of events is reflective of the way many Christians live. With their citizenship in God's Kingdom secured, they live like illegal aliens incarcerated by sin. They refuse to exercise their resident benefits.[1] How about you? Do you know your status? Are you living like a citizen of heaven, enjoying its privileges? Or are you a foreigner estranged from the entitlements that come from being legalized with Christ?

Paul informed the Christians at Philippi about their status as believers. He called them citizens of heaven, reminding them of their temporary status *here* and their eternal state of glory *there.* What was it about Paul's analogy of heavenly citizenship that spoke directly to them causing their thoughts to turn to their earthly citizenship?

First-century Philippian Christians understood colonial life and lived with a high regard for their fellow brothers and sisters in Christ. Philippi was an outpost colony of Rome in Macedonia, and though they lived in that state, they were considered Roman citizens. Many inhabitants of the Philippian city had served over twenty years as soldiers, and though they were morsels of Rome, they never forgot to whom they belonged! They dressed like a Roman, spoke like a Roman, and behaved like a Roman.[2]

As a Christian how often do you see yourself as a colonist, a person living away from your *native land* forming a temporary new settlement *down here?* Do you speak like a heavenly citizen and behave like a heavenly citizen? Citizenship carries with it an aura of pride and responsibility in connection with your home country. At the age of seventeen, I was nominated for my high school's Best Citizenship Award. Its nomination represented a person who exemplified the praiseworthy ideals of the place in which I was an inhabitant, my alma mater. As a citizen of heaven, does my earthly reputation replicate the high standards of my heavenly alma mater? Does my conduct match my true citizenship status? How can I continually be reminded that, though I am an earthly dweller, my citizenship is elsewhere: heaven! Just like the commonwealth of believers at Philippi eagerly awaited Paul's instruction for citizenship training, I, too, as a twentieth-century settler, must seek the Spirit's training in sharpening my allegiance to my true home.

As a sojourner to my heavenly state, I've discovered one avenue that pumps fresh sustenance into my citizenship. It's living in an ongoing state of correspondence with God. Whether it be in a hushed prayer or a tender entry in my journal, escaping into the realities of heaven enhances a celestial awareness that I am where He is, and He is where I am. I recall a journal entry from 2004: *I long for Heaven, oh God, because that's where my treasures lie. I long for Heaven, oh God, because that's where my parents lie. I long for Heaven, oh God, because that's where You lie. I long for Heaven, oh God!*

Oh, the wonder of believers living in two places at once, having both a present assignment on earth and a heavenly status in heaven. Paul spoke of a number of spiritual truths as mysteries, but not in the sense that they couldn't be figured out or experienced, but a mystery in the fact that the unrevealed truth of all ages had come, Jesus Christ. In Him we are enabled to accept by faith even the most complex doctrines of our new identities with dual citizenship being one of them!

"For our citizenship is in heaven…"

Philippians 3:20

36. I am An Alien and a Stranger

Has anyone ever told you that you are weird? Good. Then they have just spoken the truth about your identity in Christ! My neighbor in Euless, Texas, who was not a follower of Jesus, confirmed this truth when she told another neighbor, "Pam just acts weird!" When news got back to me, I took it as a wonderful compliment!

When my children were young I bought them the Fisher Price toy where they'd pick up a triangle and try to find the hole that matched its shape. As a Christian living in this world, do you ever feel like a square piece trying to fit in a round hole? The world, whose ruler is Satan, tells you to look and act this way, and the Holy Spirit tells you to look and act that way? If that sounds familiar, then you have just witnessed the incompatibility and the irreconcilable differences between the flesh life and the Spirit life. God Himself testified to the struggle, warning that "His offspring would be aliens in a foreign land."[1]

My friend, simply said, "You're not home yet!" Why should you expect a pain-free life when God never promised you one *here*? Why should you be alarmed that life is such a struggle? The reason you are called an alien is not because you face trouble; everybody does. The reason God labeled you as an alien is because your response to hardship should be extraordinarily peculiar. You are not a member of *this* world's society. You are a citizen of God's society whose laws constitute a diversely opposite lifestyle, making you outlandishly unlike *this* world.

The Greek word for alien, *paroikous*, literally means alongside the house. The word denotes someone who lives in a country other than his own, a foreigner. As a Christian, you don't belong to this world's system, but live *alongside the house* of those who do.[2] I hope there is a stark difference! And you are a stranger! We tell our toddlers, "Watch out for strangers!" Yes, please do. They're 'God's kind!' They are much like a visitor traveling through a country without citizenship entitlement. That's who you are, a stranger, a pilgrim, a citizen of heaven "seeking the city which is yet to come."[3]

Jesus knows firsthand the journey through this life as an alien and stranger: He was one, too. Notice what He said:

John 18:36   My kingdom is not of *this* world.

John 15:19   If you belonged to *this* world it would love you, but you are not of *this* world and I have chosen you out of *this* world.

John 16:28   I came from the Father and have come into *this* world and I am leaving this world again and going to the Father.

John 15:18   If *this* world hates you, remember it hated Me.

John 16:33   In *this* world you will have trouble, but take courage, I have overcome *this* world.

John 17:11 Father, I am departing *this* world and leaving them behind. Keep them and care for them, all those you have given to Me, so they will be united just as we are.

John 17:14–19 Father, *this* world hates them because they do not belong to *this* world. I'm not asking you to take them out of *this* world but to keep them safe while in *this* world from the evil one. They are not a part of *this* world any more than I am. Make them pure and holy by teaching them words of truth. As you sent Me into *this* world, I am sending them into *this* world. And I give myself entirely to you so they also might be entirely yours.

And finally it is written that when Jesus returns "the kingdom of *this* world will become the Kingdom of our Lord God and of His Christ, and He will reign forever."[4] Hallelujah! You won't be weird long! The day is coming when the long rebellion of *this* world against God the Father and Jesus, His Son, will come to its climatic end. Aliens and strangers will become heavenly civilians, householders of mansions, and indwellers of God's physical glory!

So until then watch out for the ways of *this* world, and beware: don't let yourself get too cozy in it![5]

> "Beloved, I urge you as aliens and strangers to abstain from fleshly lusts, which wage war against the soul. Keep your behavior excellent among the Gentiles."
>
> 1 Peter 2:11–12

37. I am Assigned to the Age of Grace

I want you to elevate your thinking and join me in a panoramic view of the history of man from God's perspective. From the beginning of time until the end, God's plan for the timing of your visitation to planet earth has been uniquely calculated. A friend of mine portrayed the image like this: "Imagine standing on the fortieth floor of a high-rise building observing a parade. Oh, the joy to see the colorful floats and marching bands in its entirety. If only the oblivious clowns and the other parade participants could see the unique part they play in the entire procession."

From the inception of time, God laid out a timetable of specific eras in history that would each play its part in His parade of bringing Him glory, whose final float would crescendo into this: the second advent of Jesus Christ to the earth, whereby He would usher in His 1,000-year earthly reign as King of Kings. As a child of God, I find the privilege of being a partaker in His pageant simply astounding! But even more fascinating than being a participant is being an observer of all the other floats that came before me. It aids me in "flourishing in my float."

God's parade of history consists of seven distinctive eras of well-defined periods, all of them pointing to man's need for a savior. Each stage of time, called a dispensation, serves as a progressive revelation of God's plan in turning the heart of man toward Him. I'm riding on float number six, the dispensation of grace, and I've discovered that in order to flourish in my new identity in Christ, it's to my advantage to know what floats preceded me. Not to study the entire parade is to leave me short-sighted in my understanding as to why He's placed me in *this* particular time period.

Listed below are the seven eras of time. Before reading them, keep this in mind: each one has its own set of rules for that particular age and each one proved the same lesson—man's failure and incapability of living up to God's holy standards. Look what God's been doing from Genesis to Revelation:

1. *Dispensation of Innocence*—God creates man, giving him the responsibility of populating the earth. Man sinned. Catastrophic results ensued: spiritual separation from God.

2. *Dispensation of Conscience*—God gives Adam and Eve no detailed code to live by but required them to acknowledge their conscience in keeping with what they knew about God.

3. *Dispensation of Human Government*—God makes a covenant with Noah, establishing a new essence of government. Man failed under the new rule of life.

4. *Dispensation of Promise*—God makes a promise with Abraham and his heirs. This era's success did not depend on human faithfulness but God's. He would be their God.

5. *Dispensation of the Law*—God gives commandments and ordinances to Moses, establishing a righteous rule. Man could now keep the laws, thereby, defining the essence of sin.

6. *Dispensation of Grace*—God accomplishes atonement for sin through Christ's blood at the Cross bringing His followers into a new age of blessings unlike previous ages.

7. *Dispensation of the Kingdom*—God grants His Son, Jesus, divine rulership on earth for 1,000 years. At the end of that time, Jesus gives the kingdom back to God, thereby, entering eternity and the New Heaven and the New Earth.[1]

As you can see from viewing the entire parade, God is a God of purposeful planning, order, and sequence indeed, the One who has calendared every individual for every age. It is no accident that you are living in the Age of Grace. He has placed you here during this dispensation as a significant part in fulfilling His purpose: the calling out of a people who will glorify the name of Christ. The church forms the body of Christ, giving this age its distinct trademark of bringing to light Jesus Christ through the empowering of His Holy Spirit.

As a baton twirler in the parade, I take immense pleasure in marching to the beat of a redemptive Savior whose grace preserves me for not only now but for the next float, the age of Christ's return! Can you imagine riding on *that* one?

"We are not under the law but under grace."

Romans 6:15

38. I am Called Out

While sitting on the back patio, I pondered the life of the ant, his little world, so confined to the pathway from the anthill to the cracker on the porch. Can his minuscule brain comprehend the bigness of the turf he treads? I wanted to say, "There's more, little ant! There's the whole front yard, and the entire town, and don't faint, there's Japan and even other galaxies." Yet, his little world is all he knows. The reality is this: my view as a human, a giant to him, is higher than his. I can see the big picture while he's cramped in his own section of the grass. I often consider myself as the ant when I read Isaiah 55:9 that God's ways are higher than mine. It forces me to consider the bigness of my God who resides outside my section of grass. Can we even fathom the scope of our purpose beyond this brief season called time? Or are we so confined to our visible realm: waking up, going to work, and driving home, that we fail to awaken the invisible glories and realities of God's richer truths.

As mentioned in the previous entitlement we are participants of the eternal parade of God riding through this life, the dispensational Float of Grace. From God's view on the fortieth floor, what's the eternal reality of His church, the followers of Christ, beyond the realm of the here and now? Just why are they here? And what is God's purpose for each one individually and for the corporate body of Christ?

Ekklesia, translated church, means the "called-out ones," the body of free citizens, the redeemed called together by a herald. The Christian community was designated for the first time as the church, stemming from a differentiation from the Jewish community who rejected The Messiah.[1] So who are you in your new identity? *You are the called out one*, and Christ resounds, "Come hither! You, march forth as the Church of the Living God!"

So what is the purpose of the corporate body of Christ in this age? Is it to make peace with the world or convert all the nations to Christianity? The divine purpose from God's fortieth floor is this: to call out those who will form His body as a witness of Christ's grace. Yes, you should seek peace and evangelize, but the higher purpose from God's everlasting view is 'the calling out' of Christ's followers, His Bride. And for what reason are you summoned forth?

You are called out as a witness to this present generation. Your purpose is two-fold: soul winning and then making disciples of the nations. Jesus said, "Go into all the world and preach the gospel to all creations."[2] What is your part of the world? Joe's Diner? The Coca Cola Company where you're employed? You've been *called out* that you might *call out*! You're a transmitter of the Gospel, one infectious with the living message of Christ. God's seed of salvation is sown on the soil of men's hearts through you. In every dispensation God has preordained a unique purpose, and seed sowing defines this one. When you pray for others to come to Christ and they do, you thrust laborers into the harvest. And don't forget your other commission: "So encourage one another day after day, as long as it is still called today."[3] Consoling and comforting strengthens the body to once again *call out* to those in need of Christ.

You are called out as a witness to the heavenly host. God is now making known His wisdom to the angelic hosts. In you, they see the manifold power of God, manifold power that abounds in multifarious ways.[4] God works to make a spectacle out of you, showing what His grace can do. "The heavens are telling of the glory of God, and their expanse is declaring the work of His hands."[5] The angels bring glory to Him, and the *called-out ones*, the redeemed of God, simply enrich their praise.

You are called out as a witness to all eternity. God calls you out now "in order that in the ages to come He might show the surpassing riches of His grace."[6] The called out ones will forever be a portrait of God's goodness through the grace of Jesus Christ. The whole heaven will glorify God because of what He has done through Christ. It is, indeed, an exhibition worthy of praise that God could take sinful man and bring glory to Himself through the saints' redeemed natures! Hallelujah! We are the *Called-Out Ones*!

"And you are the church (called-out ones) of the Living God."

1 Timothy 3:14

39. I am A Member of the Body of Christ

I asked a group of friends last week to give me a one word synonym for the word Christian. I heard the words 'follower' and 'saint,' but no one said 'member!' Friends, isn't it amazing how we've overlooked the best part of being a new creature? We're family! You are a member of Christ's community, weaved together in the bond of fellowship by the golden thread of redemption.

When you received Christ as your Savior, the Holy Spirit instantaneously baptized or placed you into the body of Christ, that living union of all believers in this present age. The *body* is a description of a group of members in Christ referring to either a local congregation or to the universal church. Regardless of race, culture, or church affiliation, if you've yielded the control of your life to Christ, then you are spiritually initiated into and become a distinct part of His worldwide and local community of followers. Together you function as *one* living organism with Jesus Christ as the Head, celebrating the oneness created by the initial baptism of the Spirit. In this chosen race of believers, God brings together His celebration of *oneness:* there is "*one* body, *one* Spirit, just as also you were called in *one* hope for *one* calling, *one* Lord, *one* faith, *one* baptism, *one* God and Father of all who is over all and through all and in all."[1] The foundation for unity is *one* body in whom everyone is a member, *one* Spirit in whom everyone is indwelt, and *one* hope in whom everyone is rewarded eternal life.

I remember the first time I understood the benefits of membership. I walked the second grade halls wearing an odd-shaped apparel on my head: a Brownie hat. We clumped together at lunch enjoying the friendship of our newfound club. Certainly membership in an organization bestows a variety of fine benefits: a sense of belonging, a connection of like-mindedness, a common purpose promoting unity, acceptance, personal growth, and diversity. Some of those qualities come to life in a couples' group of intimate friends my husband, Rich, and I fellowship with every Monday night. I love them immensely! We're "The Monday Night Group." As members of Christ's family, we connect on a deeper level of honesty, Christ-centered love, and a commitment to pray for each other, our nineteen children, and eight grandchildren. We laugh; we cry, and sometimes we change our name from 'The Monday Night Group' to 'The Moaning Night Group.' Life is hard! We need encouragement. Like Diane, one of the members, cited, "We're foxhole friends!" When you're in the ditch, you need company! Amen? Friends, you are a community in Christ's body. If you can't find a small group, start one!

Membership! It's an astounding privilege, indeed! Never in God's history before the church age have His people been given the privileges of sonship. Yet, through the Cross of Christ, you have a unique one-on-one relationship with God unlike any other dispensation of time. For example, in the Old Testament His beloved Israel only related to Him through their high priest, but you relate to Him as an adopted son and daughter through the Agent of Connection He's granted to make that possible: the Holy Spirit. Praise God. You're family with God, having been given an exalted position as a joint heir with His Son!

And membership grants another benefit! Upon placement into His body, God gave you a function and a gift that would serve as a useful part in edifying His church. Like an orchestra contains diverse instruments forming a concerto, your giftedness is crucial in accomplishing God's plan for that particular body. You're indescribably significant! 1 Corinthians 12 uses a metaphor of the physical body in defining your giftedness as a hand or an eye, an indispensable unit in bringing beauty to the whole. Friend, you might be the leg! So shake it, and use it for His glory!

And who is the head of this body? Jesus Christ! I recall seeing at carnivals comical cardboard characters with the head cut out, just beckoning me to place my head in the hole. I wonder, if someone took my picture with Christ as the head, would my actions, language, and disposition compliment the character or make a hilarious statement?

You are a member of His body: significant and choice!

"Now you are the body of Christ and members individually."

1 Corinthians 12:27

Chapter Seven

My Significance

How does God see me?

40. I am God's Delight

Smelly, dumped, and left for dead on the side of the road, cast out as the scum of the earth, that's what *she* was all right. At least that's the way the Lord found her. My heart coils with repulsive sadness and at the same time it cries in speechless amazement at a God whose impassioned love poured itself out on His first love, the nation of Israel.

My friend, no other chapter in God's Word sickens my heart more than Ezekiel 16, the allegorical portrait of a provocative God who knew no bounds in lavishing His most exorbitant goodness on His sought-out lover, Israel. He found her as a helpless baby girl, without care, destined to a life of sordid rubbish. Out of His compassion for her feebleness, He rescued her, brought her into His palace as a queen, bestowing on her His most luxurious favors: coddling, raising, demonstrating His endless fidelity, even marrying her. It's a true fairytale story like none other. I wish the story ended there, happily ever after, because no one likes a broken heart, especially if it's God's.

Why would Israel turn from God and exchange her possessions of generosity for the fleeting cheap trinkets of this world? Yet that's what Israel did. She betrayed her loyalty to God becoming a whore to other nations, and in His fury He pronounced, "You made the beauty I gave you abominable and you spread your legs to every passer-by to multiply your harlotry making me angry; you bold-faced harlot! I will stretch forth my hand against you."[1]

I often wonder as a person who has been given a second chance with God by the sacrifice of His Son, do I ever forsake my devotion to God putting the cares of this world above my adoration for Him? Does God ever catch me off guard, adulterating my affections for the treasures and pleasures of the world? I'm afraid He does; yet in His goodness afforded me though Christ, I've been granted ongoing opportunities for a restored recommitment to Him through confession and obedience. Even when I'm faithless, He is faithful. I'm grateful that through repentance I receive a daily cleansing of all my wrongdoings. Such a refining allows God the opportunity to affirm His unconditional love for me, as one day He will ultimately reign in His covenant of grace with Israel. Make no mistake in knowing this: He loves you with such purity and magnitude that it's beyond our comprehension or reason. In you He is outrageously delighted! You unmistakably enchant His heart! Do you really believe that?

It was April of 2005 when God's magnificent obsession whispered sweet words of affirmation to me. I was visiting my precious niece, Amy, in London. My sister, Vicki, and I stood like wide-eyed tourists as we visited The Crown Jewels, the building that housed the crowns, scepters, swords, and additional artifacts worn by The Sovereign of the United Kingdom during the coronation ceremonies of the past centuries. Exceptionally dazzling, without a proper vocabulary to describe it, lay The Imperial Crown of India. Such magnificence; indeed, the heaviest crown in the collection with over 6,000 diamonds! As my mouth gaped open in response to its exquisiteness, I felt the Lord softly nudge, "Pam, that crown of radiance fails in comparison to how scintillating you are to me! Because Christ dwells within, you outdazzle, outshine, and outvalue all these exquisite vestments combined. These diamonds and jewels will perish, but your beauty will sparkle with me throughout all eternity." And did He not say the same thing through Isaiah: "And you will be a crown of beauty in the hand of the Lord, a royal diadem!"[2] It's true; a crown is meant to be worn on the head, but He was saying you have been secured in His hand, that supreme shelter of care and protection. You are *regal dignity* in the hand of the Lord, His select crown of glory, and your outward expression of the character of Christ makes you even more lustrous than the Imperial Crown of India. Isaiah concludes in speaking the words of God: "No longer will people call you 'Forsaken or Desolate' for *all my delight is in you!*"[3]

I'm sure you've heard the saying, "Life is not all about you." Well, guess what? To God it is!

> "Behold, My Servant, whom I uphold; My chosen one in whom My soul delights."
>
> Isaiah 42:1

41. I am Adequate

It was early in the history of Israel's judges that a poor farmer found himself abandoned in a forsaken winepress threshing wheat. Fear of being discovered by his enemies and having his crop stolen had forced him into seclusion. Gideon quaked in his sandals, praying he could finish his labor undetected.

Suddenly a light illuminated the entire cavern. A voice announced, "The Lord is with you, O valiant warrior."[1] Gideon glanced around, questioning, "Valiant warrior? Me? The man who lives so petrified he has to hide in obscurity from his enemies?" The angel's voice revealed Gideon's purpose in being chosen by God to deliver His people out of the hands of the Midianites. Gideon's response echoed from a soul trapped in inadequacy, "Why me? I'm the weakest of my family." Yet the Lord reassured him, "I will be with you."

Therein lays the secret to overcoming inadequacy. We are adequate because God is *in* us and *with* us. By His almighty power He has declared it so. If we look around (by comparing) instead of within (by recognizing who lives inside), we instantaneously minimize our ability of seeing our God-empowered potential. No other lie of Satan has more effectively crippled the body of Christ than this one: you are inadequate. Its voice whispers in the reservoirs of our minds making us feel inept, defective, and imperfect for the task. When you follow these thoughts, you'll quickly drown amidst insignificance because someone else will always appear more popular in their social life, more glamorous in their physical life, and more holy in their spiritual life. But God has placed His sufficiency in your heart, anticipating what you will become as you exercise faith.

Throughout Gideon's adventures to free Israel, he continued to doubt himself and his abilities, but God accomplished His plan, not with 32,000 men or 10,000 warriors, but with an army that numbered only 300! God's presence in your battle or task will always place you on the victory stand. His promise in Job 23:14 brings assurance that He will perform what is appointed for you. If He assigns a work, then He's obligated to see it through to completion. That's why we can never boast or become prideful of any noble work. We are totally incompetent of doing anything apart from Him and only competent because He displays His attributes through us. That's why Paul could profess in Philippians 4:13 that "I can do all things through Christ who strengthens me." Paul was weak and it was through his limitations that God proved Himself strong. For that reason, Paul discredited his ability to rightly judge the truth of God or perform any acceptable act apart from God's divine revelation and intervention.

From the beginning, Gideon's awareness of his shortcomings became perfect fodder for the demonstration of God's strength. It was through God's empowerment that a lowly young Israelite stepped out of his hiding place, subdued his enemies allowing his countrymen to live in peace for forty years. It was Gideon who saw his unlikely success through self-doubt, but it was God who saw his unlimited capabilities through divine enablement.

Like Gideon, you've been completely qualified to perform any service of God. His strength has been placed in you through Christ that you might dismantle the devil's craftiness, exhibit confidence during your greatest fears, accomplish tasks you never thought possible, and all the while publish to the world what God can do through a soul fully yielded to Him.

It was God who called Gideon to step out of his comfort zone and exercise His might. What has God asked you to do? You are adequate for the mission. So come out of your forsaken winepress and respond to God's invitation. The Lord is with you, O Valiant Warrior!

> "Not that we are adequate in ourselves to consider anything as coming from ourselves, but our adequacy is from God."
>
> 2 Corinthians 3:5

42. I am Confident

It was the early 1980s when she encountered the most profound shopping trip of her life. Just one more errand and she would be on her way home. Scurrying to her car as she left K-Mart, she reached for her keys and unexpectedly felt a sharp jab in the side of her back. As she turned, her greatest fear became a ghastly reality. There he stood: the greasy headed, serial killer whose wanted posters clearly revealed his identity. What ensued was a nationally publicized kidnapping that riveted the nation of a woman who knew who she was in Christ. It's the story of Margy Palm, and I had the privilege of interviewing her for the television series "Heroes of the Faith with Peter Pam." For ten hours she faced an invisible spiritual war, a stand-off between the forces of darkness and the forces of light, fighting not only for her own life, but the eternal life of her killer. After telling him about God's love, her kidnapper eventually not only received Christ but turned himself over to the police.

Who of us has not experienced fear to one degree or another? It comes so naturally! We don't have to work hard at being afraid. Fear is that emotional foreboding or dread of impending danger or risk that promotes paranoia, or clouds our judgment, or cripples our ability to fully rely on God. A person fears when he faces people or circumstances that have the ability to control us, or even in the most severe case like Margy, murder us, for goodness' sake! Maybe you haven't been kidnapped by a serial killer, but you are experiencing right now financial fear, or the well-being of my child fear, or what am I going to do fear.

Where is God in your fear? Listen, friend, He's wherever you want Him to be. He's actually *in* your fear, waiting for you to call on His mighty name so He might emerge as your Rescuer and Redeemer. Jesus, by His sacrificial death, is the liberator of fear and He bestows His supernatural peace so that you can relax in His strength. He promised in Isaiah 26:3, "I will give him perfect peace whose mind is fixed on Thee because He trusts in Me." Perfect peace: it's an expression whose Hebrew translation means *shalom*–"tranquil contentment."[1] How is it that a criminal can be positioned in your backseat, yet the tranquil contentment of God resides in the front seat? How is it that one's confidence in the trustworthiness of God's character can overpower even the most threatening foes? Either Margy was half crazy or totally compelled by the Spirit to trust Him because at one point he had her enter a convenience store, buy beer, cigarettes, and a newspaper and return to the car. I asked her, "Why didn't you signal for help once inside the store?" Her response, "God wanted me to bring him to Christ." It is possible to take off your fear and put on your confidence in God. As a follower of Christ, you have right now all you need to cast out that fear! How do you break the bondage of being afraid and find release?

When crouched down in the front seat of her car with his gun secured in her back, she quoted the Word of God: "Greater is He who is in me than He who is in the world."[2] At that moment, she had a choice to make. Either she would run from what God was compelling her to do, or she would step forward and put her life on the line and trust Him. In the midst of her most trifling fear, the Holy Spirit reminded her that in Him she had supernatural courage. At that moment, she released her life to the Lord, turned to her killer, laid hands on his head, and commanded the demon of murder to come out of him in Jesus' name. It's true: when you speak God's Word into your crisis, you set in motion the enemy to flee and the power of God to perform His work.

Margy's story serves as a courageous testimony in God's gallery of the Heroes Hall of Fame. Why do we live like spiritual midgets when God has given us His boldness to live like spiritual giants? Any spirit of timidity or apprehensive cowardice does not originate from God. Through Jesus, we have the same power that raised Christ from the dead. I ponder the most thought-provoking question of Adrian Rogers, "Why are we so inhibited, when we are so inhabited?"[3]

> "For the Lord will be your confidence, and He will keep your
> foot from being caught."
>
> Proverbs 3:26

43. I am Inseparable from God's Love

I love the Apostle Peter. Maybe it's because I can identify with his weaknesses. Peter: he struggled over the issue of forgiveness; he failed to watch and pray for Jesus in his most excruciating hour before the crucifixion; he cut off the ear of Malchus, the high priest, in a moment of uncontrollable anger. And most humiliating of all, Peter denied he ever knew the Savior. Why does it sometimes feel good when we see that the champions of our Christian faith act like infants? Perhaps it's because it affirms the possibility that there's still hope for us, that God overlooks the pitiful smallness of our own flesh and sees the bigness of our desire to be more yielded to Him. Peter, he's a man just like you and me. Perhaps it was in reminiscing over his life with Christ and desiring to leave a legacy of inspiration that he wrote a final letter to his friends in Asia Minor. He knew his death was very soon. And what was his motivation during his final days? "And I consider it right, as long as I am in this earthly dwelling to stir you up by way of reminder"[1] of life's most vital priority: staying close to the Master, and staying close to Jesus He did. Tradition has it that Peter was crucified upside down for His love for Christ, but I somehow believe that it wasn't so much that He stayed close to the Master, but that the Master stayed close to him.

How about you? Can you identify with Peter? What are your greatest life mess ups, ones you'd never want published on the front page of the Sunday paper? Who hasn't felt ashamed over sin or remorsefully unworthy of God's love? Such times make us feel dreadfully separated from God. But the celebrated truth beyond our own capacity to understand is this: you might feel disgracefully disappointed in yourself, or estranged from God, but nothing can dislodge God's love from you. In fact, He wants you to know personally His love. You might lose your grip on God, but it's impossible for Him to lose His grip on you.

In Romans 8:35–37, Paul explores every possible reason that might motivate God to *drop you in the dust*. He poses this question: can *anything* come between you and Christ's love? Is there ever a situation where Christ will abandon your presence? What in this created universe can thwart God's decree of security for His own? Will emotional stress blockade God's love connection to you? Can hardships or times when you feel trapped leave you without hope? Will afflictions suffered for the sake of Christ spoil God's plan? Did the martyrs of your faith feel a loss of God's love when they starved to death, or will you feel the absence of His love when you're starving for a need to be met? Will the nakedness of circumstances when you feel completely vulnerable leave you without God's covering? During grave danger or unwanted mistreatment will God's defense break down? Or if you're put to death by a sword or murdered by someone's remarks, will Christ's comfort be discarded? Can the enemy steal God's presence through death, or will the disappointments of daily living leave you unaccompanied by His righteous right hand? Will the spiritual forces that rule the nations and bring opposition to God's people dismantle your security? Can powers beyond your control hurl you into a state of helplessness? Or when the present things of this world come crashing in upon you, are you without His aid? Nothing as high as the farthest star or deep as the ocean floor can separate you from God's indissolvable covenant to never leave or forsake you.

What are you facing today concerning your belief that God is not there for you? Can you say like Timothy, "For I know whom I have believed, and I am convinced that He is able to guard what I have entrusted to Him until I see Him."[2] Like the Apostle Peter, we, too, must confess our sins to God and make the choice for the rest of our lives to stay close to the Master, knowing nothing can disconnect us from Jehovah-Ahavah, the God of love. Such a portrait of indivisible devotion reminds me of a precious little dog.

Near Greyfriars churchyard in Edinburgh, Scotland, there stands a memorial fountain and statue to a little dog named Greyfriars Bobby. A man was buried in the churchyard in 1858. His dog for the next five years until his own death virtually lived on top of the tomb day and night. The little Skye Terrier left the site for only an hour at a time to visit his two friends and the restaurateur who fed him. Strangely enough, on Saturdays, he would wait for an extra dinner. On Sundays he never left His Master's tomb. Thousands visited the yard to see this faithful little dog. In tribute to his lifelong loyalty and devotion, they buried him beside his master.[3]

Love! It's an inseparable force!

"Who shall separate us from the love of Christ? Shall tribulation, distress, persecution, famine, nakedness, peril or sword? For I am convinced that neither death, nor life, nor angels, nor principalities, nor things present, nor things to come, nor powers, nor height, nor depth, nor any other created thing, shall be able to separate us from the love of God, which is in Christ Jesus our Lord."

Romans 8:35, 37

44. I am A Friend of God

In the Bible numerous figures are used as an illustration revealing the relationship between Christ and His church: Shepherd to sheep, Vine to branch, Cornerstone to living stones, Head of the Church to the body, and the Last Adam to the church as His new creation. But there's one that's indescribably precious, one that finds me incapable of even comprehending, one that dashes right to the heart of Jesus' love for you and me: friend to friend!

I agree with David in Psalm 8, "When I consider the Heavens, the work of your fingers, the moon and the stars, who am I that you would give thought of me?" How could it be that the Creator of the universe desires a warm friendship with His very creation, the infinite God to His finite creation? He entered earth as the Savior of the World, the Suffering Servant, the Son of Man and will return to Earth as the Victorious Warrior, the Ruler of Nations, and The Judge of the Living and the Dead. And *He* wants to be *my* friend? Yet don't forget: He came to this earth as a baby so that His humanity would appeal to you as a friend!

What does it mean to be called Christ's friend? In the first century the disciples of a rabbi were considered servants. But Jesus repainted the picture calling them friends. They would no longer be objects of slavery but recipients of the divine revelations from His Father. In the Roman world the word for friend meant "a friend at court."[1] Anyone who was called a "friend of Caesar" held an honored position in the palace, one of trusted favoritism and privacy. To be a friend meant you were placed in the inner circle privileged with the king's secrets. And Jesus assented, "I do not call you servants any longer, because the servant does not know what the Master is doing; but I have called you friends."[2]

What does it look like to be a friend to Christ? We know how to be a friend to our earthly friends. But how do you befriend a friend who is physically not here? As our High Priest Friend, Jesus is in heaven right now interceding for us that our friendship might grow strong and robust through the enabling work of the Holy Spirit. Jesus told us how to be His friend on earth and gave us the umbilical cord of the Holy Spirit to perform it.

To be Jesus' friend is to follow His commandments. John 15:14–"*You are my friends if you follow my commandments.*" Real friendship demands a face-to-face interaction with Christ. Jesus commanded us to talk to Him. Prayer is a commandment equaled in importance to other commands of God like "Thy shalt not steal."[3] Of course, you wouldn't do *that?* But do you pray? Prayer is friendship with God. The degree of your desire to know Him through prayer is the degree of your friendship. You show me a believer that has a weak prayer life, and I'll show you a believer that has a weak friendship with God. John Mark said, "The longest journey is the journey inward."[4] How true that is! Prayer is time consuming, sometimes not convenient, and often hard! But it's the yeast in your friendship.

To be Jesus' friend is to abandon your self-life for His-life. In John 15:13 Jesus said, "*Greater love hath no man than this, than to lay down one's life for his friends.*" Jesus knows about laying down a life, and He asks you to reciprocate. Christ doesn't ask you to die for Him but to live for Him in an abandoned fellowship. Such a comradery snuffs out all other competing affections that emerge from self-pleasure and selfish ambition. How intentional are you about being Christ's friend? What do you think about first thing in the morning? That's the litmus test of separating Christ's casual acquaintances from His intimate friends. Abandonment is simple; it's a crisis of the will.

Your friendship to Jesus Christ and His friendship to you is a covenant commitment to unity, portrayed best as one spirit living in two souls. It's characterized by intense loyalty and honesty, one whose transparent nature induces into the partnership a spiritual fervor and vision that launches no impossible missions. It's a humbling responsibility being Christ's friend. Just think. You carry His honor, and He carries yours.

"You are my friend."

John 15:13

45. I am Free From Condemnation

What a glorious truth we can all embrace! Who among us has not found ourselves in a situation where we have felt criticized, rebuked, renounced, shamed, or even damned! That profound sense of disapproval and blame havocs devastation not only in the silent hush of our own souls, but in the very core of our personhood! To have adverse judgment slapped on us is not a rejection easily erased! It sticks like Velcro to Velcro! Since the desire for approval is one of our basic needs as humans, condemnation's poisonous sting pierces deep.

Criticism! It hurts! There's no pretending! It comes in various forms: neglect, the silent treatment, tactless words, verbal abuse, ridicule, and even the truth spoken can cause condemnation. It hurts because we desire others to treat us the way we want to be treated. We have expectations of how people should respond to us, and when they don't meet our standards, we get our feelings hurt. Whether the assault is verbal or nonverbal, the blow to our self-esteem brings a severe sense of loss, sadness, and sometimes anger! I can't help but recall the day Mary, the

sister of Martha and Lazarus, received her own back lashing! She wants
to tell you her story:

It was six days before the Passover in Jerusalem and Simon the
Pharisee was having a feast. All the big shots of town would be
there: Lazarus, my brother whom Jesus had raised miraculously
from the dead, Judas, the other disciples, and even Jesus! It was
a party of all men, except for Martha, my sister. She had been
asked to cook in the kitchen. Some things never change! This
would be my last chance to see Jesus. The riots in the town
market were escalating. The chief priests and the elders of the
people were gathered together with Caiaphas in a plot to kill
Him. I knew the sense of doom and felt His death drawing
near! I had to find Him and express my love. He'd raised my
brother from the dead, delivered my own life from devastating
promiscuous sin, and befriended my family. I just had to find
a way to get into Simon's house. All I wanted to do was praise
and worship my beloved Jesus one last time. So I crept in the
house and crawled up behind Jesus, and when I got to His feet,
I began weeping out of sheer joy and remorse. What were they
going to do to Jesus? And what could I give to Him for all he
had done for me? "I know," I thought. "I'd give Him my entire
bottle of perfume, the most treasured possession I own, the
ointment I would use to anoint His body." So with tears and
adulation I poured the perfume over His feet. As I was swishing
His feet with my hair, I heard Judas snidely remark, "Why
hasn't that perfume been sold to the poor?" And Simon, the
arrogant, joined in, "If this man Jesus was a prophet, he'd know
what kind of woman was touching him." Oh, I know criticism.
I know the arrows of disdain, repulsion, and humiliation. But
I didn't care. Nothing would stop me from loving my Savior.

> And then Jesus stood up, defended me, and renounced, "Leave
> her alone. Quit bothering her!"

In just a matter of hours Jesus would yield His life at the Cross. Mary would treasure for the rest of her days that gallant, yet self-effacing moment at His feet. Little did she know that for all eternity to come such a modest presentation of her affection for Jesus would ripple into the hearts of all the Jesus lovers to come?

What can we learn from Mary when hurtful words and reproaches come our way? We can exercise extravagant worship; it takes the edge off of insult. We can know that self-giving sacrifice yields a high return in obtaining personal honor from Christ. We can remember that the people God infuses with His glory understand cost, and we can be comforted that the kind of worship that pleases God comes from a forsaken heart.

When Jesus died on the Cross for you, all judgment was removed: past, present, and future. Christ, who knew no sin, became your sin on the Cross in order to negate any form of belittlement that either you or others would place on yourself. God graciously extended a pardon from all incriminating fault and shame through Christ's resurrection. There is now and never will be any indictment of condemnation against you for, indeed, "If God is for us, who can be against us?"[1]

You have passed from accusation to acceptance, blame to belonging, disapproval to approval, judgment to justification, harassment to honor, disgrace to grace. Hallelujah! "It's for freedom that Christ set you free!"[2]

> "Therefore, there is no condemnation for those in Christ."
>
> Romans 8:28

46. I am His

I remember what God gave me a few years ago on Valentine's Day. As I was thumbing through the sack of little heart candies reading their inscriptions, I found one that was simply too delicious to eat. Its painted words jumped off the heart into mine: *I'm His*. Oh, such potent and poignant little words! What an endearing reminder to whom I belong! What does it mean for you to know that Jesus is yours and you are His? How does your silent communion of kindredship surface when you least expect it?

I can't help but recall an image I saw at the zoo not long ago reflecting such a union. A husky ol' gorilla cuddled his baby in his arm, perfectly snuggled in the crease of his elbow! All I could see was an itty-bitty gorilla head, tucked away in the gorilla-down comfort of his parent. I could hear the baby's lullaby as he gazed at me through the glass - "He is mine and I am his."

Every morning before I start my day, I nestle in the goose-down arms of Jesus. I meet with Him in a quiet bubble of adoration and meditation. Who knows what my day will hold? If inconveniences come my way, it's okay: I am His. If disappointment comes my way, it's okay: I am His. If a crisis comes my way, it's okay: I am His. Do you know who your "His" is? I do! For years I have searched for titles and images that bring to light the person of Christ. When I find one, I add the name to my alphabetized list in the back of my Bible. Before I roll out of bed, I often run through my memorized registry of over 100 titles and ask the Holy Spirit to enthrone each name over my day. I'm elated to announce to the world: "He is mine and I am His!" May I share a portion of my list of who my "His" is?

My "His" is an *Advocate*. 1 John 2:1- *"We have an advocate with the Father."* Jesus pleads my cause before God in a spirit of intercession through the Holy Spirit. He prays.

My "His" is the *Carpenter*. Mark 6:3- *"Is this not the carpenter, the son of Mary?"* When my life needs a lift, Jesus rebuilds my walls of faith and supplies the materials I need. He repairs.

My "His" is a *Diadem of Beauty*. Isaiah 28:5- *"...the Lord be...a diadem of beauty, unto the residue of His people."* The radiance of Christ's elegance continually fills me with His joy. He beautifies.

My "His" is the *First-born from the Dead*. Colossians 1:18- *"He is the first-born from the dead."* He was the first to rise in an immortal body and today reigns victoriously. He lives.

My "His" is a *Guardian and Bishop*. 1 Peter 2:25- *"He is the Guardian and Bishop of my soul."* Jesus allows, protects, and accomplishes His plan for my benefit and His glory. He oversees.

My "His" is the *Apostle and High Priest of our Confession*. Hebrews 3:1- *"Consider Jesus, the Apostle and High Priest of our confession."* He intercedes for us before God. He represents.

My "His" is the *Lifter of my Head*. Psalms 3:3- *"But Thou art the One who lifts my Head."* When I am emotionally discouraged and physically empty, He rekindles promised hope. He consoles.

My "His" is the *Lord of the Harvest*. Matthew 9:38- *"Beseech the Lord of the Harvest."* Christ is not a reluctant giver but a bountiful blesser. He's ready to yield a healthy crop. He bestows.

My "His" is the *Potter*. Isaiah 64:8- *"We are the clay; He is the potter."* I can accept the pressure of His hand in allowing sorrow. Through suffering, I become like Christ. He shapes.

My "His" is a *River of Water in a Dry Place.* Isaiah 32:1, 2-"*A King will reign...be like a stream of water in a dry country.*" When spiritually parched, He quenches my thirst. He revitalizes.

My "His" is a *Scepter.* Numbers 24:17-"*A Scepter shall rise out of Israel.*" Jesus is the sovereign rod of imperial power that accomplishes His predetermined good plan for me. He conquers.

My "His" is the *Tender Grass.* 2 Samuel 23:4-"*...the tender grass springs out of the earth.*" Like sheep feed on the grass for refreshment, I feed on His presence and the grass of His Holy Word. He satisfies.

My "His" is the *Wall of Fire.* Zechariah 2:5-"*For I,*" *declares the Lord,* "*will be a wall of fire around her.*" Jesus is my defense. I call on Him, and no foe will prevail against me. He barricades.

Begin today a sacred "His-Is" list of your own. It will become one of your favorite Bible Study discoveries.

> And Jesus said, "Father, keep them safe, all of those you have given to Me."
>
> John 17:11

47. I am An Expression of the Love of Christ

Jesus Christ was the only perfect man to ever walk the face of the earth, and He alone received the accolades of God His Father. For it was God who declared that Christ would be His firstborn, the One who would reign in heaven as the Ruler of the Kings in earth. It was Jesus, the Faithful Witness, who embodied the untarnished nature of God. It was Jesus who lived the flawless will of God. It was Jesus who verbalized the divine passion of God. And it was *this* Jesus who came into your heart at salvation, indeed, an embodiment of His own essence granting you His royal blessing of grace.

Whatever Jesus was in nature, God put in you. If Jesus was gracious, then so are you. If Jesus was loving, then so are you. You carry the very life of Christ. In fact, Paul told the Corinthians that the life of Jesus was manifested in his own body. Therefore, he could say, "For me, living is for Christ and dying is even better."[1] That being the case, our lives should mirror one image, the life of Christ. We are an expression of Him, a manifestation that comes forth from our own redeemed natures.

While many of us don't see ourselves as imitators of Jesus, we often see it performed in someone else. I know a woman over ninety years of age that serves as the supreme example of one whose life mirrors the reflection of Christ. She is an esteemed example of one deserving the crown, "I am an Expression of the Love of Christ."

Joy Jefferies is not just any ordinary ninety-one-year-old lady. She is a sublime ornament of grace in the prestigious hall of fame of the "Most Godly Women Alive." To know Joy is know Jesus Christ. To see Joy is to see Jesus Christ. To love Joy is to love Jesus Christ. I had the opportunity to have Joy in my home, as well as interview her on my radio broadcast. Her baby son, Rich, and his precious wife, Cindy, are two of my favorite friends.

It was December of 1990, when Joy received the call that her daughter, Marilyn, had been murdered by her own husband. This wasn't just another story capturing local news. Its gruesome conspiracy found its vile plot splashed on the front cover of American magazines, as well as a national movie recreating the violent act of one man's most decadent nature. Marilyn's husband had taken a business trip out of town, all serving as a comfortable alibi for him to fly home between meetings, shoot and strangle her, and then return to Washington to carry on "life as usual."

To see Joy is to see the genuine manifestation of Christ, a woman who lives not according to what life has done to her, but according to how she can use life's tragedies as a vehicle to magnify the power of her inborn Living God. It was the spring of the following year when Joy was taking communion that she knew she could not partake in the Lord's Supper without genuinely forgiving the man in whom she'd entrusted her daughter's hand in marriage. And genuinely forgive him she did. For years she wrote back and forth to him in prison encouraging him to make a difference for Christ in the lives of his fellow inmates. It was Joy who wrote to the dean of the prison endorsing his request to treat other patients medically.

To observe Joy is to observe a woman who will fight the good fight to the very end. At ninety years old, it is Joy who approached the founder of the juvenile detention center asking permission to bring encouragement to teenage boys. Always having a positive word about everyone, she tells Cindy, her daughter-in-law, "Those are just such precious little boys. I don't know why they're in jail!"

Joy possesses what every follower in Christ received at conversion: a new lifestyle that through Christ's power can rise above the mundane, the mistreatings, and even murder. She lives: "For me to live is Christ, and to die is gain."[1]

Joy's "gain" knocked on her heart's door on March 1, 2007. People waited three hours outside the viewing hall just to pay respects to the image of God's glory that she left behind. To imagine Joy now is to envision her in the arms of her husband; her daughter, Marilyn; and the One she most emulated, her Jesus.

> "When Christ who is our life is revealed, then you also will be revealed with Him in glory."
>
> Colossians 3:4

48. I am Valued

My two and three-year-old, Jason and Sara, were playing in the backyard. I was washing dishes at the sink when my former husband walked
through the garage door and announced he didn't love me anymore.
Time stood still in that kitchen at 803 Glenn Drive, and today its memory stands as a pillar of those momentary emotions: shock and the gro-
tesque humiliation of being devalued.

That was over twenty years ago. From the reverberations of that day
God has allowed my ministry, *Arise Ministries*, a privileged opportunity
to lead an Oklahoma, statewide single mothers' conference, *Survive 'N'*
Thrive. With the Governor's endorsement, countless volunteers from
authors, professionals, and counselors in the area, *Arise* has accepted
the calling to minister to not only single moms at our statewide conference and surrounding regions, but single moms all over the country.
God is now taking the *Survive 'N' Thrive* conference to other states, and
we pray to the nation. Indeed, He can use our greatest life heartache
and devastating sorrow for kingdom purposes.

I know women who feel devalued. Their sense of significance and
worth has suffered one too many blows of "I don't love you anymore,"
or "You don't measure up," or "You're not pretty enough, smart enough,
thin enough, or sexy enough." As women, we hate the word *enough*,
because for many of us, that's what we're not. Because of rejection,
betrayal, living a lie, harboring anger, nursing grudges, and more, many
have lost the capacity to enjoy the freedom of who they are in Christ.
Rather than living in unfurling and extensive purpose, they suffocate
in insignificant despair. Yet it was God who said of His new creatures,
"I have clothed you with the garments of salvation, and covered you in
the robe of righteousness."[1] He chants, "You are My handiwork, cher-
ished, loved unconditionally, enriched by My desire of you, free from all
condemning charges against you, lavished with the riches of My grace,

and qualified to partake in spiritual blessings. Beloved child, won't you receive My benefits and your rightful inheritance? Will the real you please stand up and see yourself as you truly are: one adorned with My merit, appraised by My edict declaring you exceedingly valuable!" Oh, friend! Glory to God for His truth shed abroad in our parched hearts!

You are a new creature of immeasurable worth to Christ. What is true of Jesus is true about you. If the enemy can keep you from knowing that truth, then he has won the battle for your self-worth and victorious Christian life. Genesis 1:3 is the first time you see the word *said*: "And God said," *amar* in Hebrew, meaning to declare in the heart.[2] God's spoken words released the energy stored in His heart concerning the status He would place on His people: valued! You are who He says you are whether you see, believe, or feel it or not. So why not enter the richness of His declaration? Isn't it true? A violinist must practice, practice, practice to perfect the skill of melodious tunes? And you, as a new creation, must practice, practice, practice to perfect the skill of believing that His declaration applies to your own tunes. Personal wholeness comes from appropriating the truth about who God says you are. It's true: you progress no farther than your perception, so stretch your perception factor.

+ Affirm the truth about God's character. Your enjoyment of the real you parallels your belief about who God is.

+ Review every morning the alphabetized list at the back of the book of your "100 I Am Blessings." Move your thoughts out of park and beyond neutral, into drive. Don't leave home without the list tattooed and activated in your mind.

+ Press forward in the new you. Refuse to allow your past to cripple your present or determine your future.

• Choose. You get to pick moment by moment: freedom or bondage? If you don't choose faith, then you've outright chosen the pathway to frustration, fear, fretting, faultfinding, failure, and fiasco.

Of what value are you?

> "Look at the birds of the air, for they neither sow nor reap nor gather into barns; yet your heavenly Father feeds them. Are you not more valuable than they?"
>
> Matthew 6:26

49. I am Enlightened

One of the greatest blessings of Christians remains the inborn ability they receive at conversion in being enlightened by the Word of God. The natural man, that person physically born under the corruption of his soul apart from Christ, cannot comprehend God's ways nor understand the newfound nature of the spiritual man, that person having become spiritually reborn by the Holy Spirit. As followers of Jesus, we carry the capability of receiving from God His divine wisdom, not for the purpose of knowing Him intellectually but rather experientially. We are enlightened, meaning we have the Holy Spirit within us, the One opening our eyes to the spiritual realities of God, pointing us to Jesus, the One who alone inhabits all truth and knowledge. It is the Spirit who renders evidence that God's Word is true, causing us to supernaturally receive illuminated insight into His power and ways. Have you noticed that the closer you grow to Christ and walk with Him, the more your spiritual eyes see the vast difference between the lifestyles of those who know Jesus as their Savoir and those who don't? I wonder where such revelations originate.

When I was young, my favorite companion accompanied me to bed every night: my glow bug doll. Perhaps you had one, too. If you pressed on its tummy, the battery inside ignited the face causing it to light up.

Like no other doll on my shelf, *this* one possessed enlightened power. Much like the battery in the doll, when you asked Jesus Christ into your heart, you received an implanted divine battery making it possible to connect with God's electrical current of spiritual truth, enabling you to light up with His joy, reflect His glory, and illuminate with the glorious revelations imparted in His Word.

Recently, the Holy Spirit has quickened my thirst for a deeper understanding into Paul's prayer in Ephesians 1:18–20 concerning the saints in Ephesus. I'm captivated by the vast resources and treasures God's made available to those who rely on His Son. It's become my favorite daily hobby in asking the Spirit to show me exactly what Paul had in mind when He prayed that the eyes of their hearts would be enlightened. What lay on Paul's mind?

Paul prayed for them to know what is the hope of God's calling for the saints–We get so enmeshed in the ways of the world that we forget we're heaven-bound earthlings moving toward an eventual destiny or eternal position that we already obtain. Our present hope abides in the fact that we are currently sharing in His authority on earth, having been "seated with Christ in the heavenlies."[1] Our hope comes from our position in Jesus and that one day we will reign with Him; however, for now, we're placed on this planet to enforce the victory of Christ over Satan's domain through prayer, discipling others, and evangelism. How does bringing to mind your glorious calling affect your view of life? Does it expand your spiritual insight that God's plan for you extends beyond your present circumstances? Do you find support in knowing that God's finale encompasses an eternal hope, one stupendous, secure, and steadfast?

Paul prayed for them to know the riches of the glory of God's inheritance in the saints–We understand the word inheritance. It's an endowment passed to an heir. Did you notice in Paul's prayer whom God declared as His greatest treasure? It's you. You encapsulate the richness of His wealth. In you resides His Son, the one who displays to the lost world the portrait of Christ. William MacDonald adds, "It is certainly an exhibition of unspeakable grace that vile, unworthy sinners, saved through Christ, could ever occupy such a place in the heart of God that He would speak of them as His inheritance."[2] Friends, you are indescribably valuable! Paul prayed that your heart would be enlightened that you would know this truth and see yourself the way God sees you.

Paul prayed for you to know the surpassing greatness of God's power toward the saints. When Jesus raised Lazarus from the dead he commanded, "Unbind him, and let him go."[3] Like Lazarus, Jesus has untied the wrappings around your old, dead life and liberated you to live in resurrected strength and might. This power was great enough to fight off all the forces of hell that pressed against Christ's tomb in an all out hellacious war to keep Jesus in the grave. But He came out in resurrected valor and force! In you resides that same capacity of greatness. There is nothing you face today, not death, depression, or despair that God's raised supremacy in you cannot defeat. Jesus was the first to rise in power to an endless life of glory and in you resides that same working of strength that overcame what looked impossible to those who never imagined Jesus would once again come to life![4]

So take courage! And may "the God of our Lord Jesus Christ, the Father of all glory, give you a spirit of wisdom and revelation in the knowledge of Him"[5] in all that concerns you today.

"I pray that the eyes of your heart may be enlightened…"

Ephesians 1: 18

50. I am Clean

"Wake up, Rebecca!" her mother scurried. "I heard that Jesus will be in the Temple this morning. There might be a crowd. I want us to hear the Teacher!" So with eager hearts the family of four made their way to find the Lord to glean from His unusual stories and wisdom. While find-ing Him seated near the steps, Rebecca made her way to the Master's feet, but when He was telling a story, a group of scribes and Pharisees butted their way into the crowd, dragging a shamefaced woman behind. "Teacher, this woman has been caught in adultery, in the very act."[1] The very scene defines the meaning of humiliation!

Do you recall your most embarrassing moment? I remember a day in high school when a teacher dragged me in front of the class to make a fun-loving remark. Obviously, it impacted me greatly. Like the adul-terous woman at Jesus' feet, we all know the feeling of being pointed out in an uncomfortable fashion. But who was this Judean lady that found herself paraded through the mob like a used rag and thrown at the feet of Jesus for a whiplashing of disgrace? And if she was found in an adulterous act, why didn't the "Police Squad Against Sinners" drag her partner to Jesus as well? Doesn't adultery take two? We can only imagine the abhorrence on her face.

Shame. It's a hideous, hopeless, never ending pessimism that defines a person's identity. It's that unpardonable emotional feeling that arises from the consciousness of something disgraceful. It comes from any-thing in our lives whether it originates from past sins, something done to us, or anything concerning our physical makeup. It screams one mes-sage: you're disgusting and unworthy of God's love.

I've counseled women with shame issues. I can spot them a mile away. It manifests itself in a sense of self-pity or inferiority and a hatred for self-appearance. Those trapped in its web withdraw, refusing to invest any part of themselves in others. Or they attach themselves to another needy per-son feeling they can rescue the individual. But the message is the same: I'm a sinful person. I can't forgive myself. I'm dirty before God.

One of my respected heroes is my step-daughter, Amber. I love her! She is an inspiring woman of God. Having graduated from Dallas Theological Seminary, she leads women through Celebrate Recovery classes. I've seen a transformation in her life. She's God's butterfly of beauty to so many of us, a breath of fresh air. She teaches that your new identity in Christ frees you from the prison of guilt and shame. While it's true we have all committed sins or even had acts of sin done against us, they don't have to define our personhood or contentment. Jesus nailed not only our sins but their effects on us at the Cross. So receive His message: You are clean! You are forgiven! You are valuable!

I love the origin of the pearl. Initially trapped inside the shell-forming mollusk remains an unwanted tiny parasite or bit of shell. With time, the mantle cells begin to wrap sheets of nacre around the intruding particle until the foreign body is enclosed in a shell-like substance forming a pearl. What began as an irritant becomes a jewel of inexpressible worth! Won't you allow God the same miracle of transforming your "parasite" into a gem of His healing power? *You are a pearl!* So take personally what God says about His love for you and believe the truth.

+ *Believe the truth about justification.* Because of being declared not guilty, your conscience can stand before God shielded from the tormentor of humiliation and regret.

+ *Believe the truth about reconciliation.* Because you have been brought back into a right standing with God, there is no unclean act that can separate you from God's acceptance.

+ *Believe the truth about the resurrection.* Because Christ rose from the dead, the continuing effect of sin's disgrace is dead; you are wholesome on the inside.

+ *Believe the truth about regeneration.* Because of your new birth, you are not the old you! You are permanently free from the debilitating effects of remorse and degradation.

Jesus forgave the adulterous woman, and He's forgiven you too. Now press on and walk forward in fresh life. Put on your imaginary pearl ring, and never forget that you're clean by His Word, clean by His will, and clean by His wonder!

> "You are already clean because of the word I have spoken to you."
>
> John 15:3

51. I am Loved

When Jason and Sara were tiny tots they loved for me to read them Bible stories. Not an evening escaped that the miraculous heroes of the Bible didn't accompany their thoughts to bed. I recall the first time the children took a trip to the mall at Christmas. Bible characters must have been dancing like sugar plums in Jason's head because when he saw Santa, he pointed in fascinated wonder and said, "Look, Mommy, there's Noah!"

I wonder if God chuckles at us. Do we delight His heart by the cute things we say and do? Do you think He ever looks down and just wants to squeeze us to death? I do! How deep, concentrated, and vast is God's love for His beloved! As much as we adore our children, it pales in comparison to God's insatiable attraction for His. Someone once said that being in love is temporary insanity whereby you idiotically act in ways that go beyond the boundaries of what's reasonable, momentarily emerging as a mad man!

It was 755–715 BC that God placed what appeared to be a mad man on the horizon of the Northern Kingdom of Israel. Actually, I'm not sure who was more insane, Hosea, the prophet, or what appeared to be God Himself. God asked Hosea to perform a bizarre act of marrying the prostitute Gomer in an attempt to parallel God's love for his wandering wife, Israel. In this symbolic drama, Hosea was to represent God and Gomer was to play the part of Israel.

So God spoke to Hosea, "Go, take for yourself a wife of harlotry, and have children of harlotry."[1] Was God telling Hosea to marry a prostitute and that some of his children would be born to him from other men? So Hosea followed God's orders and took Gomer for his wife, and together they raised three children. But Gomer continued in her promiscuous ways, and God commissioned Hosea with yet another peculiar request: "Buy her back for fifteen shekels of silver and a lethek of barley."[2] So he did, and Gomer was, thereby, redeemed by the amorous love of her husband.

Hosea wasn't insane; he was just out of his mind in love with Gomer and willing to follow God's command. I know what you're thinking! Why would God ask Hosea to marry an unfaithful woman? Good question. I've researched the question myself; some believe the story stands as an allegory of God paralleling His unquenchable love for His wife, Israel, while others take it literally, that even over 2,300 years ago, God's ways were higher than man's. Make no mistake, friends, the outlandish point is this: God loves you with an inexplicable passion hungering to bring you into His fortress of possessive care! Such a display of the redemptive love of Hosea and Gomer serves as a foreshadowing of God's desire for an abandoned love affair with you, His church.

I simply cannot comprehend a God who desires nothing more than to have that kind of relationship with us, to spoil us with His eternal provisions of magnificent love, even though we've been spiritual fornicators ourselves, seeking the pleasure of other interests above Him. And just like Hosea bought Gomer for a price, God did the same in that He "extended His own love towards us, in that while we were sinners, Christ died for us."[3]

How comfortable are you in receiving God's erotic love? How often do you silence your heart and listen for His love song, letting it caress your deepest nature?

How beautiful are you my darling, how beautiful are you! You make my heart beat faster with a single glance of you.

Song of Solomon 4:1,9

And I will betroth you to Me in faithfulness, then you will know Me as your Lord.

Song of Solomon 2:20

You are beautiful and there is no blemish in you.

Song of Solomon 4:7

And anyone who touches you, touches the apple of My eye.

Zechariah 2:8

I will establish with you an everlasting covenant.

Ezekiel 16:60

And I pray that you, being rooted and established in love... may grasp how wide, long, high, and deep is the love of Christ for you.

Ephesians 3:16–19

God's love entrenches itself in His fascination of you. Oh, friend, His love exceeds no bounds! You must read Hosea chapter 11 and see for yourself! I'm speechless!

"For God so loved...that He gave His only Son."

John 3:16

52. I am Complete

For almost ten years I taught a Bible class of women. We named ourselves 'Blended Blessings' because, indeed, we were a blend of women experiencing unique transitions in life. What began with five single moms grew into a class of over 200 women of all ages and stages of life. Sunday after Sunday the underlying heartache of so many was this: "I feel so lonely and incomplete. If only I could find someone, I wouldn't feel so alone."

Loneliness hurts. I recall a time in my own life living alone in Albion, Michigan. I experienced a distressing emptiness probably for the first time in my life. You know it's bad when you go to Walmart just to hear yourself say hello. Let me repeat myself: loneliness hurts, and those who suffer from its pain would resound in a hearty, "Amen!"

Max Lucado writes about an encounter he had strolling through the cemetery reading headstones. How could he forget the tombstone of Grace Llewellen Smith? No words on the stone revealed anything about her, when she was born or when she died. Who was this lady? The only inscription about her was this: "*Sleeps, but rests not. Loved, but was loved not. Tried to please, but pleased not. Died as she lived - alone!*"[1] How very sad! What a disgrace for Grace! Wasn't there anything pleasant her family could say?

Loneliness! Grace Llewellan knew about it, as well as a host of Bible characters: Jeremiah, David, Paul, and even Jesus Himself. And that's not all. Maybe you should be added to that list! Loneliness is that hollowness in your stomach, that isolated silent partner within who shares your secret. It's that sickening reality that at the end of the day it's just *you* again, vacant of anyone who cares to know the real you. We were created to love and be loved, be understood and needed. Loneliness is its direct antithesis.

Oh, precious friends, praise God! He made you, and He knows your great need for someone else. Your circumstances don't have to define, limit, or destroy you. In Him is the someone else, The Divine Completer, The Source, the One able to soothe and remove whatever causes estrangement from Him. Life's crisis can result in a cancer of hopelessness and emptiness, but He is El Shaddai, the All Sufficient One, the One capable of repairing your damaged emotions. In Him is "everything you need for life and godliness."[2] Everything? Everything!

What is your *everything*? It's already been met! At conversion God gave you everything you would need pertaining to Christian growth. Nothing needs to be added. Though some traits may be undeveloped, you have it all. You've been made whole, complete, and filled with the inherent character, disposition, and mind of Christ Himself. All the power and attributes of God were poured into Christ physically, and now they have been supplied to you by the command of the Holy Spirit. You embody a storehouse of provisions through Him. Are you appropriating the richness in your own well? You are not incomplete and void of help in time of need for "of His fullness you *have received!*"[3] You have unlimited access to His supply of divine life, a reservoir that never diminishes. It's rendered continuously—grace upon grace, supply upon supply, favor upon favor, need upon need. You possess in Christ Jesus a precious companionship, one of unconditional love overflowing with comfort, acceptance, approval, and forgiveness. You've been restored to inner wholeness. He dwells within to settle down and be at home in you, incessantly serving as a resident healer of your deepest heartaches. Corrie Ten Boom said, "There is no pit so deep that He is not deeper still." When the All Sufficient Completer restores you in the pit of life, you emerge testifying of His supremacy that there is no crisis, no loneliness, no illness, or no relationship heartache that will ever supersede Christ's promises and provisions concerning you.

I'm sorry Grace Llewellen Smith never understood the beauty of her own first name. I wonder, what would have been her epitaph had she partnered with Christ and His grace?

> "For in Him all the fullness of Deity dwells in bodily form; you have been made complete."
>
> Colossians 2:9–10

Chapter Eight

My Benefits

What personal acts of God's favor became mine as a new creature in Christ?

53. I am Upheld

During the initial stage of building the Golden Gate Bridge, more than twenty construction workers fell to their death in the freezing waters connecting the North Pacific to San Francisco Bay. Engineers and superintendents could not find a solution to the ominous problem that threatened security for the workers. Finally, one foreman suggested placing a gigantic safety net beneath the bridge. Surprisingly from that point on less than ten men fell, all saved by the net. When fear of death no longer existed, the crew's productivity rate increased over twenty-five percent, causing greater effectiveness in the project.

Isn't it amazing what happens when fear no longer stands as an obstacle in our lives? How would your life be different if you no longer wrestled with the fear of failure, or the fear of running out of money, or the fear of your children's well-being? What kind of freedom would you experience if you knew no matter what kind of endeavor you encountered, you would not be permanently toppled over, crippled by hopelessness, trapped in depression, or fall into destruction?

Just like the net served as a comforting device for the men on top of the bridge, God has stretched beneath you a net that extends from the beginning of time well into the millennial years of eternity. Never will there be a danger, a thought, or an unwanted situation that His covering of grace will not bring a sense of protection. How reassuring to know that you are always in a position to be upheld, bolstered up, and kept from permanent failure because of any weakness or unexpected circumstance.

It was during the reign of King Hezekiah, a time in Israel's history when the people felt abandoned by God, that He stretched forth His comfort, bringing solace to their troubled souls. Because of God's covenant made with Abraham, He fostered His love for them through His net. In Isaiah 41:10, God extended His love and pacified them by saying:

- *Panic not*–Take a deep breath on the inside. You can rely on His faithfulness. He's not only within reach, but His very presence is with you silencing your worries or woes.

- *Do not be distraught, for I am your God*–He is fully engaged in all that concerns you, so put away your downcast spirit enthroning His name: El Shaddai, Almighty God.

- *I will fortify and assist you*–God labors to comfort and support your cause. He'll never permit a permanent state of defeat or entrapment beyond His ability to rescue.

- *I will uphold*–He extends a firm grip with His righteous right hand, that lifeline of hope that anchors your safety in times of anxiety, unsettledness, and apprehension.

Today, that same covenant-keeping God who watched out for their well-being watches out for yours. What threatens your sense of peace? What circumstance has God allowed that creates a desperate need for His sustaining power? Does it feel like God has abandoned you and conditions will never change? How can you be certain God is with you? To sustain or uphold means to place an object on another by actually touching the two. God places the person of the Holy Spirit in you as a linking device, making it possible for you to connect with God. It's through that union that He sees every whimper of doubt, every lament of sorrow, and every quibble of despair. He stretches forth His righteous right hand to gird up your trust in His grace.

I don't know about you, but my heart welcomes God's desire to rescue me from my sorrows and insecurities. I've been promised an invisible underpinning that upholds me, securing God's faithfulness to reinforce my stamina to carry on. When I'm standing on a tall bridge outside my comfort zone or worried about a circumstance beyond my control, I can look to my net and be comforted in knowing that no matter how far I fall, I will never descend beyond His grace.

It's no wonder the men building the Golden Gate Bridge increased in their productivity, and you can too!

> "Fear not, for I am with you. Be not dismayed for I am your God. I will strengthen you, I will help you. I will uphold you with my righteous right hand."
>
> Isaiah 41:10

54. I am A Trustee of God's Promises

Some people refer to God as the big man upstairs whose arm must be twisted in order to receive a favor. Many see Him like a heavenly gumball machine; you do a good deed or say a prayer, and He might coerce one of His angels to roll down a piece of bubblegum; and even at that, you'll likely get liquorish! But nothing could be farther from the truth! "No good thing does God withhold from those who walk uprightly."[1] He longs to exalt His children with profound blessings. He is not a reluctant giver, but the generous bestower of boundless kindnesses. This Supreme Blesser whose earth is His footstool and calls the clouds the dust of His feet is referred to as The Majestic Glory, and out of His unthinkable love, He's entrusted a most potent aid to those who seek Him: His promises.

Because you are a partaker of His divine nature, you instantaneously become an heir of promise, given rightful unlimited access to all of God's fathomless grace and unceasing favor. You are a beneficiary, one receiving advantages from your Giver, one taking possession of all God's property. You possess the promises of His message, pledges divinely powerful for immediate release from all that encumbers you, words of covenant that penetrate the unseen spiritual realm evoking God's response on your behalf. His promises are not some "mamby-pamby" declarations of good luck, but potent mandates securing spiritual strength! You have all God's power to set in motion the guarantees you already own. The question is, "Are you activating what you possess?"

Are His words of spiritual fortitude and might being formed in you by the practice of calling on them? How cognizant are you of your enemy's tactics? Satan works out of his own set of vows, promises to destroy. Is there an inner vigilance in your spirit ready to activate His oaths you already possess? You have all you need in Christ! All God's promises are yes in Jesus.[2] So activate in your belief system what you've inherited in your spirit by not allowing Satan's lies to rob you of who you are in Christ. Notice the lies he plants in your mind. Replace them with the truth you own!

I'm without hope.	I will not leave you comfortless. John 14:18
I can't live like this.	I will supply your needs. Philippians 4:19
I'm too tired.	I will give you rest. Matthew 11:28–30
I'm not smart enough.	I will give you wisdom. 1 Corinthians 1:30
I'm in bondage.	My truth shall make you free. John 8:32
I feel all alone.	I will never forsake you. Hebrews 13:5

I can't do it. You can do all things. Philippians 4:13

I'm a failure. I began a work in you; I will finish it. Philippians 1:6

I'm worried. Cast all your cares on me. 1 Peter 5:7

Nobody loves me. I love you. John 3:16

I can't get through this. All things are possible. Luke 18:27

I'm afraid. I have not given you a spirit of fear. 2 Timothy 1:7

I don't know what to do. I will direct your steps. Proverbs 3:6

I can't go on. My grace is sufficient. 2 Corinthians 12:9

I can't make decisions. You have a sound mind. 2 Timothy 1:7

I am ruined. I work all together for good. Romans 8:28

I can't handle this. You possess My risen power. 2 Timothy 1:7

I'm without help. I am your Shepherd. Psalm 23:1

I can't forgive myself. I forgive you. 1 John 1:9

This is too big for me. I called you; I will do it. 1 Thessalonians 5:24

I'm permanently unsettled. My peace I give to you. John 14:27

I have no help. I am a present help in trouble. Psalm 46:1

I'm depressed. Believe you will see My goodness. Psalm 27:13

I am crushed. I heal broken hearts and wounds. Psalm 147:3

I am confused. I will instruct and teach you. Psalm 32:8

I am tempted. I deliver out of temptation. 2 Peter 2:9

I am a nervous wreck. Trust and lean on me. Proverbs 3:3–5

Friends! Friends! Beware of despair! Use its venom as a divine opportunity to trigger the truth of your inherited promises! David Nicholas
said it quite well:"God's promises are like the stars; the darker the night,
the brighter they shine."[3]

"He has granted to us His precious and magnificent promises…"

2 Peter 1:4

55. I am A Beneficiary of God's Perfect Timing

They were disheartened! What they had hoped for and believed would
happen, didn't, and they were left with questions and serious doubts
concerning the words of Jesus. Had He deceived them in what He had
testified? Was He really the Son of God? If Jesus was the Christ, how
could God allow Him to be crucified and taken from them? Things had
not turned out the way they had envisioned, and they were stranded in a
cesspool of unanswered questions. These were the thoughts that Cleopas
and his friend pondered as their feet shuffled the dust on the road to
Emmaus, a little community seven miles northwest of Jerusalem.

Upon entering this quaint village, they encountered a stranger on the
path. Actually, it was the glorified Jesus who had concealed His identity
from them and returned to earth for a short visit after his resurrection, but the two men didn't recognize Him. The fever in Jerusalem
had reached a high pitch! Outbreaks of tears filled many hearts, for
Jesus, the future King of the Jews, had been crucified. It was in this
kind of atmosphere that The Messiah appeared to the men on the road
inquiring why they were so sad, questioning what the ruckus was about
in Jerusalem. I find humor in Cleopas' somewhat cynical remark to
this stranger: "Are you the only one visiting Jerusalem, and unaware of
the things which have happened here in these days?" Can you imagine
scolding The Almighty for being unaware?

Well? Is He? Have you ever wondered if The Almighty is unaware? Are you facing a situation where things haven't turned out the way you had planned? Are your eyes prevented from understanding God's ways? What solace can be found when you're slumped in the hospital of God's waiting room? I'm going to ask Jesus when I see Him in heaven what was the saints number one request on earth. I wonder if it will revolve around the word, "Why?" I'm certain one day every why will find glorious exposure as to God's higher ways, but for now we can take courage in *this* pledged promise of hope: God's timing is perfect.

When you pray and pray for a person and nothing *seems* to be happening, God's timing is perfect. When you pray and pray for God to perform something in your own life and nothing changes, God's timing is perfect. When a crisis comes knocking at your door with an unwanted illness of a mother, or an untimely death of a child, or an unexpected "you're fired" from a boss, or an unmanageable alcoholic son, or an unruly mouthy daughter, or an unwarranted announcement of a divorce, or an unseen diagnosis of prostate or breast cancer, or an unnerving heartache you never dreamed possible, God's timing is perfect! And though God might not have "caused" these things to happen, He always has a redeeming purpose. As new creatures in Christ, our circumstances remain sealed in the sovereign bubble of His spotless will. Never will there be a resolution to your request that comes too late, or too early, or not at all. In God's providence, He hears, calculates, and prepares for the execution of His timing in every detail concerning you. Ecclesiastes 3:11 assures, "He has made everything appropriate in its time." Appropriate (*yapeh*) means beautiful, comely, pleasant, fitting.[1] Just as snug as Cinderella's glass slipper, your circumstances fit in conforming you to His image. And though the fit squeezes at times, feeling terribly uncomfortable and certainly anything but pleasant, you can know that in its proper time it will be altogether lovely. Always lurking behind every disappointment, stands this entrenched principle:

God's guardianship, control, and eternal best interest concerning His beloved new creatures never fails.

It must have been superbly shocking when Jesus unveiled His identity to Cleopas. Jesus had been invited to his house for dinner: "Sir, would you stay with us for it is getting toward evening, and the day is now nearly over."[2] Certainly this man had no idea who would dine at His table that night. Their meager meal would serve as a timely communion and revelation as to the necessity of why Jesus had to die on the Cross. His conversation to them on the road to Emmaus explaining how the events of the Old Testament led up to the Savior's crucifixion and resurrection would soon make sense to them.

So Jesus took the bread and broke it and "their eyes were opened and they recognized him!"[3] Do you suppose they noticed the nail prints in His hands? Do you suppose they had flashbacks of their conversation with Him on the road and felt totally stupid and embarrassed? Do you suppose their hearts fainted in inconceivable shock, unbelief and frivolous delight?

What are you waiting on today? In God's perfect orchestration, He will open the eyes of your understanding. So take heart; it's a promise: "He performs what is appointed for you,"[4] and it will come to pass in His perfect timing.

"My times are in Your hands, O Lord."

Psalms 31:15

56. I am A Cultivator of a Grateful Heart

The dawn broke over the horizon in the Valley of Jezreel into a Judean village that housed ten men whose life embossed the invisible mark on their forehead: the living dead. These segregated men, whose skin disease classified them as lepers, awakened morning after morning to yet another dust shuffling day of the announcement of their identity: "Unclean! Unclean!" Yet it was not just another mundane afternoon, for *this* day *one* of them would weave himself into the pages of Scripture as a celebrity of grandeur proportions of what happens when Jesus transforms a dismal attitude into a heart of gregarious gratitude. It was Christ who heard their sheepish voices from a distance, "Jesus, Master, have mercy on us."[1] And have mercy He did. And as they followed His command to make their way to the priest, they were healed; yet only one of them acknowledged the greater miracle, an encounter with God Himself, and it was he who returned to Jesus to build an altar of praise at His feet. Could he ever have imagined that the very instant he turned back to Christ, his reputation would catapult into epidemic proportions? One day in heaven I will meet this cleansed leper. In considering him, who among us can escape the nudge of examining our own response to the Master's hand of mercy?

I love this story. I used to be a leper. It was before my moment of salvation that I, too, joined their pathetic chorus: "Unclean! Unclean!" Yet Jesus removed the infectious cells that would permanently confine me as prisoner trapped in my own uninvited circumstances. My new position in Christ gloriously sets the stage and creates the atmosphere for my heart to cultivate a lifestyle of expansive thanksgiving.

Are you a grateful person? When others think of you do they hear affirmations of God's goodness? Is your level of contentment based on what happens to you or who you are in Christ? Are you more obliged to respond to what you feel or who you know? And why are some people more grateful than others? Is it because they are naturally more thankfully oriented or is gratitude a matter of choice? Do you practice Paul's instruction: "As you therefore have received Christ Jesus the Lord, so walk in Him, having been firmly rooted and now built up in Him and established in your faith,...and overflowing with gratitude?"[2] Overflowing means to have excess and be firmly rooted, to be strengthened and constantly fixed. Do you exude with an excess of thanks abounding out of a cemented reservoir of strength? To be grateful is to acknowledge past mercies from God. Willis King said, "Gratitude is from the same root word as grace—the boundless mercy of God; and thanksgiving is from the same root word as think, so to think is to thank!"[3] Is your mind a think tank looking for avenues to give God glory?

What a hero! It was the leper whose heart established a firm resolve to turn around and thank Christ. What about you? What about-face choices do you need to consider?

- *Gratitude expands from a clear conscience.* What keeps you from being a grateful person? The conscience was installed by God as a transmitter letting you know when your thoughts and deeds break His laws. To ignore the voice of the conscience is to retard His promptings that lead to praise.

- *Gratitude expands from intentional alertness.* Do you purposefully nurture a vigilant heart? Start recording your benefits one by one in a morning journal. Doing so transports your thankfulness to a higher floor.

- *Gratitude expands from living outside yourself.* Self-absorption induces pride and comparison, so refocus on others and the benefits they bring. God's installed in your sphere dispensers called others. Who are your others? Have you told them they greatly impact your journey?

- *Gratitude expands from giving thanks for hardships.* It's easy to be grateful when all is well. But remember Job: "Naked I came out of my mother's womb, and naked I shall return....the Lord gives, and the Lord takes away; blessed be the name of the Lord."[4] It's remarkably true: suffering grants gratitude its greatest exposure.

Now exactly what was the name of that one leper? And better yet, who were the other nine who missed the mark?

> "...since we receive a kingdom which cannot be shaken, let us show gratitude..."
>
> Hebrews 12:28

57. I am Granted an Intercessor

I love to hear stories on the power of prayer, and even much more see them demonstrated in my own life. I have a very private closet in my home. It's just an 'itty-bitty' thing, so small I can barely crouch down in it myself, but I am certain, it's one of the most anointed spots in my house. It's my prayer room, and while it's true the Holy Spirit resides *in me* and not that closet, I still love the strength of fellowship the Lord brings to me when I enter my cubby hole of solitude. It's decked out with what I know the Lord loves the most: me and prayer requests. I have hundreds of petitions on post-it notes stuck to the wall with pictures of people I lift up in prayer. It's my get-a-way with Jesus. Under the carpet on the concrete, lays magic marker scriptures I penned when the house was being built. I know when I'm in there, I'm covered on all sides. Stupendous answers of prayer have come out of that corner of the world. And though I can't stay in my closet 24–7, my prayer notes can! It's thrilling; I'll be cleaning house and someone will call asking me to pray for them. It's become my favorite pastime to jot their request on a note and dash it to the prayer wall. I wonder if the Lord is as amused with my love of running to Him with another post-it-prayer, as I am tripping over myself in getting there.

I love it when someone calls: "What cha' doin'?" Have you ever thought about asking Jesus, "What cha' doin,' Jesus?" Or does that sound weird to you. Maybe you fail to think of Jesus in terms of being a live person on the other end of the receiver, but He is alive, right now in glorified form, just as alive as you and I are this very moment.

While it's true Jesus had an earthly mission with His disciples, He's now been assigned another operative ministry, an eternal ministry. "What cha' doin', Jesus?" He's presiding over the universe, having been granted full authority over it; He's performing as our High Priest before the Father; He's preparing a place for us in eternity; and He's praying for His children as an Advocate, the One who upholds and defends. How often when you're finishing a prayer do you perceive the prayer is over? No, the prayer's activity is not over; it's just begun, for Jesus takes the request and *continually* entreats God's throne, for He "*always* lives to make intercession for you."[1] Always! The only thing we *always* do is breathe, but He *always* thinks of you; in fact, He lives to do so! What do you live to do? Eat? Find pleasure? Build a career? Raise the kids? Find a mate?

Jesus lives to intercede or appear before God on your behalf, not to plead for God's acceptance or forgiveness of you; His earthly atonement settled that issue at the Cross. He now lives to represent you before the Father, to intercede meaning, "to meet, or appeal, or intervene"[2] for the purpose of overseeing and preparing you for eternity. I love this oldie-goldie hymn: "He lives! He lives! Christ Jesus lives today!" It's true: He lives to embrace the saints' requests; He lives to remind the Father that all your sin has been laid on His account; He lives to strengthen your faith in prayer; He lives to provide eternal security; He lives to bring completion to your salvation; He lives to present your petitions to the Father as the "High Priest over the house of God;"[3] He lives to answer all the accusations from the enemy and defend any charges against you; He lives to restore your fellowship when you sin; He lives to provide the grace needed to overcome temptation; He lives to bring you home. In fact, His very life in heaven serves as one continual prayer petition. While I place my prayer wall before Him, He places His prayer wall before the Father.

So what does all this have to do with your new identity? When Jesus prayed for His apostles, He included *you* in that list! "I am praying not only for these disciples but also for all who will believe in Me because of their testimony."[4] That's you! How does it bring comfort in knowing Jesus' prayer spelled out *your* name before His Father? How often do thoughts of His intercession bring strength and hope?

Friends, we are privileged beyond measure to be His. May we approach our own prayer wall, or prayer journal, or prayer request humbly, knowing we serve a Jesus who lives to intervene in every stage of our earthly pilgrimage.

"Jesus intercedes for us."

Romans 8:34

58. I am A Participant in Prayer

Edward V. Rickenbacker, a World War I pilot, and seven friends drifted twenty-four days after their plane crashed in the Pacific. Their only food was four oranges, a seagull, and two fish. Can you imagine surviving on so little? Yet the alarming truth is this: some born again believers with the unlimited resources of God have tried to survive on less than *that* in their spiritual lives.

Do you ever wonder why your walk with Christ feels malnourished and weak, or ponder why your desire to serve Him lacks robust vitality? Could it be in the last twenty-four days you've only yielded yourself to four fleeting thoughts of Him with little to no follow through in activating the most potent force you possess: prayer! Imagine God granting you His golden key to power begging you to use it. "Here," He pleads, "I'm placing in your possession an extraterrestrial cell phone that dials into my heavenly powers granting you unrestricted liberty in asking whatever you need according to My will. Here, I'm giving you the means to enforce My program in your sphere in working your cir-cumstances for good. Here, I'm granting you divine entrance into the domain of Satan, that through Jesus Christ you might thwart his lies that harass your soul. Here is the most potent force on earth today, a stimulus that establishes My best for you and simultaneously boomer-angs into the ultimate purposes of My glory. Would you please, please, please use it?" Friends, when you don't like what's happening outwardly, change what's happening inwardly. Pray! Just pray!

How would you answer God's entreating? Are you using this most formidable instrument? How many would say, "I'd use it more often if I believed in its power." Or, "I'd use it more often if I understood what it was." What is prayer anyway?

Prayer's not primarily what you think it is. While it's true that prayer gives us a means to lay hold of His promises, it's ultimately a means to lay hold of His sovereignty. Its usefulness goes far beyond our elemen-tary understanding that it's solely a vehicle in asking God to give us what we want or make our pain go away. True prayer centers on God's glory and not man's requests, so that when the answer comes, it's received as a part of His overall blueprint in which you will one day surely agree.

Prayer is an open and honest dialogue with God that allows you to take part in two worlds: His and yours. It's an exchange of thoughts using normal, everyday words from your heart, forgetting the verbiage like "thou art and thou knowest not." It's an exchange of confidence where you come to Him as a child, and He responds as a loving Father. It's the means by which you get everything in your life out in the open before God. Prayer's the place where you transfer your will to God's, releasing your agenda and preconceived ideas of how He should respond. Psalm 84:5 portrays prayer as a pathway to God: "Blessed are those whose hearts are found on the highways to Heaven." Watchman Nee cited, "Prayers are railroad tracks. Our prayers lay the track down on which God's power can come. Like a mighty locomotive, His power is irresistible, but it cannot reach us without rails." It's rather thought-provoking, isn't it! I wonder how many railroad tracks we're laying these days?

Prayer's power makes a difference! It's the training of the soul that promises results. Unlike the Old Testament saints who had no direct access to God, you have entrance into His presence continually! Can you imagine pushing aside such a gold mine? Satan would have you think prayer doesn't work because you don't see immediate results. He would have you think your prayers aren't holy enough, or you're not good enough, or God's not faithful enough. But those are lies! Mary and the church of God prayed for Peter, and as a result he walked out of prison. Cornelius prayed, and God brought the Holy Spirit to the Gentiles. The apostles prayed, and the number of disciples continued to increase. Peter prayed, and Tabitha was raised from the dead! Paul prayed, and Ananias was sent to restore his eyesight. And I prayed, and God delivered me from an excruciating heartbreak of the loss of my first marriage. I say, "Yipppeee, God! You perform miracles. Prayer works!"

And most of all, prayer is not just an exercise you do, but a life you live. It's not just a Sunday morning duty. Rather, prayer is marked by a prolonged attitude or an uninterrupted communion with God that's carried in your heart continually. It's God's presence that lingers. James 5:16 confirms that a life wrought in prayer induces a catastrophic impact in the sphere of the believer! "The earnest, heartfelt, continual prayer of a righteous man makes tremendous power available."[1] Don't' ever underestimate the force of your prayers! You do not have a worry or weight or a pain or a problem that fervent prayer cannot soothe and remove, heal or help! Someone said and I agree, "Nothing can stand against a saint who can pray because prayer can do anything God can do, and God can do anything." Indeed, there's no more fruitful ministry available to the child of God than prayer.

> "And they were of one mind and continually devoting themselves to prayer…"
>
> Acts 1:14

59. I am Attended by Angels

Angels! Angels! Angels! Who doesn't want to know about these spirit beings? Are they real? What do they look like? Has anyone ever really seen one? As for me, one thing I have asked of the Lord for years is this: "Lord, before I die, would you let me see an angel on this side of heaven?" Some days I'm wide-eyed wondering if today is the day!

Angels find their name on the pages of Scripture over 270 times and in thirty-four biblical books. These exotic and stunningly invisible beings were created by God to live forever, glorifying Him. God calls his angels messengers, swift as winds, and servants made of flaming fire.[1] Innumerable in number, they directly report to the throne of God as His personally assigned messengers carrying out the bidding of The Almighty. Who knows where God will send them? They arrived at the birth of Jesus announcing to the shepherds the babe wrapped in swaddling clothes; at creation they hovered in attendance and "thus the Heavens and Earth were completed and all their hosts."[2] On numerous occasions they appeared to earthlings granting heavenly aid. These agile intelligent beings, displaying tremendous joy and desire, flit from one location to another and one day will join all believers in the heavenly city of the New Jerusalem.

As astonishing as they appear, the most striking fact remains: they don't partake in the benefits of redemption or testify of grace through faith; nor do they have the capacity to be filled with the Holy Spirit for they never sinned. They have their own position in the royal order and worship in God's creation. As mysterious as it seems, though some angels have fallen, God made no provision for the salvation of fallen angels, only man.[3] Since angels are not joint heirs with Christ, they will step aside in glory one day as the redeemed of the Lamb take their place of prominence alongside Christ. They'll rejoice with celestial songs, having awaited the moment when the fullness of Christ exposes itself fully in the heirs of salvation.

As God's secret agents, they do one job really well: they minister and attend to the saints on earth, and *you* are one of their subjects! How often do you see with your heart the invisible realities of God's glory about you? Such keenness of belief and expectation evokes a wealth of spiritual power and blessings! I wonder what heavenly hosts have assisted you in your path and you didn't know it? I wonder how often His angels hovered near in bringing assistance and you failed to recognize its source? I wonder if God would open your eyes to their whereabouts if you would ask Him.

In 2 Kings 6:8–13, Elisha's army camped at Dothan awaiting the arrival of the Aramean enemy. Elisha's helper rose early observing on the hillside an army encircling the city with horses and chariots. The prophet's helper responded in fright, "What shall we do?" And Elisha responded, "Do not fear, for those who are with us are more than those who are with them." Then the Lord opened the eyes of Elisha's servant to see the *more who are with us!* God had summoned to the hills of Dothan a dispatch of countless angelic hosts on chariots of fire. What would you recognize in times of fear and overwhelming circumstances if you asked God for x-ray lenses in order to see into the invisible world? What comfort would it bring in times of need if you remembered God had "given his angels charge over you, to keep you in all your ways, bearing you up lest you dashed your foot against a stone?"[4]

You are insurmountably valuable and precious to God! His watchful eye over all that concerns you commands the heavenly hosts' attention to bring to you sustaining power and divine assistance as you walk the turf of earth whose rulership belongs to God's arch enemy, Satan. God's protective nature surrounds you, charging His hosts with the job of superintending the events of your life bringing to light His highest and best! Angels persistently watch and wait for God's go-ahead in rendering heavenly house calls.

When's the last time your car ran out of gas and a stranger stopped to help you? Did you look closely: are you sure it was a stranger?

> "But angels are only servants...spirits sent from God to care for those who will receive salvation."
>
> Hebrews 1:14

60. I am A Rider on the Heights of the Earth

No other bird captivates our sense of awe like the eagle. What a majestic monarch of the sky! What is it about an eagle that stirs in us a sense of pride, poise, and prestige? We're attracted by its grace in flight and fascinated by its crest of power. Oh, to rise up above the mundane and soar to new heights of discovery.

Do you ever want to stand on the edge of a cliff and jump? What would it feel like to leap off the ledge, setting yourself free to experience life outside yourself and your daily encumbrances? Oh, the ecstasy to arise! Where does that innate craving to soar come from?

God placed in us at salvation an aspiration to seek a higher calling above our own capabilities, a passion that would propel us onward and upward into the sphere of riding on the heights of the earth. That sphere is a state of being, a real place we have access to every second if we choose to live there. It's a vacuum in our hearts that only the Holy Spirit can fill. It's called the Spirit-filled life, a choice to breathe in spiritual air where Christ's emotions released within us can abound in unreserved peace. It's living in the invisible sanctuary within us, that place where we feed on Christ's thoughts and His ways. It's the place where the Holy Spirit elevates our human existence above the atmosphere of our own problems to see the landscape of our circumstances from God's perspective. It's a life of infectious purpose and joy.

"Is that possible?" you ask. And I respond, "Are you made in God's image? Will God empower you to do what He does?" Psalm 104:3 declares, "Oh Lord, you lay out the rafters of your home in the rain clouds. You made the clouds your chariots; *you ride upon the wings of the wind.*" If He rides on the wings of the wind, then you can ride on the heights of the earth. As a wind rider, you've been endowed with supernatural capabilities from on High.

A wind rider is full of strength. "He gives strength to the weary and to him who lacks might He increases power."[1] In your fatigue and brokenness, He grants His force in girding up your fainted spirit. He increases His abundance on your behalf, causing your field of vision to extend beyond the present. In what area of your life do you need the strength of The Almighty? God will lift you up! Like the eagle who rises sometimes 10,000 feet to catch sight of the view, God will exchange your weakness for His strength, giving you a renewed outlook.

A wind rider is full of power. He will "mount up with wings like eagles"[2] and put forth fresh feathers. God will lift you emotionally and make your wings sturdy and secure. The eagle's body is strong. It can knock over kangaroos and small sheep from cliff tops. As a wind rider you've been gifted with unusual force. You can make it through the most difficult times! The same resurrected power and nature that dominated Jesus dominates you. What possible kangaroo in your life could be bigger than His might?

A wind rider is full of hope. He will "run and not get tired and walk and not become weary."[3] God's gift of the Holy Spirit enlarges your courage to meet the task ahead with poise. He uses your difficulties as a tool to lift your confidence in His promise to overcome. As proven with the eagle, one of the first rules of aerodynamics is that flying into the wind increases altitude. With each shear of the wind, the eagle is able to use the storm to his advantage and hoist himself above the turbulence. God will renew your velocity with each gust of wind and give you energized hope.

Like the eagle, you are a marvel! God has made you to soar to new heights with Him. What's keeping you from lift off? Place your hope in Him, and depend on His strength. Go ahead! Step off the cliff. Inflate your wings. Dare to ride high and throw yourself to the wind!

> "Then you will take delight in the Lord, and I will make you ride on the heights of the earth."
>
> Isaiah 58:14

61. I am Well Content with Difficulties

The world's way of dealing with difficulties compared to God's way remains an alarming contrast! The world's system says when you face trials and insults, live by your emotions, be stressed and frazzled; but God's ways confess, "In weaknesses, distresses, and persecutions, be *well content*."[1] Well content? In Greek *eudokeo* means pleased or delighted.[2] How can we be thrilled when life doesn't go our way, happy when we're ridiculed, content when our heart breaks, and satisfied when we suffer? Does God know something we don't know? Obviously, He does!

When you received Christ, you became a partner of His entire divine nature. All that He's expressed, you've been invited to experience: love, joy, and peace. We like *that* part of our command to exercise His nature. But there's a flip side where we don't like to go: "Rejoice, as you are partakers of Christ's sufferings."[3] There's not one of us who *initially* jumps at the chance to wear His crown of thorns, yet our new identity is the sum total of all that He is, and because He had a nature that suffered, so shall we. Somewhere along the way, our concept of suffering must melt into His. Obtaining God's perspective of suffering is key to successful Christian living.

Why would a God who loves us so magnificently allow us to enter the darkness of misfortune and loss? What eternal purposes does God have in our pain? And why does sorrow even exist? John Piper offers insight on this highly misunderstood doctrine:

> Suffering displays the greatness of the glory of the grace of God. The highest, clearest and surest display of that glory is in the suffering of the best Person in the universe for millions of undeserving sinners. Therefore, the ultimate reason that suffering exists is so that Christ might display the greatness of the glory of the grace of God by suffering in himself to overcome our suffering and bring about the praise of the grace of God.[4]

That being said and being a reality hard to grasp, what tangible benefits come from suffering? And how can we more positively utilize our sorrows since they are monumental necessities in our new identities? Know this: as casualties of suffering, there's hope. Observe from A-Z how God wastes no affliction in accomplishing His purposes, not only in our lives but in the lives of others as they observe the manner in which we yield to hardship.

Christian Suffering:

A- *Allows one to know God more intimately.* Watchman Nee cited, "We never learn anything new about God except by adversity." Nothing drives us more to God than when it hurts too deeply to carry on as usual. We move toward God through the path of pain and suffering.

B- *Brings an eternal weight of glory.* Our rewards in heaven are far greater than what we lose on earth caused by disappointment. Our afflictions afford a future reward.

C- *Creates comforters.* Endurance through suffering makes us conduits of His mercy. J. H. Jowett added, "God does not comfort us to make us comfortable, but to make us comforters." Only great sufferers produce truly benevolent servants.

D- *Decentralizes self.* Heartache dethrones confidence in the flesh, removing self-centeredness and self-promotion. The only hope of decreasing self is increasing Jesus Christ.

E- *Equips one for future rulership.* "If we suffer with Him, we shall also reign with Him."[5] Followers of Christ are in training for eternity's economy of love. Our greatest heartaches become mandatory channels through which God shapes us for our careers in glory. Suffering qualifies us for rulership.

F- *Forces attention toward eternity.* The greater the heartache, the more appealing heaven's perfection! God's goal to disengage us from this world is part of the separation process making us adaptable for our future home. Indeed, God's retirement plan is "out of this world." Hallelujah!

G- *Gives God glory.* Suffering affords opportunities to display the works of God. When we place our pain on the altar of God as an act of worship, we prove to be His disciples in that our well-being is not tied to the visible circumstantial realm, but the invisible spiritual realm.

H- *Harkens the opportunity to endure for Christ's sake.* For Jesus' sake we celebrate our weaknesses, endure fires of affliction, and persist through trials. If it's not for Jesus' sake, it's for self-pity's sake.

I- *Initiates brokenness.* God's greatest purpose in dealing with His people is to reduce them to the place where they desire nothing but Jesus Christ. Suffering induces brokenness, and brokenness yields dependence.

J- *Jump-starts the recommitment of a surrendered will.* Suffering collapses your own independence. Jesus prayed, "Father, take this cup from Me; not My will but yours."[6]

K- *Kindles humility.* Adversity removes a spirit of pride and instills a spirit of poverty. Our effectiveness in building His kingdom will travel as high as our neediness is low.

L- *Launches conquest.* Once we've passed through one of the many schools of suffering, we emerge as conquerors fortified in the experiential proof of God's faithfulness, ready for expanded territory in spreading His name.

M- *Matures godly character.* Without Christ living His life through us, how would others see Jesus? Mahatma Ghandi quibbled, "I'd become a Christian if I could ever meet one." Who failed to let their season of suffering finish its work?

N- *Never emerges without a divine purpose and a predetermined timetable.* God calculates a limit on our sorrows. Each one comes camouflaged in an eternal gold nugget of God's timing and higher purpose. No pain is random or allowed without a specific beginning and end.

O- *Overturns the cycle of making ungodly choices.* The Law of the Harvest is this: you reap what you sow, more than you sow, and later than you sow. In some instances suffering comes as a consequence of our sin.

P- *Patterns itself after the life of Christ.* Christ became a curse for us in order to bring us back to God. John Piper makes the point, "All we possess came through His suffering, and all we will ever enjoy will come through our suffering."

Q- *Quickens obedience.* Hebrews 5:8 teaches that Jesus learned obedience through the things He suffered. Christ's humiliation served as a model for us to seek our Father with intentional submission.

R- *Rouses the compassion of God.* Judges 2:18 states: "For the Lord had compassion on them as they groaned under those who afflicted them." Mark 1:41 adds, "And seeing the leper, He had compassion on him." God loves; God sees; and God cares.

S- *Substantiates a witness to unbelievers observing Christianity.* Through Paul's hardships he carried the gospel to others; they stood amazed. He proclaimed, "I rejoice in my suffering for your sake."[7] And many responded and came to Christ.

T- *Tests the strength of our faith.* God disciplines through suffering with the goal of abandoned reliance on Jesus Christ. Pain is an essential ingredient in building the muscle of faith. The overused adage remains true: no pain, no gain.

U- *Unfolds an opportunity to live on God's terms.* I interviewed in person Joni Eareckson Tada, a quadriplegic and precious ornament of grace among believers. I asked, "Joni, how do you love the Lord with all your strength?" She conceded, "I wake up and live life according to His agenda."

V- *Validates God's character.* How will we know God's goodness if we never experience anguish or sadness? God tries our faith through our suffering so we can try His faithfulness through our surrender.

W- *Weans us from the world's appetites.* God's jealous nature finds offense with other rival passions. Our friendship with the system of this world murders the abiding testimony of God.

X- *X-rays what's in the heart.* Suffering exposes what we really believe about God. Trials force your unbelief in God's providence to the top for confession and removal.

Y- *Yields opportunities for God to prove His sufficiency.* We learn His sufficiency to the same degree that we comprehend our insufficiency. He allows our dilemmas and often appoints them that we might know that God is enough. He never allows more than His grace will uphold.

Z - *Zooms in on the blessing of prayer.* Prayer is not learned in the dining room of celebration but in the closet of suffering. Prayer pours out our deepest need to God; it is there that His presence becomes a shield for our soul.

My friend, take heart. You never know in times of difficulty what God is doing or how He will use your pain. But *this* you can always know: He will never waste a heartache that He will not put to use for His glory. I agree with Ron Dunn, "If God subtracted one pain, one heartache, one disappointment from my life, I would be less than the person I am now, less than the person God wants me to be, and my ministry would be less than He intends!" Indeed, every sorrow is significant. Who knows? God may use your suffering to bring others to Christ, or He may allow your crisis to reveal the authenticity of your faith. Whatever the case might be, you can rest assured that when the season has passed, the lessons learned from the experience will not only benefit others, but will cultivate spiritual maturity. And ultimately, when suffering's goal is finally accomplished, you will enter eternity's glory dressed in your eternal state of perfection.

So praise God! Jesus Christ, the Alpha and Omega, the One who is the entire alphabet of God, abides in your suffering, making you someone you could never have been without it.

> "I am well-content with weaknesses, insults, distresses, persecutions, and difficulties for Christ's sake; for when I am weak, then I am strong."
>
> 2 Corinthians 12:10

62. I am Afforded Sabbath/Salvation Rest

Where do you turn when you're deeply disturbed or overwhelmed with worry and stress? Our human nature gravitates toward something to make us feel better. According to a recent article, approximately 40% of the American women turn to shopping, suffering from what specialists call the upcoming mental disorder of our day.[1] Other reports show that another 30% of adults turn to food. [2] We each have within us an unhealthy addiction of choice if we yield to its lust. God, our Maker and the One who owns the manual on how humans function best, knows that if the vacuum He's placed within us desiring deep satisfaction is not yielded to His Spirit for filling, then we have reason to fear. God's Word tells us over and over to *fear not*; however, Hebrews 4:1 states that we *should* fear one thing: the failure of entering His rest.

If you could go to the nearby filling station and fill up with a deep satisfaction and a fresh start to relax in His control, would you? At creation, God granted the patriarchs a filling station such as that, a place of inner rest found in Him. But because of their unbelief, this "Sabbath-rest" remained unfulfilled. Now it comes to you through salvation in Christ and keeping His promises. You've been granted "salvation rest."

What unsettled issues do you face? Is it truly possible to experience God's undisturbed peace in the midst of your greatest turmoil and find restoration of lost strength? It is not only possible, but it's guaranteed. God has renewed the appointment for you to come and receive His provisions.

Of all the promises in God's Word that have served as my filling station of fuel when I've needed to replenish my supply of hope, *this* one has proven most faithful: Hebrews 4:16, "Let us therefore draw near with confidence to the throne of grace, that we may receive mercy and grace to help in time of need." In it contains the image of a God who anxiously awaits my arrival in order to supply me with whatever I need to persevere in the Christian faith.

+ *Let us therefore draw near:* You have a direction to turn when you're stressed. God supplies your need when your heart is close by. To turn toward Him for help requires a letting go of all the substitutes you run to for relief. To enter His presence puts you visibly in His sight, exposing before Him every crevice of your deepest desire for rescue. There is no sin you could ever commit that would prohibit your invitation to draw near. God throws out the welcome sign for needy seekers. You don't need visitation rights; just come!

+ Let us therefore draw near *with confidence.* What's your attitude when you draw near? Doubtful? Ashamed? Tied in knots? You are summoned to come with the freedom to be completely honest about every secret thought and emotion. You're approaching the One who understands your greatest frailty while bearing the heaviness of your burden. He sees; He knows; He understands. What difference would it make in your rest if you entreated Him with the assuredness that you can rely on His loyalty?

+ Let us therefore draw near with confidence *to the throne of grace.* You draw near to the Almighty's throne! When you pray, do you bring to mind the Bible's description of its appearance and motif of power: flaming with fire, glittering with sapphires, flashing and crashing with lightning and thunder, dazzlingly white gushes of living water protruding from its presence, a rainbow of emeralds encircling its glory while surrounded by a crystal-clear sea of glass. Close your eyes. Envision that! And consider one more thing: it's not a throne of condemnation, but a throne of charitable favor. This blessing is known as God's grace, a condition that grants a reprieve from anxiety, acceptance, and joy. It's a kindness not deserved or earned but a favor given without any expectation of being repaid. It's an absolute free expression of God's generosity with His only motive being an opportunity to act as the supreme Giver. Who wouldn't want to approach a place like that?

✦ Let us therefore draw near with confidence to the throne of grace that we may *receive mercy and find grace to help in time of need.* God has something for you when you come there. Countless times I have approached this audacious seat of power and received a transformation in my unsettled emotions, gripping sadness, or paralyzing fear.

Because Christ sits at the right hand of God the Father, you've inherited a plentiful supply of compassion or whatever you need. His throne bubbles over with continual excess! Never will you be stranded in the desert of need with a pitiless God who has run out of provisions.

My friend, you are expansively blessed with God's greatest gift of extravagance: Sabbath/salvation rest! What's keeping you from "filling-up?"

"There remains therefore a Sabbath rest for the people of God."

Hebrews 4:9

63. I am Abounding in Hope

Years ago off the coast of Massachusetts the S-4 submarine found itself tragically rammed by a passing ship. As it began to sink, the sailors were trapped in the coffin of their own deaths. We can only imagine their frightful attempts in clinging to their masks of oxygen, praying that their greatest fear wouldn't come true. A nearby scuba diver placed his helmeted ear to the side of the vessel and listened for any signs of life. Someone inside tapped a message in Morse code, relaying the frantic atmosphere: "Is…there…any…hope?"

Hope: it's is an indispensable virtue and one of the most distinctive marks in the Christian life. For the believer, hope is unlike the world's definition. Hope is not merely an inward wish that by coincidence your desire comes true; rather, it's an aspiration of rock-solid faith knowing something is certain to happen. It's accompanied by an expectation rooted in confidence that God will do what He has promised. We pray for hope; we live for hope; and we'd die without it. Someone once said if you could convince a man there was no hope, he would curse the day he was born.

In what ways do you need hope today? Do you feel trapped in regret over a mistake you made? Will you ever be able to rise above your physical handicap and let go of the lies you've believed from your enemy? Are you tired of trying to fix a problem and nothing you do seems to help? Do the scales ring out the same disheartening message that the weight will never drop off? Are you weary from praying for a child who has strayed from God's truth? And how long will you look behind every pair of eyes you meet and wonder if that person might be God's spouse for you? Meshed between these lines lies your own secret struggle, your own issue that gropes the outer limits of hope, that place where you wait for your deepest dream to come true.

Where does one look for hope? The Bible says to look inside the Author of Hope, Jesus Christ. Christians must therefore learn to persevere and be patient in the difficulties they meet. How do they do that? Peter gives the answer, "Blessed be the God and Father or our Lord Jesus Christ, who according to His great mercy has caused us to be born again to a living hope through the resurrection of Jesus Christ from the dead."[1] You have a surplus of hope in whatever you need to get you through the difficulty and lift you in the process. This *Living* Hope supports you! This *Living* Hope sustains you! This *Living* Hope stabilizes you! Jesus is not a mysterious hope in a mysterious future. He is a present, resurrected *living* hope in a stable future.

And this Living Hope is *in* you. Peter continued the message to sanctify Christ in your heart always being ready "to give an account for the hope that is in you."[2] When your faith falters, prepare to give an account on how you will respond but letting the Living Hope that's already in you, rise up and abound in excessive measures. The real you carries the Real Hope. Whatever it is you need, call upon the Living hope *within* you!

Throughout the gospels we find Jesus calling attention to his own personhood and not to some far off coming Messiah. He repeatedly gave the remedy for lack of hope: "Come unto Me." To the burdened He beckoned, "Come to Me all who are weary and heavy laden." To the children He invited, "Let the little children come to Me." To the spiritually thirsty He offered, "Come to Me, whoever is thirsty." How well Peter remembered the echoing over the waters of Jesus' bellowing commission of faith, "Come unto Me."

In the Old Testament, Hosea describes hope as a door. In the New Testament, Jesus Christ is the door, and it is through Him that you find hope. John MacArthur defined hope as an unbreakable spiritual lifeline reaching past all appearance right up to the very presence of God where Jesus has taken up His permanent post. You are never without help! For the hope you have in Christ is "the anchor of your soul, a hope both sure and steadfast."[3]

> "Now may the God of hope fill you with all joy and peace in believing, that you may abound in hope by the power of the Holy Spirit."
>
> Romans 15:13

64. I am Enriched in Speech and Knowledge

Satan is the father of deception. Ultimately, one of his most destructive lies is this: you are deficient. To be deficient means you lack some element to carry out the job with success; it's the idea that you lack what it takes, or you don't quite measure up, or you missed the mark. And, by the way, while Satan's at it, he adds one more insult, "It's not that you fall short, but no one else misses the mark quite like you. You're just defective." If he can get you to believe that you are flawed, impaired, or not up to snuff, then he has won the battle in derailing you from activating your most blessed privilege from God: you are abundantly supplied and richly furnished in every way in living a fruitful Christian life, an existence that thrives in the fullness of His wealth. "For you have been given everything pertaining to life and godliness."[1] Indeed, you are a saint with no lack from God, given every divine resource necessary in developing into the person that God has ordained you to become. In Christ, you have it all, enriched by His magnanimous favor and endowed with His enablement to obtain the desires He puts in your heart. There is no inclination put there by God that is not up to date with His ability to fulfill it! You are garnished and graced with all you need in living a holy life, a mission whose purpose is to be an effective witness for Him.

Paul addressed the Corinthians reminding them of the benefits they had received through grace. They were without excuse if they chose not to testify to the truth of the Gospel, for they had been granted two gifts: speech and knowledge.

How often have you thought, "I can't open my mouth and tell my neighbor about Christ. I don't know what to say. I'm not good with my words!" Yet Paul said, "You have been enriched in speech." God, through the Holy Spirit, has put His words in you. All He needs is your willingness to let Him speak. You might be shy by personality, but you are courageous through the Holy Spirit's might as you yield to His development of confidence and boldness. I know a pastor who serves as a prime example. By his inborn personality he's a very shy person, but by God's reborn power he's a valiant crusader of God's Word. And how about Moses? Exodus 4 speaks of his tremendous fear. He pleaded, "Please, Lord, I have never been eloquent. I am slow of speech and slow of tongue." Yet it was God who said, "I will be with your mouth and teach you what to say."[2]

What's God asking you to do, but fear of what you will say is holding you back? You can be sure that if you're willing to speak for Christ,

He will be faithful to put the words in your mouth. God promises, "Do not become anxious about how or what you are to speak, for it shall be given to you in that hour what you are to speak, for it is not you who speak, but it is the Spirit of your Father who speaks in you."[3] God has never failed me with words needed when I've trusted in Him. They are His words, and thereby, the natural consequence is this: transformation, lives changed, touched, empowered.

Or maybe you've said, "I have confidence to tell others of my love for Christ, I don't have the knowledge." I understand. When I was asked to be Peter Spencer's radio co-host and later television co-partner in "Heroes of the Faith with Peter Pam," I thought, *Lord, I don't know enough to be a partner with Peter.* Listen! There are no adequate words in describing the brilliance of this precious man of God! I fussed, "Lord, he teaches apologetics to a hundred million homes in Russia; he's been trained as a theologian since he was five years old; And you want *me* to partner with *him*? What in the world do I have to say? I don't know Greek! Lord, I'm *grossly* deficient!" Yet, God reminded me that He'd use the knowledge He had already revealed to me for the glory of His name. I would have all the speech and knowledge needed whenever I opened my mouth in completing God's assignment in spreading His fame. Indeed, I'm not Peter, but praise the Lord, I am Pam! And you are not like someone else who is "more this and that" in certain areas than you, but you are *you*, uniquely invested with gifts for a God-ordained purpose that only *you* can execute! If you fail to acknowledge your spiritual uniqueness, then you deprive yourself of spiritual power. Believe the truth: you are valuable, complete, and fully adequate for whatever task God asks of you because He enables whom He calls. You are not deficient, and you are *not* without! You are immensely adorned with the riches of all God's grace in accomplishing His assignments. The greater the stretch, the greater the power! And the greater the exploitation of faith, the greater the depth of insight in both speech and knowledge, and so the glorious cycle continues!

"That in everything you were enriched in Him, in all speech and all knowledge."

1 Corinthians 1: 5

65. I am Grace Filled

Grace! It's the most glorious news that could ever hit the front page cover for mankind. Grace! It's the solid base of the new creature in Christ. You read about it; you hear about it; you journal about it. You even sing about it: is not the song "Amazing Grace" one of the most celebrated hymns of all times? Honestly, just how amazing is grace? Its significance to the Christian faith is so unparalleled, we often find ourselves totally inept in even defining it. As a new creature in Christ, your very essence is defined by it! So what is this amazing thing called grace?

Amazing grace: First of all, it is the gospel of Christ as distinguished from the law. While that may sound horribly boring, pay attention! It's the gift from God establishing your release from trying to fix all your old patterns of pleasing God to embracing His new pattern in Christ, whereby, you are fully accepted and made complete by Him.

God deals with His people through arrangements called covenants. The often called Old Covenant is known as the Law, whose purpose was to define the problem of sin while pointing to man's inability in meeting its standards. It primed man for a solution: Jesus Christ. Through the atonement of Christ's Cross, God established a New Covenant whereby God could pour out His unfathomable riches on His people of obedience. Notice the stark difference *from* the Covenant of the Law *to* the Covenant of Grace. Man's existence went *'from and to'* in many ways:

• *from* being enslaved to do what was right (law), *to* being set free to be released to do what was good (grace)

- *from* having a set of rules with limitations to live under (legalism/law), *to* a person to live through without measure (Christ/grace)

- *from* a ministry of condemnation, shame, and guilt (law), *to* a ministry of reconciliation and restoration (grace)

- *from* a system that led to weakness (law), *to* a system that led to confident hope through the Holy Spirit (grace)

As a reborn saint in the New Covenant, you thrive in a plan whereby God released His fullness without restraint. Christ had fulfilled God's requirement at the Cross! So embrace grace!

Amazing grace: It's God's ultimate Christmas present given to man unto salvation on the basis of His goodness alone, having nothing to do with man's good works. Paul confirmed, "God saved you by his special favor when you believed. And you can't take credit for it; it is a gift from God. Salvation is not a reward for good things you have done, so you can't boast about it."[1] Grace is God's voluntary favor given to all who receive His Son. The dying remark of John Allen of the Salvation Army summed it up: "I deserve to be damned. I deserve to be in hell; but God interfered."[2]

Amazing grace: It's the kindness, friendship, and favor of God deposited in your account upon salvation: not just riches, but unfathomable riches, meaning they are untraceable in discovering an end to their wealth! Are you reveling in your endless fortunes: His Word, His patience and forbearance, His wisdom, knowledge, assurance, mercy, and great love? In addition, you've inherited a never-ending supply of whatever you need through prayer. "And my God shall supply all your needs according to His riches in Christ."[3] In ancient Greek, to supply (*epichoregia*) described how a choir manager would provide for all its members in a Greek drama. In short, he took care of all their living expenses; he had a full supply of any kind.[4] What are your living expenses? You generate God's supply through prayer. Grace! It's God's hug to His Son's beloved! You are caressed with the squeeze of God!

Amazing grace: It's the glory to be revealed throughout eternity. There's more grace still to come! Peter exhorts, "Fix your hope completely on the grace to be brought to you." He speaks of your future enjoyment of Christ's riches when He returns. You did nothing to deserve your earthly redemption of grace, and you will do nothing to deserve or complete your future state of grace: eternal perfection, heavenly ecstasy, and communion with the Father. How gloriously extravagant is the truth? God, in His goodness lives to extend His loving-kindnesses throughout all eternity. "*Amazing grace, how sweet the sound!*"

> "May grace…be yours in abundance."
>
> 1 Peter 1:2

66. I am Empowered

Alisa and I have been very close friends for a long time. In junior high her mother tutored me in seventh grade English. Alisa won numerous honors in high school. You name it, and she probably received it. She had it all: stable home life, popularity, yes, and even all the boys. She was Cinderella at the ball, only without the mean ol' stepsisters. She skipped that part of the story. At thirty-five years of age, I got a call from her. She lay under the rubble of a humiliating betrayal and gasping for air to save her life, she came running to me for help. After ten years of marriage to her high school sweetheart, he was leaving, resulting in a heart-wrenching two-year separation ending in a divorce. While her two baby toddlers rallied under her feet, I remember her saying, "Pam, I'll love him until I die. What's God going to do with my life now?" To add to it all, during the time of the divorce, her father was hospitalized in seven institutions within two years with a brain dysfunction, leaving her fully responsible for his care. Her mother was on the verge of a nervous breakdown, and her only sister was moving to Atlanta. For years, I consulted with Alisa, what appeared to be all day long! Trust me, I intimately shared her burden. Actually, let me tell you the truth about Alisa. She doesn't exist. I'm telling my own story.

What does one do when sorrows grow horrifically unbearable, where life as you knew it is no more, when the goose-down feathers in your pillow become your tears' best friend? Where does one turn in times of betrayal and despair? Paul faced the same questions from behind the bars of a Roman prison, and he said, "I can do all things through Christ who gives me strength."[1] *All* things? What's your *all*? What threatens your sense of peace? What defines the way you respond to unwanted circumstances you can't fix?

At salvation a supernatural supply of God's strength was placed in reserve specifically for times of crisis. Gaining access to this reserve works much like a car battery when you turn on your car. When you place the key in your car's ignition and turn the switch to "on," a signal is sent to the car's battery. It then takes the energy that's been stored in chemical form and releases it as electricity. Paul was saying no matter what the crisis, you have the battery of the Holy Spirit inside of you, ready to infuse His reserve of electricity, thereby, releasing His chemical of divine power in whatever you need. To be strengthened is to be empowered by another, to have someone else's might put in you, giving you supernatural capabilities beyond your own potential. Paul was saying as long as you yield yourself to the "on" position and rely on Christ alone as your only source of power, He will impart not only what you need for the moment, but He will give excess energy to overflow into other areas of your life.

I recall the days as a single mom falling on my knees beside my bed to the "on" position. Not only did God tell me that one day He would use my disheartening loss to further the gospel, but He would instill

His joy in me on a moment-by-moment basis, enough spirited electricity to overflow into the lives of my two children. Oh, my! God's faithfulness leaves me speechless!

What secret supply do you have in reserve for your days of despair? Warren Wiersbe alleged, "All nature depends on hidden resources. The great trees send their roots down into the earth to draw up water and minerals. Rivers have their sources in the snow-capped mountains. The most important part of the tree is the part you cannot see, the root system, and the most important part of the Christian's life is the part that only God sees."[2]

What does God see in your roots of anguish and hopelessness? Are you *using* His *infusing*? Through Christ you have all you need. It was Mother Teresa who said, "I can do all things! I know God won't give me anything I can't handle. I just wish He didn't trust me so much!" And Mother Teresa became known as one of the most empowered women of God who ever lived!

> "I have strength for all things in Christ who empowers me. I am ready for anything and equal to anything through Him who infuses inner strength into me. I am self-sufficient in Christ's sufficiency."
>
> Philippians 4:13 (TAB)

67. I am Assured That God's in Control

Perhaps no other promise in Scripture finds a more welcomed place in believers' hearts than this one. It takes the question mark out of our lack of trust in God and replaces it with an exclamation point of solidified courage to press on in the hardest of times. For my children and me, it served as an anchor in our single-parent family. To this day I have a note from my son when he was seven. It's taped to the back of my Bible: "Mom, it's amazing to me when things went wrong how you trusted in God. You told me it would be okay. After the divorce you kept repeating Romans 8:28 over and over again."

Precious friends, I am a passionate witness that this promise from God is gloriously true in overwhelming and extravagant measures! You can rest in the sovereign and utmost control of God. Paul writes in Romans 8:28, "And we know that God causes all things to work together for good to those who love God, to those who are called according to His purpose."[1] Let's break down this promise section by section and glean from its celebrated, magnificent message of hope.

"*And we know*"–When your world turns upside down, you don't know what you know! The life that used to be comfortable now becomes a world of overwhelming insecurity. God says that you can know that He is your *El Roi*, the God who sees you in times of tragedy, bereavement, and disappointment. The Greek word to know, *oikeios*, means a family relative, one belonging to the household of God, as opposed to its opposite meaning: a stranger, one from another group.[2] As a relative-child of God *from His group*, you can have confidence in Him because you are in the household of faith, a dominion the enemy cannot touch. You can rest assured that there is nothing that will come your way that God has not allowed. You can 'know that you know' that He knows! John MacArthur adds, "We can know beyond all doubt that every aspect of our lives is in God's hand and will be divinely used by the Lord not only to manifest His glory but also to work out our own ultimate blessing."[3] To know is a statement of faith and not feeling. God does not always deliver what we want, but we can know it serves a higher purpose. We express to God that even though we cannot see the whys, we know the who!

"*that all things work together for good*"- All things? Even divorce, loss of a child, cancer, rape, betrayal of a friend, financial disaster, unemployment, rebellion of children? These things are sometimes in our *all* list, and we don't like them. We want a life of ease and comfort. You ask, "How could a loving God let these 'all things' on *my* list?" First, let's remember God's ways are higher than ours. God says in Psalm 20:2, "And you thought I was just like you?" Second, God's ultimate purpose is to shape you into the likeness of Christ. It is our destiny to be like Him. I'm sorry, but it takes a village of hurt to do that. Some things on your list are *not* good! God didn't say everything would be good, but that He would work them together for a higher profit. Works together translates *synergeo*, meaning "to cooperate together continuously for the end goal as a fellow worker." [4] The English term is synergism: the cooperative action of elements working together to produce a greater effect than before. "In the physical world, the right combinations of otherwise harmful chemicals can produce substances that are extremely beneficial. For example, ordinary table salt is composed of two poisons, sodium and chlorine." [5] I don't know how He takes the poisons in our lives and makes table salt out of them, but He does! I suppose being called "the salt of the earth" has a new meaning now?

"for those who love God and to those who are called according to His purpose" - This magnificent miracle of making salt out of our trials is not for everyone. Only those who have been born of God by means of a spiritual rebirth become shareholders of this promise. Indeed, God has "blessed us with every spiritual blessing in the heavenly places in Christ," [6] and God's providence in our lives of working everything together for our good is one of them. It is our love for Him, the outpouring of our deepest affections that enable us to praise God regardless of the trial. Indeed, those who remain true to God's perfect will, Jesus Christ, will find comfort, hope, sustaining power, and even joy!

> "And we know all things work together for good for those who love God and to those who are called according to His purpose."
>
> Romans 8:28

68. I am Disciplined

It happened in church. One young girl was misbehaving in the morning worship service so the dad exercised his role by quickly escorting the child down the aisle and into the foyer. On the way out the door, the congregation heard six words of a desperate plea from the toddler's mouth as she turned toward the crowd, "Pray for me! Pray for me!"

Discipline! It's not a word most children invite into their lives. Yet as adults, we see the need to execute corrective training, knowing a child's spirit left to its own nature will destroy itself, reeling totally out of control, developing into a grown-up who never learned how to submit. We understand the need for discipline in a child, that is, until it is *us* and our Heavenly Father escorts us into the foyer for a little visit.

Just like an earthly father disciplines his child for the purpose of harmony and balance, our Father disciplines us for the purpose of godliness and holiness, and though we might fight the idea at first, its outcome makes it one of the most prosperous favors of God on our behalf. After all, it's not just *anyone* the Lord chooses to admonish. Can you imagine sitting in church and abruptly approaching the back row to spank an irreverent child? You'd never do that! They're not your own! But because *you* are 'God's own,' becoming an adopted adult son or daughter at conversion, given a family position guaranteeing joint ownership to *all* His riches as a joint heir of Christ, shouldn't He have the right to train you in order that you might enjoy to the max His highest benefits now and throughout all eternity?

Perhaps you'd more readily embrace the idea of God's discipline if you understood its root meaning, (*paideuo*) to chastise, to train, to educate, to equip.[1] All of God's born again children enlist in His boot camp, 'God's Gold Gym,' a program designed for a makeover called transformation: a process where a person's disposition, character, and behavior models a holy life. In the early ancient world, a Greek boy was often expected to work out in the gymnasium until he reached maturity. God enrolls us in His program, a working out of our salvation, complete with the treadmill of disappointment, the weights of adversity, and push-ups of 'life isn't fair,' all a part of exercising their usefulness in causing us to *sweat out* everything we turn to in getting our needs met apart from Christ.

Have you ever thought when you're sweating in the throws of hardship that God's watchful hand of training rests intentionally upon *you?* Do you reckon it as from the Lord and embrace the lesson to be learned by "despising not the chastening of the Lord, nor fainting when you are reproved by Him?"[2] How can you benefit from God's activity if you don't recognize its presence? How can you know when He's extending His purposeful hand of chastisement your way?

God's discipline comes through conviction. Just like an earthly father, a warning comes first. For God, it's the quickening from the Holy Spirit who works to relate you properly to God. Confession's response releases the chastening. If repentance is ignored, God continues with more serious consequences, such as silencing His response to your prayers, withdrawing His protection, removing opportunities, or ultimately taking your life. Don't continue in the progressive discipline of the Lord! "God will not be mocked. Whatever a man sows He reaps."[3]

God's discipline comes through protection. Often God allows an inconvenience that actually protects you against danger. Just like a parent erects a fence in the yard to protect a toddler from the dog next door, God might set limits or not say yes to a prayer knowing its fulfillment could dismantle your humility or threaten your dependence on Him.

God's discipline comes through affliction. God educates by a means that is not eagerly embraced: pain and suffering. Every hardship is an allowed discipline of God whose ultimate result brings a God-ordained profit to those who are trained by it. Such a belief comes only from a faith that believes no matter what, God is good! It's through adversity that discipline's purpose achieves its eventual goal: a destination not to grieve but to improve, indeed, an outcome that "yields the peaceful fruit of righteousness."[4]

> "He disciplines for our good that we may share in His holiness."
> Hebrews 12:10

69. I am A Receiver of Eternal Life Now

In studying the discipline of joy, I asked a doctrinal question of 100 women concerning their understanding of the concept of eternal life. 100% of them alluded to the fact that eternal life was a future reward, a culmination of God's favor to be enjoyed with Christ in heaven forever, a final result of their salvation from sin. Though that is ultimately correct, it is minutely incorrect. When Jesus announced "I have come that you might have life, and have it abundantly,"[1] was the prosperous life He promised merely reserved for some *future* experience with Christ in heaven? When we are regenerated and come into the eternal plan of God, are we placed in a holding tank, biding our time until the upcoming big day of bliss? What is eternal life? When does it begin? Let's ask Jesus since He's its cofounder.

John chapter 17 explores the concept of eternal life. What is it? It's a process comprising three stages. Phase one takes place in the ancient past before time began. Romans 16:25 speaks of it as "being a secret from the beginning of time." Phase two takes us into the present, a time that began when we entered into personal relationship with God through Christ. Jesus defined, "And this is the way to have eternal life: to know the Father, the only true God, and Jesus Christ, the one the Father sent to earth."[2] Eternal life is *knowing* God intimately, (*ginosko*) referring to a Jewish idiom of sexual intercourse between a man and a woman.[3] It's to experience the deepest level of covenant. How personally you are experiencing eternal life in your day-to-day happenings? Meister Eckhart affirmed, "People who dwell in God dwell in the Eternal Now."[4] Paul warned that *not* to live in the eternal now leaves nothing but a life of loss and rubbish. And finally, phase three in the eternal life plan relates to the future, an endless duration of blessedness in all eternity! It's for *that* reason that Jesus went to the Cross that lost sinners might have everlasting life.

Many today maintain life insurance policies that pay substantial bonuses after death. God granted you a life promise whose benefits begin not at death but at birth, spiritual rebirth. Eternal life is your present possession! What are you doing with it? Are you daily cashing in on your heavenly settlement enjoying the blessings of His graces: support from fellow brothers and sisters in Christ, contentment, undisturbed peace? Why not? They're yours! How can you more intentionally cultivate your eternal now dividends? Jesus' dialogue with God in John 17 gives ideas:

> And Jesus rejoiced, "I brought glory to you here on earth." Making Christ the center of your life is like leaven in bread. It raises the eternal now experience. There is no better tombstone epitaph than to say your life goal was to give God the honor and glory due His name.

> And Jesus celebrated, "I did everything you told me to do." Obedience: it's the burial of your self-will and the resurrection of His. It's the prince of virtues. What has God told you to do that sits in the pocket of procrastination? Jesus finished the work the Father gave Him to accomplish.

> And Jesus applauded, "I manifested your name to men." Do you play the "Show and Tell" game with the names of God: El Elyon- My God reigns; Immanuel- My God Abides; Intercessor- My God maintains; Jehovah Jireh- My God provides; Rabbi- My teacher?

> And Jesus exalted, "I perfected men in unity." How purposely

do you chase after peace? How dangerous is the spirit of contention, criticism, stubbornness, division, or vengeance? What would enhance harmony in your sphere: a rewiring of the tongue or a letting go of the heart?

So activate what's yours. Why not enjoy a pinch of heaven on earth? God not only stores up riches in His future Kingdom, but He dispenses them on an ongoing basis as you let His eternal now bust open. Today is a gift. That's why it's called *the present*. Open it!

> "And this is the way to have eternal life, to know you, the only true God, and Jesus Christ, the one you sent on earth."
>
> John 17:3

70. I am A Recipient of God's Cleansing

What are the similarities we share with these Bible characters?

•David–And his heart condemned him, "Lord, I have sinned greatly in what I have done, but now I pray, O Lord, take away the iniquity of your servant."[1] Seriously? David, the one the Scriptures quote as a man "after God's own heart?"[2]

•Paul–"It's a trustworthy statement, deserving full acceptance, that Christ Jesus came into the world to save sinners, among whom I am foremost of all."[3] Seriously? Paul, the chief of sinners? Paul, one of the most influential men in the Christian faith? Worst of sinners?

Do you ever feel like the lowest sinner? Did you know the name for Paul in Latin means little? As a result of your sin, have you ever felt small? I have! Friends, that gives me hope. If God can forgive and use an adulterer and murderer like David and the most "little, chiefest of sinners" like Paul, then there's hope for me! Perhaps we all feel that way! I'm reminded what the message of God confirms: "For all have sinned and fall short of the glory of God."[4] But praise Him, through Jesus Christ, we're all granted God's highest goodwill for, indeed, His Spirit labors to provide spiritual tools enhancing ongoing opportunities to receive renewed fellowship through prayer and confession! Praise the Lord! Truly, for me, no other verse in God's Word is more heartily needed and celebrated than the privilege of prayer and confession that comes through a heart of sincere repentance.

Why would I pick confession as a significant blessing? I suppose it's because it's the door opener that launches God's power into all the other entitlements. While it's true that you might have received Christ and become a recipient of the "100 I am Blessings," unless you allow His will to be implemented in you through the acknowledgement of and the turning from any known sin, you will never fully experience the joy of your identity in Christ. It's a fact; we come to God first on the level of our wills, being truthful about the real me. Confession brings an end to self-deception and all the false coping mechanisms we hide behind that keep us from dealing with our pain. It forces unconfessed offenses toward ourselves, others, and God to the top for removal and cleansing. I often picture myself coming to God, sitting next to Him on a couch covered in the warts of a critical spirit or selfishness. I place each sin on the floor in front us. As I breathe in the merciful air of His forgiveness, I ask Him to lead me to see each sin's root: pride? lack of faith? prayerlessness? And with each discovery, He applies, one by one, the ointment of His blood, dissolving their hideous sting.

Will the real me please stand up? Its initial step comes through confession. Just what is confession? And how should we see this most significant discipline from God? Confession is an acknowledgment of a heart willing to lay low before the Father. Douglas Steere says confession is a time "where a soul comes under the gaze of God and where in His silent and loving Presence this soul is pierced to the quick and becomes conscious of the things that must be forgiven and put right before it can continue to love the One whose care has been so constant."[5] To confess is to acquiesce to the aspiration of God, acknowledging openly and honestly the sorrow of all sins by naming them one by one. To confess is to come together with God against your own flesh in agreement about your sin. Confession is the means in which God transforms the inner spirit. It's asserting one's willingness to turn from ungodliness, pleading for His takeover in the very core of your soul. True confession is an invitation for God to examine the deepest conscience, followed by a humble allegiance to yield to the inner workings of the Spirit as the sole rule of life. Sometimes this process can be very painful. But remember, while it's true that it might take years of repentance to blot out a sin in the eyes of men, only one tear of repentance suffices with God.[6] There is no getting around it; in God's economy, the only way up is down.

So often repentant children come to Him totally oblivious to the setting in which they enter His presence. Many approach His Highness with an aura of shame, seeing it as their turn for the Holy whippin', feeling it will take an act of Congress to coerce God to forgive their offense. Nothing could be farther from the truth. How do you feel when your children come to you in order to confess a wrongdoing? Aren't you thrilled to see them come in the door? The Holy Spirit works in union with God in drawing you near, and when they see you coming, it's a heavenly celebration! You enter His presence as a child of light, a rightful son or daughter of the King! You come not into an environment of sullied condemnation, but sacred communion. No need to plead for His forgiveness, rather confess your sin. Your sin debt was paid. Christ nailed the source of your unfaithfulness to the Cross, purging all unrighteousness. You simply need to be renewed to enjoy its benefits. So celebrate and receive God's cleansing! True confession grants spiritual power and vision.

Confession's finale brings joy by granting one cleansing after another. Oh, how my heart loves taking a bath!

"If we confess our sins, He is faithful and just to forgive us our sins and cleanse us of all unrighteousness."

1 John 1:9

71. I am Renewed

Are you stuck in a pattern of unwanted negative thoughts where you feel like you're losing your spiritual *umph?* Then welcome the good news: you are renewed in Christ. On a practical basis, no other benefit you received as a born again Christian is more welcomed and needed than this one! If you can learn the principles of living a renewed life, then you are well on your way to expansive living!

Your victory in the Christian experience comes from the mastery of renewing your mind. To rejuvenate your thoughts is to replace corrupted beliefs with the truth of God's Word. It's to ask God to work through you until you think what He thinks. Someone said, "It is to let the mind of the Master be the master of your mind." Renewing your thoughts is to break free from the world's way of thinking. It is to be changed on the outside into conformity with the inside redeemed nature. But how does that happen? Thank goodness one of God's greatest gifts is the power of choice.

As you know, controlling your thoughts remains an ongoing battle. You have two sides that sometimes fight like a civil war within you. On one side there is the soaring eagle, the Spirit-dominated life. Everything it stands for is majestic and good, where it aims high in flying above the clouds, and even though it dips down into occasional valleys, it rests on the mountaintops. The other side is the untamed tiger, the flesh-dominated life, that inside growling that represents your very worst. He eats upon your unresolved anger and inadequacies and justifies himself when you're living apart from God. The question over the battle that rages is this: who wins the battle? It's simple; the one you feed.

To renew your mind is to change your "feeding" habits in the way you think. Will you bite into the thoughts that enhance courage, perseverance, and hope, or will you nibble on the morsels that trigger defeat, drudgery, and despair? Until you participate with God in the process of exchanging your thoughts for His, you will continue to live in a downward spiral.

God's goal is a renovation of your character, a change in your outside behavior brought about by an inside transformation. Your choice to *step off* of the destructive track of diminishing thoughts and *step onto* His track of rejuvenating truth sets into motion the renewed mind where right thinking leads to right acting. Never do you have to remain trapped in decayed thoughts. You have the tools to renew your mind because you have a new kind of mind to renew. You have Christ's mind, and when you feed on Him, changes occur, attitudes lift, dispositions shift, and hope returns. Your redirected mind-set begins to expose the power you possess in breaking demonic strongholds that have entrenched themselves around your thought life. When you replace your thoughts with His, God brings out the best in you, reestablishing a deep sense of peace and restored direction.

But Satan, your enemy, does not want you to know this invigorating truth! He wants you trapped and warped in your thinking, a captive of hopeless misery. How can you battle such a foe? Take charge! Reverse the curse by renewing your mind. Recall the essence of his nature: he's a *liar*! Stand ready to blast open the truth!

L= Listen for his lies. He'll hurl insults like, "You are inadequate and unloved." Be ready to recognize what's not true.

I= Invalidate the lie. Renounce what cripples, shames, and debilitates. If what you're hearing brings condemnation, then get rid of it.

A= Act! Exchange the lie with the truth. If he says, "You will never get out of this hopeless condition." Agree with Job: "God does unsearchable wonders without number."[1] Remember Jeremiah: "Nothing is impossible with God."[2]

R= Redirect your actions to line up with your new beliefs. By faith put into motion what you know is true.

So be restored and replenished. God will grant you reinforcement to live in His inexhaustible revitalizing miracle of renewal.

"...but be transformed by the renewing of your mind..."

Romans 12:2

72. I am Blessed with Spiritual Blessings in the Heavenly Places

With each entitlement studied and written, I've become increasingly more enamored by the goodness of our God and the wealth of His graces! The glorious inheritance of His benefits that came to us in our new identities can only be described as God's unfathomable favor toward us! Unfathomable? These blessings of His unsearchable kindnesses remain so far beyond our ability to comprehend them that they cannot even be traced; our finite beings remain inept at grasping the magnitude of God's love and generosity toward us! With that being the case, how can I explain the phenomenon that the God, whom we bless, praise, and eulogize, would turn from His position of blessedness and become 'The Blesser' toward His creation? Yet, that's what He did! To imagine the Creator stepping into His own created environment and becoming one of them through the physical body of Christ is incomprehensible, and for what purpose did God become man? So that we might receive eternal blessings. In modest gratitude I say, "Hallelujah to 'the One True God' whose sole nature thrives to bestow favors on His children." For, indeed, he rescued us from the domain of spiritual death and placed us in the sphere of spiritual life, that place where His blessings abound and await our pleasure!

It is God who is *The Blesser*. To bless another describes an act where one gives favor and good tidings. *The Blesser* holds the recipient in a position of honor with the motive of invoking on him a measure of prosperity. To bless one is to enable him to succeed, while the opposite would be to curse. It is God whose divine nature of perfect holiness has chosen that "those of faith shall be blessed,"[1] and He shall, thereby, enhance His children's relationship with Him.

Do you often wonder when life brings nothing but pain and suffering, where the blessings of God have gone? Unfortunately, we gravely misunderstand the nature of God's blessings. While it's true that "every good thing bestowed and every perfect gift is from above coming down from the Father of Light,"[2] it's also true that the nature of His blessings are not always material but primarily spiritual. What are these blessings and where do they originate?

We are so conditioned to minimizing our temporal life into this earthly existence called time that we fail to see the real life; it's the spiritual me who actually lives "raised up and seated in the heavenly places in Christ Jesus."[3] The real you actually resides in two abodes: the visible realm, the earthly; and the invisible realm, the eternal. A story was told of Queen Victoria of England. As a young girl she was shielded from the fact that one day, she would be queen of England for fear it would spoil her. Finally she was told, and her response, "Then I will be a good one." Her life was controlled by her position, and though she did not often sit on her throne, her life was governed by the fact that her power came from that position. In her heart no matter where she roamed in the country, her attitude never left her throned position, that place of her identity's origination.[4]

Likewise, all of our identity and blessings remain in the heavenlies surrounding God's throne, and it is through Christ, our mediator, that we receive every blessing or spiritual enrichment needed to live the Christian life. In Christ, we have every spiritual blessing. What is it you need today? Did you know you already have it? Do you need more faith, more peace, more joy, more strength to endure? It is yours as you appropriate it by faith. Some might say living the Christian life is hard; not so, it's impossible! Who among us can love perfectly and live sinlessly? Yet God has granted us divine enablement to live a supernatural life, one marked by the seal of His power that we possess through the Holy Spirit, God's witness within us.

To receive His blessings now would be enough, but there's more! When He blesses us, He actually glorifies Himself, for one day all of heaven will worship Him for His benevolence! Every creature will bow: "Amen, *blessing*, glory, wisdom, power, and might be to our God forever and ever!"[5] He blesses us, and forever we will bless Him!

> "Blessed is God…who has favored us with every spiritual blessing in the heavenly places in Christ."
>
> Ephesians 1:3

73. I am Compelled to Walk in God's Statutes

God gave a glorious promise to the children of Israel in Ezekiel 36: 26–27, one whose fullness would come to light in the Messiah, a promise that every Christian richly enjoys. "Moreover, I will give you a new heart and put a new spirit within you, and I will remove the heart of stone…and give you a heart of flesh. And I will put My Spirit within you and cause you to walk in My statutes, and you will be careful to observe My ordinances." Such a promise serves as the foundation of your new identity: God implanted a pliable and soft nature, one where your heart's desire would be persuaded to follow God's laws and ways. The only reason you desire the things of God is because He put in you the holy mechanism (the Holy Spirit) causing you to thirst for Him. You have within you a magnet that's bent toward God. These divine inclinations give proof that you are not the person you used to be and not yet the person you are becoming. Your former inside vacuum of self-centeredness has been replaced with God-centeredness. Such a miracle testifies of God's initiative to conform you into His image. Your new position is living proof that you are a new creature drawn by the Spirit to walk in His commands. And how did God package His commands? They're enclosed in the pages of your Bible.

The Bible: it's God's heart dissolved on paper; a record of God's revelation to man, an instrument able to totally transform the soul written by those divinely inspired by His Spirit. It's God's roadmap for an abundant life; the Message Bible says it's a manual to teach the inexperienced the ropes and give young people a grasp on reality.[1] It's God's tool of judgment, a perfect discerner of man's heart: *perfect (kritikos)* suggesting the idea of a critic. The Bible critiques the inner man.[2] It's God's love letter to those new hearts regenerated by Christ. Hebrews 4:12 describes the Bible as living because its author, God, is living. Its content records the resurrected life of Christ, which quickens a response from those indwelt by the Holy Spirit; it's active by dealing with the conscience, bringing it to a complete awareness of God's activity; *it's sharper than any two-edged sword, piercing as far as division of soul and spirit, of both joint and marrow;* it cuts incisively revealing sin; *and it's able to judge the thoughts and intentions of the heart;* it's like a dagger that cuts to the innermost part exposing all to God's light. The Bible! Every human being on the face of the earth will be judged or blessed by its content, and I'm instructed to walk after its statutes.

We have this holy compelling within us, but we need boosters in keeping His voice within us easily heard. What are ways you can enhance your love for Christ's teachings? How can you assert the privilege and joy of getting to know God on a more meaningful and regular basis? Your upward development depends on a solid root system. God's shown me effective ways in deepening our love connection. If you need a fresh lift in rekindling your attraction to His Letter, try these:

+ Ask for the Holy Spirit's guidance to rightly appraise the Word before you begin reading. (This is crucial, crucial!)

+ Devote a specific time and place each day to pray, read, and journal.

+ Approach your Bible study with an intentional expectation of an encounter with Almighty God.

+ Memorize the scriptures pertaining to your needs.

+ Rewrite in your own words what God tells you.

+ Ask application questions: What is God saying to me about His character, my sin, what He wants me to do?

+ Draw pictures beside verses illustrating what the text implies. (I draw stick figures!)

+ Read a verse emphasizing different words: *God* loves me: God *loves* me; God loves *me*.

+ Record on a post-it note how God spoke to you in the morning. Place it on your steering wheel, bathroom mirror, or computer screen.

+ Meditate on what you read, knowing reading is not meditating. Dwell on Him all day in your thoughts.

+ Don't just read the Word, incarnate it. Put it into practice.

+ Record your voice on tape reading scripture and play it over and over in the car. It's a great tool for scripture memory: play–rewind ; play–rewind ; play–rewind.

So enjoy God's Word and the next time you're sitting in the doctor's office and you see the Bible on the table, don't just sit there. Pick it up; put it to your ear and listen. It's alive and active! You will hear the heartbeat of God: ba-boom, ba-boom, ba-boom.

> "And I will put a new Spirit within you and cause you to walk in My statutes."
>
> Ezekiel 36:27

74. I am Afflicted but Not Crushed

In September 1957, a song released by Elvis Presley became a top-selling record for the next twenty-five years. It sold two million copies in the United States alone, earning a Double Platinum Certification. Remember the song? Who doesn't recognize "Jailhouse Rock?"

Have you ever had one of those weeks where you felt locked in a jailhouse of problems? Circumstances crowded in like a captive trapped in a prison cell and there seemed to be no way out! Everywhere you turned, there stood another bar of steel locking you in? Perhaps you need to join Joseph in Genesis 39. One day he ended up in prison for a crime he did not commit. Injustice at its peak barged into his day and for two years he remained locked behind Egyptian bars. When's the last time you were treated unfairly and found yourself surrounded by the dust of despair? When's the last time you wondered what possible purpose God could have in the unwanted incident?

The Bible says that it was *there*, behind prison bars, that the Lord extended kindness to Joseph. Maybe you are thinking what Joseph might have been thinking: "Excuse me, Lord. Why couldn't you extend your kindness to me while laying out in the sun on the Mediterranean beach?" But God had a plan. Stretching and sharpening Joseph's capacity for service was birthed in the isolation of that jail. One day soon

Joseph would serve in the Pharaoh's palace as the second most important man in the world! Only by preparing him in the prison would he be equipped for usefulness in the palace.

As true with most of us, lessons in spiritual maturity come out of the cell of adversity, discouragement, and betrayal. Suffering gives spiritual growth training. God, in His sovereignty, brings you into circumstances that induce dependence on Him through the intercession of the Spirit in you. It is in that pain that one's response to misfortune will either qualify or disqualify him for the next opportunity of spiritual growth. Why is it that we have a false notion that life should be all about financial excess, spirit-filled children, a faithful spouse, or no untimely deaths? Why do we feel we've received a "raw deal" when bad things happen, when Jesus Himself declared "we enter Heaven's glory through many tribulations?"[1] Why should we expect a pain-free passage through planet Earth whose jurisdiction temporarily belongs to Satan and his demons? That would be like entering a bee-infested cage and expecting not to get stung. Jesus knew that suffering was inevitable, that life would sting at times. Just because it's unavoidable doesn't mean Christ won't give you strength to endure the pain and sustain you in the process. You are not permanently crushed, defeated, perplexed, or destroyed through the trials of this life. Jesus said, "I have overcome the world."[2] Oswald Chambers said, "God does not give us overcoming life. He gives us life as we overcome. The strain of life is what builds our strength. If there is no strain, there is no strength."[3]

Have you maximized your injustices and asked God to match His delivering power to your willingness to trust Him in the process? Are you ready to yield in surrendered patience to what He has allowed, knowing that pain nurses courage? Joseph was ready, for he refused to be defined by mistreatment. Rather, he chose to hand over his mishandlings to God as an act of worship and trust the character of God to sustain and support his plight. As a result, God's favor promoted

Joseph's reputation and success followed his path "and whatever Joseph did, the Lord made him to prosper."[4]

As so it came to pass, one fine day, the prison gate swung open, and Joseph emerged from that cell stronger than any bar of steel. Who would have thought that behind the prison walls, that God, the Rock of Ages, would prove to be Joseph's "Jailhouse Rock"?

> "We are afflicted in every way, but not crushed; perplexed but
> not despairing; persecuted, but not forsaken; struck down, but
> not destroyed; always carrying about in the body the dying of
> Jesus, that the life of Jesus also may be manifested in our body."
>
> 2 Corinthians 4:8–9

75. I am Lavished with the Riches of God's Grace

I believe there are some things in life that should flabbergast us to the outer edge of insanity, and beholding the unfathomable riches of God's goodness and lavish grace toward us is one of them. The deeper I dig in trying to lay hold of the magnitude of who I am in Christ, the more dizzy I become in celestial drunkenness. Who can begin to hold inside all these magnificent treasures we received upon our initial salvation experience? Our little hearts just can't take it. In fact, sometimes I think mine is going to bust! The Apostle John knew what I was talking about: "See how very much our Heavenly Father loves us, for He allows us to be called His children."[1] We can't even imagine what we will be like when Christ returns. But we do know that when He comes, we will be like Him for we will see Him as He really is. No wonder He's so good to us! We're His children, and He knows what treasures lay ahead of us for all eternity. How does He do it? I know for myself when I have toys and treasures for my family on Christmas morning, I can't wait for them to see what I have prepared for them.

Out of God's goodness He has awarded an inheritance *according* to His grace. If you were to receive an inheritance *according* to my riches, you wouldn't receive much, but it's according to *His* riches. And just how wealthy is God? His riches exceed the limits of excessiveness, standing profusely extravagant to the same measure of everything He owns! How much of His wealth are you spending these days? Are you praying big? Believing big? Asking big? God's wealth is not necessarily monetary endowments but rather spiritual endowments extending into all eternity. But you don't have to wait until eternity to cash in. He's purposed blessings to accompany your eternal reward, gifts to be enjoyed now.

What are these grace gifts He's given? They are the spiritual resources and pleasures He's granted in strengthening your spiritual maturity. They are gifts in aiding your understanding of Him, helping the process of being transformed into His image. They flow from God's grace. And what is God's grace? It's His goodness, His holiness, His perfect attributes of love, joy, peace, and faithfulness. Our whole lives fall under His awning of grace. We live in the atmosphere of His grace. Every breath we inhale and exhale comes from His grace. All this goodness comes through one source, Jesus, God's greatest demonstration of grace. Notice these grace gifts given:

God's Word - The Bible is God's instruction manual in how to experience an abundant life. In it the Holy Spirit leads you to obey. Day by day by day He transforms you into the person He has already declared you to be throughout all eternity.

Wisdom and Insight - Through God's Word you learn and develop practical wisdom, leading to a lifestyle of spiritual consciousness. God grants a penetrating discernment in the execution of His affairs. Such wisdom and insight serve as instruments in showing others what God looks like while deepening your own sensitivity of Him.

God's Seal - When you received Christ you did not instantaneously receive all God's fullness since you still await the redemption and perfection of your physical eternal body. But you did receive God's seal promising your eternal inheritance to come. That sealing mark that identifies your ownership of God is the Holy Spirit. He's your down payment of eternity's glory. You now possess through the Spirit not only security for eternity, but rightful ownership and authority benefits concerning God's plan for you now.

Joy - It accompanies the life of a believer. How often does Christ's joy within you paint a picture on your face? Would others notice by your countenance that your source of life is the risen Christ? I believe Charles H. Spurgeon said it best, "When you speak of Heaven let your face light up; let it be irradiated with a heavenly gleam; let your eyes shine with reflected glory. But when you speak of Hell—well, then your ordinary face will do." Oh, friends, let your demeanor mirror the lavish graces of God you've received, a gladness of heart that beams out of your very face. So take off the ordinary you and let the real you shine forth!

"In Him we have redemption through His blood…according to the riches of His grace."

Ephesians 1:7–8

76. I am Bestowed with the Mind of Christ

My daughter, Sara, is a "chip off the ol' block." She thinks much like I do. I don't have to say a lot to her when I'm trying to tell her something of significance. She's spent time with me, and she knows me well! Just one word spoken sends the message. For example, when she was dating her husband, Jess, I would say as she left the house to go on a date, "Antenna!" That would mean to keep the antenna of her life up because the Holy Spirit wanted to talk to her while she was out with him. And often we even laugh at the same time when a word is spoken because we think alike; she's shared my joys, shared my sorrows, sat at my feet for words of wisdom, and telephoned for prayer. She knows me. Because the Holy Spirit is in both of us, He enables us to think His thoughts, which means we think the same things. She, in a unique kind of way, has my mind.

What happens when one who is not a believer comes to Christ? God gives His beloved creature a brand new radar receiver, the Holy Spirit, the One who makes it possible to know the Father's mind if only he will exercise the privilege of activating its power through meditating on God's Word and prayer. God speaks to His children today through His Spirit. When the believer yields himself to the instruction of the Bible (the mind of God) and to the control of this newly implanted power, the Holy Spirit, a transformation begins. One's thoughts, emotions, and actions begin to mimic God's thoughts, emotions, and actions. Such a change continues as the person falls under the influence of the Holy Spirit, the One who continually seeks the mind of God.

It was out of Paul's concern for his beloved friends in Corinth that he wrote his first letter hoping they would grasp the glorious miracle of one of the most magnificent realities they had received as a new creation: they housed the mind of Christ. What? Can you imagine how difficult that was for them to comprehend? They lived in an age where the Greek gods were distant and not interested in the matters of mere mortals. How could such a God through Christ not only come to them, but also give them the capacity to know His mind, to partake in His reasoning, to become privy to His divine revelations? Friends, I often ponder the same shock! Think about it. Think about having access to someone else's mind. How would your life be affected if you had access to the mind of Charles Manson? What if you could act upon the mind of the president of your country, or what if you could experience the mind of Jesus? I'm utterly flabbergasted what took place at the moment of salvation. Never has a brain transplant been more miraculous! What happened at that moment?

My inner-self abandoned that natural condition in which I was born, a state dominated by my lower nature. Formerly, my soul remained void of any possibility of relating to God. I had no inborn faculties to experience the things of God. I was like a car with a dead engine. And just like it is impossible for a human being to fly, it was impossible for me to comprehend the workings of God. For the unsaved person, the Christian life seems foolish. He has no capacity to discern spiritual matters or perform services pleasing to God. His nature remains under the state into which it was born: a condition of decay. Such a person avoids the teachings of Christ.

But upon receiving Jesus, I abandoned the *natural* man and became a *spirit* man, receiving the Holy Spirit, thereby replacing my dead car engine with a new one. Now I'm capable of understanding the Bible and rightly evaluating God's ways. I now have the mind of Christ or His supernatural reasoning power to discern His Word, a revelation taught not by human wisdom, but by the words of His Spirit.[1] Is that a miracle? You and I possess the likemindedness of Jesus and can unite with His thoughts of divine insight, while exercising clear thinking and common sense.

What day-to-day impact should it have knowing you have the mind of Christ? Listen to this: never will you be without discernment in knowing what to do: You have the mind of Christ. Never will you face a circumstance permanently paralyzed by fear: *You have the mind of Christ*. Never will you remain trapped in past bondage unable to break free: *You have the mind of Christ*. Never will you be unable to disregard old patterns of behavior and start anew: *You have the mind of Christ*. Never will you exist without hope:

You have the mind of Christ.

You *have* the mind of Christ.

You have *the mind of Christ!*

> "But a natural man does not accept the things of the Spirit of God, for they are foolishness to him and he cannot understand them because they are spiritually appraised (judged), but he who is spiritual appraises (judges) all things..... for we have the mind of Christ."
>
> 1 Corinthians 2:14–16

77. I am Favored

She was a first century mother of a celebrity, a Hebrew woman by birth, living in a quaint community located on the southern plains of Lower Galilee. She was a concoction of mysterious wonder: ordinary but extraordinary, normal but abnormal, common but rare. No one knows much of her background or parentage, where she was born or the nature of her death. She was unknown in the Galilean village, having made few appearances in the gospels, but has become well-known in today's Western culture, having inspired the most exquisite artwork in the world. Who was this woman? Ask Jesus. She was His mother.

Mary! Her life eulogizes the virtues of a God-devoted woman, a Jewish maiden admired for her spotless virginity and humbleness of heart, obedient and subservient to the will of God. Many esteem her as an object of veneration, and many set her apart in a class all her own. Though there is certainly a merit of honor due her name, I've found a common bond with Mary, and together we share one of God's greatest gifts: we are *blessed* of God. Was it not Elizabeth who pronounced to her, "You are blessed *among* women."[1] Among? That means there's more than one. I'm among 'the among!' And Mary recognized the blessing of the blessed: "My soul exalts the Lord and My spirit has rejoiced in God my Savior...From this time on all generations will count me *blessed*."[2] She was, indeed, blessed; she carried the Savior of the world! And you are blessed; her Son said so!

Over thirty years had passed since Mary's initial visit by Gabriel foretelling the coming of Christ, and news spread like wildfire on the grassy hills of Judea. Jesus, the healer, traveled on the hilltop beside the Sea of Galilee curing every kind of disease and pain, indeed, everyone from the demonic to the epileptic, even to the run of the mill townsman suffering from a downtrodden heart. It was Jesus, and it was He who would bestow His followers with the same 'one word pronouncement' His mother had received from the Father: *blessed!*

To be favored is to inherit God's Empire into your heart, a permanent condition where one's satisfaction and joy lies outside this material world. God says when we get our new identities we are marked with His abundance. I imagine from heaven's viewpoint the heavenly hosts gaze upon those earthlings who've been branded with the insignia OBC- Owned By Christ! Friends, we're tattooed with a distinct emblem that leaves a permanent imprint: *favored!*

Are you receiving strength from your most hallowed status? When you're driving down the road or walking into the grocery store, do you sometimes fall to your knees in your heart thanking God for His merciful favor? I know what you're saying, "But I don't feel blessed. Life is hard for me right now!" Yet, to feel the blessing is to reckon your position above the circumstantial realm where God invokes His welfare on your behalf, even though you might remain temporarily blind to His workings. Is that strange? It is, indeed! God's ways are peculiar. He views life from a higher altitude. Just look at His reasoning with the disciples:

> You're blessed when you're at the end of your rope. With less of you, there is more of God and His rule. You're blessed when you feel you've lost what is most dear to you. Only then can you be embraced by the One most dear to you. You're blessed when you're content with just who are you, no more, no less... You're blessed when you care. At the moment of being 'carefull,' you find yourselves cared for. You're blessed when you get your inside world, your mind and heart, put right. Then you can see God in the outside world. [3]

I wonder if Mary felt God's goodwill when she endured the town's gossip and snickers after Christ's crucifixion. I wonder if Mary felt God's blessing when she visited the Polaroid snapshot in her mind taken at the foot of the Cross? And how about you? Do you reckon yourself smiled upon by God when you feel not? There resides in all believers a power able to transcend every human emotion, thrusting one into a spiritual reality of being fully satisfied no matter what. How could that be? Better yet, how could it not be? God's Kingdom resides within.

"Blessed be God.....who has blessed us...."

Ephesians 1:3

78. I am Comforted

The 23rd Psalm, known as the Shepherd Psalm of David, remains one of the most celebrated scriptures today. Why is that? Its words resound with the invitation to know a God who protects by providing green pastures and still waters. It appeals to anyone's personal desire for a God of serenity and grace. Who hasn't heard the psalm about the Lord being the Shepherd and how He tends His beloved sheep? God compares us to that particular animal, and knowing their nature, I'm not so sure that's a compliment. Though soft and cute, they are basically ignorant little critters, stepping right off cliffs and wandering astray in obstinate rebellion against their master's care. Foolishly, they think they can handle the wilderness just fine on their own. And God compares us to them? We, indeed, need a Shepherd! Life outside the pasture's confines promises despair, destructive fear, and destitution of hope. But for those whose hearts have been made new by the indwelling Spirit of Christ, they find the Shepherd as a compassionate protector and provider, One who asserts His abiding presence bringing a consolation that stretches deep into the sheep's most throbbing sorrows.

When I am in need of the immediate TLC of my Shepherd, I find comfort in the Hebrew translations of the 23rd Psalm. Their richness provides a tranquil solace of God's guardianship over the soul of this little sheep. Who is this Shepherd, and what does He do?

The Lord is my Shepherd. Lord (Yahweh)[1]- Jehovah, the one true self-existent God; Jesus Christ (*Yeshua*)-God saves, the anointed one.[2] He is *Jehovah Rohi*- "the Lord, my shepherd" described by Isaiah as the one who feeds his flock, gathers the lambs in His arms, and carries them in His bosom, gently leading them.[3]

I shall not want: 'want' (*haser*)[4] indicating lack. The Shepherd withholds nothing that is needed. It's to say, "The Lord is my caretaker. I have all I need."

He makes me lie down in green pastures: 'Lie down' (*rabas*)[5] a reclining position, resting but ready for action. He stretches you out in fresh vegetation void of fretful calculating, anxiety, or fear.

He leads me beside quiet waters: 'leads' (*nahal*)[6] to be divinely guided to a station of rest, to sustain. The shepherd guides to a place of satisfied contentment, ease, repose.

He restores my soul and guides me in paths of righteousness: 'restores' (*sub*)[7] to render liberation. The Shepherd brings back to life refreshment of soul.

For His name's sake: 'name's sake' (*sem*)[8] to give high status to the One of renown. He is the Shepherd of His own fame and reputation. He will never let Himself down!

Even though I walk through the valley of the shadow of death: 'shadow' (*tsalmaveth*)[9] rings around the eyes, a condition of darkness, an unhealthy condition. In times of oppression, His commitment presides through the trial.

I will fear no evil because you are with me: 'fear' (*yare*)[10] to be intimidated over an unfavorable condition, to reside without reverence. God's presence promotes confidence.

Your rod and staff they comfort me: 'Comfort' (*naham*)[11] to be encouraged. His instruments bring relief from despair.

Thou dost prepare a table before me in the presence of my enemies: 'prepare' (*arak*)[12] to lay in order. Jesus lavishly calculates and provides in the midst of danger.

Thou hast anointed my head with oil, my cup overflows: 'anointed' (*dasen*)[13] to take away the ashes and make fat, become prosperous. His excessive provisions run over.

Surely goodness and lovingkindness will follow me all the days of my life: 'follow' (*radap*)[14]–to pursue ardently, to secure. His provisions chase after his sheep for a lifetime.

And I will dwell in the house of the Lord forever: 'dwell' (*yasab*)[15] a prominent seating position, to be returned to its original state of correctness. The Shepherd will restore to His flock their original position of perfection before sin: a state of perpetual bliss, fulfillment, and eternal joy forever!

Is it any wonder why the 23rd Psalm towers as the 'Statue of Liberty' in bringing comfort to His beloved?

He is the "great Shepherd of the sheep."

Hebrews 13:20

79. I am Carried

In continuing the theme of the 23rd Psalm, I've discovered why we as sheep gravitate to the image of Jesus as our Shepherd. From conception, we were carried in our mother's womb. After birth we were placed next to our mother's chest. Even today when you see an infant crying, what does the parent do to bring relief to its soul? They pick it up, carry it, and draw it close to their side. Never has there been a person born that has not possessed a desire for someone to love and hold them. I believe that inborn yearning for nurturing and protection comes by God's hand serving as a catalyst for people to seek out Jesus, the only One who can fill the longing of their souls.

John chapter 10 speaks of the wondrous relationship between the shepherd and the sheep. It's the shepherd who serves as the provider, the guide, the protector, and the supreme figure representing authority and leadership. So close is their connection that the sheep know the tones and inflections of their Shepherd's voice and readily respond to His calling. When I was in Israel, I saw it for myself. Overlooking the Shepherd's Field in Bethlehem wobbled a young shepherd boy with his sheep. As the flock began to stray toward me, just a word spoken in a strange pitch awakened an about face in the sheep, and over the hill they followed their Shepherd.

But perhaps the most endearing depiction of Christ as our Shepherd is the portrait of Him carrying the sheep around His neck. It's the tender love connection between the two that we cherish. Why? Because we want to be carried. We want someone to lift our millstones and miseries, our sickness, sadness, and sorrow. We want someone to caress our broken places, comfort our innermost sores, and carry us when we grow limp and fatigued. We long to hear the Shepherd's voice calling us by name to come to Him and drop the overworked schedules and overwhelming burdens.

Jesus Christ is our Shepherd, and while sometimes it's our nature to worry, it's always His nature to carry. He beckons, "Come to me all of you who are weary and heavy laden and I will give you rest. Take my yoke upon you and learn from Me, for I am gentle and humble in heart, and you shall find rest for your souls."[1] So turn to Him. Drop the load! And ask Him to carry you in these times:

When you are depressed Psalm 27:13–14

When you are lonely Psalm 13

When you are tired Psalm 127:1–2

When you are anxious 1 Peter 5:7

When you are abandoned Hebrews 13:5

When you lose a loved one 1 Thessalonians 4:13–18

When nothing seems to be going right Psalm 37:1–4

When someone has wronged you Colossians 3:13

When you want to take revenge Romans 12:19

When God seems distant Psalm 139

When you need to be forgiven Psalm 51

When you worry Psalm 37:25–26

When you are sick James 5:14

When you need wisdom James 1:5–8

When you feel like giving up Luke 11:5–13

When you feel betrayed Psalm 55

When you feel shamed Proverbs 28:13

When your past won't leave you alone Colossians 1:21–22

When you feel you have failed God 2 Timothy 2:13

When temptation strikes Ephesians 6:10–18

When you need guidance Psalm 25:9

When you have left God Luke 15:11–32

We can learn much from our North American Indian friends. They had no written alphabet before they met white man, yet their body language was anything but primitive. Their connotation for friend was not "the-one-who-stands-close-by," rather "the-one-who-carries-my-sorrows-on-his-back." Doesn't that define the love of your Shepherd?

> "I am the good shepherd, and I know My own and My own know Me."
>
> John 10:14

Chapter Nine

My Service

In what roles am I enabled to impact the lives of others?

80. I am A Servant

When we say the word servant, no doubt biblical personalities come to mind: like the Old Testament hero Zerubbabel who reconstructed the Jerusalem Temple, or the New Testament prophetess Anna who prayed in the temple day and night. But who comes to mind in your world? What modern day servants tread the ground where you walk? If the definition of a servant of God is one who is devoted to another at the disregard of one's own personal interest, then I have a model before me every day. My friend in ministry, Shelley Pulliam, exemplifies Paul's words, "Do nothing from selfishness or empty conceit, but with humility of mind, let each of you regard one another as more important than himself."[1] I am most thankful for her gift of service to me personally, others, and to *Arise Ministries.*

If others could give you a title, what would they say: Shelley, the servant; Megan, the genuine of heart; Ed, the worrier; Kelly, the prayer warrior; Dan, the friendly? Notice how James, Jesus' actual brother, addressed himself as he penned the first verse in the book of James. He didn't say, "James, the Head Councilman of the Church of Jerusalem," or "James, the Brother of Jesus" (though he could have impressed everyone with *that* title); rather he humbly identified, "James, the *Bondservant* of

Jesus Christ." To him, being a servant was a more prestigious honor than being a brother!

I suppose from a biblical perspective we're all subject to slavery, either as slaves to sin or slaves to God. Yet when you received Christ, you were released from sin's power over you and brought into the enslavement and care of God inheriting His nature; and what was that? Jesus came to serve, not to be served. Even though you might not feel or act like a servant, the fact remains you have a nature already pliable in taking on the role of a bondservant.

When James and Paul classified themselves as bondslaves, the believers in the first century easily understood that concept. A servant/slave, represented by the Greek word *doulos*, denoted a man deprived of all personal freedom, a person not at his own disposal, but rather under the lordship of his master.[2] Such a man had no rights of his own because he was consumed in the will of another. What happens when we see ourselves deprived of all self-interest and brought under the subjection of Christ? What happens when our wills become enslaved by our desire to wholly follow Him? We then become slaves for other fellow servants.

It was likely an exhausting afternoon when Jesus seized the moment of solitude with His disciples in a small fishing boat. Surely they needed a one-on-one visit with their Master to report to Him all that had happened while they were performing ministry in other towns. I'm certain the disciples felt an unwanted intrusion upon seeing the multitudes. Yet Jesus saw the hungry people, and feeling compassion on them, bid the crowd to sit on the grass for his next miracle. His compassion, the Greek word *splagchnizomai*, meant He was "moved from the gut."[3] How much deeper can one serve than from his gut? Perhaps the biggest miracle that day was not feeding the 5,000 but that Jesus' disciples finally caught His nature, which moved them "from the gut" to do something about the need before them. You might be thinking: how can I be a servant like the disciples? What special talent do I have?

God has gifted you like *no one else* in order to give to *someone else*. Beethoven, one of the greatest composers in history, proved the point. Upon hearing that a friend had lost his son, Beethoven visited the family. At this state in life, Beethoven was all but deaf, so he found conversation humiliating. Rather than trying to speak words of comfort, he simply stepped over to the piano and began pouring out his grief on the keys. The famed musician expressed his pained emotion through music and sought to use it as a vehicle to comfort his friend. When Beethoven finished playing, he simply left without word. His friend later noted that no one else's visit meant more to him during that time of acute grief.[4]

What can you give as a servant to someone in need? You are God's servant when you *give out of your deepest part*. What is it you do best? Then in Jesus' name, go do it!

"Serve one another in love."

Galatians 5:13

81. I am A Gifted Gift to Others

Who doesn't like to receive a gift? And better yet, who doesn't like to give one? What a great feeling to take a hot meal of roast, carrots, and potatoes to a sick friend. We associate gifts as a tangible object, something we hand over to someone else, an expression of our friendship. We love gifts, and Jesus loves gifts, too.

One of my favorite Old Testament victories of David tells of a time when the Jebusites had taken over the city of Jerusalem and begun its establishment as the new order. But not for long! David and his army marched into the city, usurped the enemy's short-lived authority, and ascended to take the seat of the throne while the defeated chiefs and commanders trailed in chains behind him. All of the vanquished armies drew near to the throne in humble submission and bowed down to the new leader. They came laying before him the plunder of battle. Then King David took the spoils of victory and shared them, distributing them equally as gifts to his beloved people.

Is that not a picture of what Christ did for us? He conquered Satan's battle for control of mankind by shedding His blood on the Cross. He was crucified and then resurrected in victory ascending to the Holy Hill where He sat down at the right hand of God. Like David, He took the spoils of His victory and gave them to His beloved as gifts. "But to each one of us grace was given according to the measure of Christ's gift. And when He ascended on high, He led a crowd of captives and gave gifts to His people."[1]

Can you envision Christ placing in your hand His personalized gift that uniquely fits His plan for you in building His Kingdom? Your grace gift was given at the time of your new birth to do spiritual work in the life of the church and the world. It contains His supernatural abilities and divine enablements that give you God-powered capabilities for service that reach far beyond your own natural talent. Do you ever wonder what God's will is for your life? I've always said, "God's will is your spiritual gift." Your life purpose and ministry evolve out of it. You cannot receive God's greatest blessings and ignore your gift. They go hand in hand. You are divinely gifted by God, useful in the body of Christ, but many find such a truth hard to believe. Don't ever feel insignificant in the family of God!

Your gift promotes the strength and health of the church. You have a particular function in which your spiritual gift is required. You've been placed in the Christian community of faith for a reason. Paul confirmed, "But now God has placed the members, each of them, in the body, just as he desired."[2] You have an assigned part in God's program that only your gift will satisfy. All the spiritual gifts listed in Romans 12 play a role in bringing fulfillment to Christ's work in His church and the world. Your giftedness is indispensable! God has placed within the church all that will ever be needed to function and grow, and your gift is a vital part of that growth. You are gifted!

But that's not all! It's not only that you *have* a spiritual gift but you *are* the gift. It's one thing to take a person a meal and say, "Here's your gift." But it's quite another to place yourself in front of them and say, "I'm your gift!" Do you see yourself as a treasure to others? Your new person-hood in Christ qualified you as a gift. If you are living a life dominated by the Spirit's control, then likely you are exercising your gift without even knowing it. You are the gift: your life is the gift!

While I was teaching my Bible class, I'll never forget the reaction on a lady's face when I mentioned their lives were gifts to each other. She said in honest shock, "I'm a gift?" I extended my point by placing a Christmas bow on top of all their heads and asked them to greet one another as God's blessings to each other. It's amazing how their coun-tenances changed in seeing their fellow classmates as they truly were: little packages from God with a bow on top. Such a visual image brings gladness and delight to our hearts.

Isn't it amazing! The Greek word for gift, *charisma*, means joy.[3] Just think, you are the charisma of God with a bow on top!

"…and He gave spiritual gifts to men."

Ephesians 4: 8

82. I am God's Workmanship

We have a hard time grasping the concept of the length of eternity. How can we conceive something that goes on and on and on without end? But have you ever turned your head the other direction and con-templated this unfathomable truth: God has always been. You mean there has never been a time when God was not, that He existed before He made heaven and earth? As staggering as *that* concept might be, I have a mind-bender that outweighs the two of those combined. As far back as "God has always been" to the boundless future that "God will never end," is the amount of time that God has had *you* on His mind! Can you even comprehend such a love? You were foreknown before the foundations of the world. His affection for *you* inexpressibly possesses His very essence. There has never been a moment in time that He has not been overwrought in His thoughts of *you*! No matter how much we love God and study His Word, we can never fathom such a mystery. We can only believe what the Bible says is true. That truth is this: your place of identity in Christ secures God's role as your Heavenly Father, as well as the Overseer and the Performer of all that encompasses His divine counsel concerning you. God has a predetermined love for those He knows will place their faith in His Son, Jesus Christ.

Just how special are you to God? Ephesians 2:10 speaks with the foreknowledge of God's sovereignty for His children. Packaged in His plan lies His preordained blueprint: *"For we are His workmanship, created in Christ Jesus for good works, which God prepared beforehand, that we should walk in them."* I am personally overcome with speechless wonder when I contemplate how He brings into fruition what's been stored in His will for ages. It's a fascinating doctrine to behold, one I'll never understand! But I can gain a mild understanding as I accept the Word of God by faith and exercise its truth through obedience. I want to look beneath the layers of this most breathtaking and engaging verse!

- *"For we are His workmanship"* - The Greek word for workmanship, *poiema*, means masterpiece,[1] one's most excellent piece of work, of which we derive the English word poem. You are His work of art, his magnificent poetic literary piece. How often do you see yourself as a work of genius, a magnum opus, a creation of God's own design? His affection is not on the basis of your good works, for they can never save you or increase God's favor of you. You are "saved by grace through faith and that not of yourself."[2] When God sees you, He sees Christ first, because you are *in* Christ. Your portrait hangs in the celestial art gallery of the Heavenly Honorees Hall of Fame!

- *"...created in Christ Jesus"*–This act of being created in Christ culminated when you received Jesus. The verb for created means "something made habitable."[3] Christ's nature inhabited your inner person at regeneration. You are not the "you" you used to be! Yippeee! Will the real you please stand up and take a bow!

- *"...for good works"*–Good deeds performed through the energy of the Holy Spirit make God look great. Paul said in you was "an abundance of good deeds."[4] You billboard the greatness of God. Your deeds accomplish two goals: they give God glory; and they prove the reality of your faith. What *workman* for God would withhold His works? If you are filled with His Spirit, then good deeds become a natural outward manifestation of the inward workings of God. I always said *not* to perform good deeds through the Spirit's power is to be spiritually constipated. Jesus said, "The Father is glorified when you bear much fruit."[5]

- *"...which God prepared beforehand"*–In God's sovereign plan He decreed what activities would bring Him glory and bless those around you. It brings me personal courage in knowing if God has appointed a good work appearing outside my comfort zone, then He is obliged to provide the power to accomplish it. My friend, God proves His might when you step out in faith beyond the boundaries of your own expertise. Living life on the edge with Jesus expands the dimensions and effectiveness of your works.

- *"...that you should walk in them."* God calls you to walk, trusting Him. You can walk in His ways by yielding your will to the Spirit to perform His deeds. And how do you discover what those deeds might be? It's simple: Just come to Jesus. C=*confess* all known sin; O=*obey* what He's revealed; M=*meditate* on His Word; E=*embrace* any opportunity for service. You are His masterpiece! Now walk like a workman!

"And you are His workmanship."

Ephesians 2:10

83. I am A Repairer of the Breach

Peter Spencer, my former co-host of the radio talk show "Lifeline of Hope with Peter Pam," coined a phrase describing the unrest in our world that characterizes the lack of peace in man's existence. He ended almost every broadcast with this phrase: "And remember, Christianity is not a religion, but a revolution against the kingdom of darkness." We wrestle against the invisible forces of Satan's powers that make peace impossible. We can never obtain permanent peace because of the fall of man and the resistance of Satan. Both battle for control and both thrive to usurp God's sovereignty. It's like Patrick Henry said, "Gentlemen may cry, peace, peace, but there is no peace."

So what's one to do if there is no possibility of tranquility? Should that give you license to fuel the chaos in your home by arguing, or succumb to fanning the flames of gossip and quarreling at work? No! Christ has given His followers an alternative and eternal plan. At the Cross Jesus made peace a reality and for those who place their trust in Him, His divine nature of rest becomes part of their natures. God's command now for believers is this: because My peace is in you, go and make reconciliation with others. Pursue a spirit of cooperation; put others' interest above your own; offer forgiveness, repair the breach.

It was 742 BC when Isaiah emerged as a major Hebrew prophet in Judah. Israel was at a crisis point in its history, and God called upon Isaiah to tell of impending judgments. Isaiah spoke words of comfort to the Jews who would be sent off to Babylon, and then predicted their return from exile. He prophesied of a future day of blessings when the broken down walls around their cities would be repaired. God would settle them again in a state of prosperity, and His favor would fall upon them. They would be called the repairers of the breach.

In today's term a repairer of the breach is a person who's been impressed by God to restore the broken walls of a damaged relationship, torn asunder by the misuse of appropriating God's principles, or torn apart because of irreconcilable differences. Christ is the Prince of Peace, translated *Shalom*, meaning wholeness and tranquility.[1] His part in mending the partnership is to instill His completeness in both parties. He is The Tranquillizer aiding in the process, and your part? You are the peacemaker.

Are you a peacemaker or peacebreaker? Are you more likely to overlook irritations bringing harmony or more likely to fly off the handle bringing discord? Christ promised in Matthew 5:9, "Blessed or satisfied are the peacemakers for they shall be called sons of God." He was relaying, "Blessed are those peaceable men who belong to Me, the Maker of peace, and favored are those who pursue reconciliation for they shall merit the blessing of being My child." Romans 14:19 adds to the thought, "Let us therefore pursue the things which make for peace." What are your *things*? As you consider yourself a peacemaker, what actions on your part would enhance the restoration?

Search for God's wisdom
> Psalm 85:8 - "I will hear what God the Lord will speak, for He will speak peace to His people and to His saints."

Show evidence of a kind attitude.
> Proverbs 3:17 - "Her ways are ways of pleasantness and all her paths are peace."

Speak well of others.
> Romans 14:19 - "Let us pursue the things that make for peace and the building up of one another."

Stay Spirit-filled.
> Romans 8:6 - "For to be carnally minded is death, but to be spiritually minded is life and peace."

Stay close to God.

Job 22:21 - "Now acquaint yourself with Him and be at peace; thereby, good will comes to you."

Precious friends, this is a difficult assignment indeed, but take courage: "God was reconciling the world to Himself in Christ, not counting men's sins against them. And He has committed to us the message of reconciliation."[2] Can you now commit it to someone else?

"You will be called the repairer of the breach."

Isaiah 58:12

84. I am A Fruit Bearer

Consider this allegory. Out of the goodness of his heart, a king one day chose a group of his sons and daughters who had committed their lives to the palace to go into a foreign country to take medical supplies to the people of a diseased land. Because such tidings were unheard of in a faraway land, the king's only way of getting the foreigners to see the benevolence of his heart was to give his children a pill that would glow in them, revealing His love. Every child of his team was assigned a unique job in accomplishing the mission: some carried the medicine, some applied it, and some performed follow up calls, but each had an assigned part. It was the king's intent for the diseased people to be healed so they could spread his fame and escape the wicked dragon's dungeon; thereby, living out the rest of their lives with the king in all His glory.

But what if the king's agents sent into the infectious land chose to keep the medicine in their own pockets, staying in their private dwellings instead of performing their task of giving their lives away in representing the king's goodness? What if the agents compromised their lifestyle, joining the foreigners' way of life putting aside the king's desire?

My friend, you have been chosen by the King of Kings to represent Christ's love to the world in saving sinners and equipping the saints. You are a fruit bearer, distributing Christ's life of love, joy, and peace to others through your attitude and actions. Jesus said, "I chose you and appointed you that you should go and bear fruit."[1] Notice three ways this happens:

1- *A fruit bearer lives by a mission statement.* Not long ago a friend asked me, "Pam, what's your mission statement?" I actually had never thought about it. A mission statement is a God-given personal motto that defines your day-by-day, moment-by-moment purpose. I asked God for one so He gave it to me: *Every day and every way, build the Kingdom of God.* I was ironing when the phone rang. Donna Taylor, a dear lady in my Bible class who has gone on to be with the Lord, asked me to call a pastor at church, requesting a visit for her sick friend in the hospital. I was about to call a pastor when the Holy Spirit nudged, "No, you go." I argued due to my tight schedule. Then He reminded me of my mission statement, *Every day and every way, build the Kingdom of God.* So I immediately dropped the ironing, and we visited her friend, Brenda. And glory to God; she prayed to receive Christ while we were there! Astounding! But equally precious and alarming to me personally was this: she died right after we left. How significant it is to make yourself available to a mission statement. God works through it as a fruit-bearing device.

2- *A fruit bearer completes the mission God sent him to do.* Did Jesus not set the example when He said to His Father, "I glorified you on earth, having accomplished the work you gave me to do"?[2] Can you say that? What is it God has commissioned you to do? What blocks your fruit bearing? *A lie from the enemy:* "My past is too shameful to represent the Lord Jesus." Then rebuke it. *A selfish sin:* "I just don't want to give up my time." Then confess it. *A worry:* "I'm too wrapped up in the well-being of my career." Then yield it. *A fear:* "I'm terrified of stepping out of my comfort zone." Then face it! Nothing lies outside your fruit-bearing capabilities unless it lies outside the capabilities of God.

3- *A fruit bearer lives in a state of readiness.* Huey Long was the controversial and scandalous politico who served as the governor of Louisiana from 1928 to 1932, and then was a U.S. Senator from 1932 to 1935. He was known as the "The Kingfish" who didn't play by the rules. In 1935, he set his sights on the presidency and announced his candidacy. Dr. Carl Weiss, the son-in-law of his longtime political opponent, assassinated him just a month later. Long's last words were, "Don't let me die. I have got so much to do." Death surprises most all of us with no regard for our list of things waiting to be done.[3]

So learn the valuable lesson: May your fruit bearing carry out the assigned enterprises of the Lord, and may your death catch you with God's mission fully accelerated.

> "Walk in a manner worthy of the Lord…bearing fruit in every good work."
>
> Colossians 1:10

85. I am An Ambassador

Let's play Bible trivia. Guess who I am. I am a city in Greece on the narrow isthmus that connects the Peloponuesus with the mainland. I am a notorious commercial area whose people are diverse and dreadfully licentious. In fact, our immoral life was so renowned that it gave rise to a verb, "to Corinthianize." Paul stayed a year and a half with our inhabitants Aquila and Priscilla. Who am I? You guessed it: I'm the city of Corinth. And it was Corinth that lay deep in Paul's heart, for he grieved over His troubled congregation there! So in AD 56, Paul wrote them a second letter from Macedonia.

2 Corinthians 5 thrives from a heart that begs the reader to stand up and take notice: wake up! Death and judgment loom in the near future; our bodies, like temporary tents, will come down, so while on this earth "live not for yourselves, but for Him who died and rose again.[1] Paul lived in the urgency of the commandment, reminding believers to rescue those unredeemed souls destined for hell. They had received the ministry of reconciliation, a God-ordained assignment to restore relationships with others and bring the lost to Him. God's voice hasn't changed today. His call still remains critically grave. Indeed, it's a tragic occurrence when we fail to tell others about the eternal staircase to Christ!

When the World Trade Center towers collapsed on September 11, 2001, 69% of the fatalities occurred with people who were at or above the entry point of those two jets. In the South Tower, 600 civilians died above the plane's impact. Unknown to them was the fact that there was an open staircase that connected the upper floors to the street below. Of the hundreds who were trapped on the top thirty-three floors, only eighteen people used that staircase to escape. The tragedy is horrible enough, but to think how many more could have been saved had they only known about the open stairway. The gospel is much like that life-saving staircase; only those who find it can escape certain death.[2]

I've discovered several reasons why many believers don't tell others about the pathway through Christ to eternal life. Either they don't know what to say, or they have failed to see themselves as authorized messengers of God. If they understood the authority that's been placed on their lives as God's diplomatic representatives, they'd know He would empower them to carry out His mission of bringing the lost into harmony with Himself. Have God's people forgotten who they are in Christ?

No doubt if the president of the United States sent his press secretary to your front door, you would roll out the red carpet and listen to his words. He's one of the highest ranking officials of the land. Indeed, that secretary has been deputized to speak on behalf of the president. Likewise, you've been given a similar position, for you are Christ's ambassador, one who's been certified as an agent from the courts of heaven. Do you see yourself dressed in His authority given the earth-bound assignment to speak on His behalf to your lost co-worker, cousin, or friend? To see yourself in such a way relieves any fear of rejection or condemnation. You're simply letting the Lord entreat Himself to others through you, thereby pointing them to the eternal staircase, the only escape from eternal punishment.

None of us likes to think about the reality of hell, and none of us likes to think that maybe we have missed opportunities to let God's voice be heard! Yet, it's never too late to gain a fresh start. It's never too late to ask God to supply energized courage to be His intermediary. It's never too late to pray for God to place you where the unsaved might find you. It's never too late to reinstate your title as an ambassador. As long as there is breath within you, it's never too late! Are you breathing?

> "Therefore, we are ambassadors for Christ, as though God were making an appeal through us; we beg you on behalf of Christ, be reconciled to God."
>
> 2 Corinthians 5:20

86. I am A Witness

Beatrice Vance died in a medical facility while waiting nearly two hours to receive treatment for a heart attack. The woman's death was ruled a homicide because she was not treated in a timely manner. After complaining of a classic heart attack, it took the doctors nearly two hours to see her! At the coroner's inquest, a jury declared that she died as a result of gross deviations from the standard of care that a reasonable person would have exercised in this situation. Someone made an alarming parallel of such negligence to the church. If physical neglect can be ruled a homicide in the medical community, the same could be said of Christians who neglect to share the life-giving gospel with people who are literally dying without Christ. If the Hippocratic Oath calls for due diligence in saving lives, then doesn't the Great Commission imply the same for saving souls?[1]

Jesus said to the eleven disciples before He ascended into Heaven, "And you shall receive power when the Holy Spirit has come upon you and you shall be My witnesses."[2] What priority did Jesus place upon the disciples until His return? They were to give an official eyewitness account of the Son of God! Christ would impart the Spirit's energy and insight, and they would take on a new role, a witness.

A witness is God's messenger, bringing to light what's been seen or experienced. In the Greek, a witness, *martus*, signified a martyr, a person loyal no matter what the cost.[3] First century Christians associated being a *witness* with one who was willing to be murdered for Christ. Jesus testified to the doxology of Christianity: "Go and make disciples of all people"[4] no matter what the cost! Let your life be one continual *going*: in the grocery store, at the office, on your vacation, with your family. Go and tell, tell, tell!

Do you tell? Are you a faithful witness agreeable in being placed where the Spirit wills? The Holy Spirit, like you, has a will of His own, too, but only one of you can be in charge. Paul and Timothy were trying to enter Bithynia in sharing the gospel, but "the Spirit of Jesus did not permit them."[5] God ordained the gospel to go to Europe, but Paul and his pal were headed to Asia. Guess which "will" won? They ended up in Europe, of course.

As a seventh grader on the track team running the fifty-yard-dash, I learned about the will. Early morning practices brought to light the meaning of commitment over comfort. "*On your mark, get set, go!*" It was the get-set stage that demanded intuitiveness of the will. Every part of my body required hypersensitivity to the elements around me. Like a runner, a witness lives in the get-set stage. It's a part of the race demanding watchfulness in order to seize the moment.

I remember seizing the moment last year as I entered a convenience store. It was a rainy day, one of those mornings where home and hot chocolate sounded like a splendid idea. I approached the counter where the clerk muttered, "What a gloomy day! I'm just waiting on the sun." I perked up and said, "Son? I'm waiting on Him, too!" What ensued was a remarkable conversation! A witness wakes up every morning to "on your mark" and leaves the house on "get set." I wonder, how conscious are you of the people God positions on your radar screen? Jesus places the witness where He wills.

Whether you like it or not, you are a witness. The question is, "What kind of witness are you?" Peter commissioned believers "to sanctify Christ as Lord in your heart, always being ready to make a defense to everyone who asks, being ready to give an account for the hope within you."[6] What an awe-shaking responsibility! If faith comes by hearing, then doesn't someone have to tell?

In the Alamo foyer hangs a portrait of a man whose inscription reads, "*James Butler Bonham: no picture of him exists. This portrait is of his nephew, Major James Bonham, deceased, who greatly resembled his uncle. It is placed here by the family that people might know the appearance of the man who died for freedom.*"

Jesus died for your freedom; no one knew what He looked like, either. Would Jesus' family place your portrait in a gallery in honor of His likeness?

> "And you shall be my witnesses…even to the remotest part of the earth."
>
> Acts 1:8

87. I am A Branch

Jesus had only a short time left on earth. Within twenty-four hours he would make his way to the Garden of Gethsemane. Often before someone prepares to die, he spends time with his closest friends, and that's what Jesus did. The time had come for His arrest, and Jesus chose the disciples' company. Soon his earthly ministry would be over, and he would begin his new mission of intercession in heaven for the believers. Would they remember all that He had taught them? Could He entrust the gospel to their safekeeping? I can see Jesus walking through the vineyards observing his disciples who remained completely unaware of what was about to happen. Perhaps Jesus took one last look peering deep into Peter, James, and John's souls and spoke of their union and communion with Him. "I am the vine, you are the branches; he who abides in Me, and I in him, he bears much fruit, for apart from Me you can do nothing."[1] The words would soon graphically infiltrate their memories, and John would document their conversation. You can eavesdrop by reading John chapter 15.

We live in a do-it-yourself world where we teach our children to be independent; if you want a job done, do it yourself; be your own boss, strong, and free-spirited. But Jesus was teaching just the opposite. Live like a branch, dependent on *Me*; if you want a job done, depend on *Me*; if you want to be strong and free in spirit, depend on *Me*. Jesus compared them to a branch, an appendage whose life source would come from remaining in Him, the True Vine. Jesus' axiom was simple: "Live a *branch-to-vine* life."[2]

Are you drawing your life sustenance from any other source than God? Like a newborn gets its vitality from its mother's breast, where do you get yours? What's your attachment? Branch to food? Branch to possessions? Branch to career? Branch to relationships? Branch to appearance? Every branch has a source, and Jesus knew if they found their needs met anywhere else, they would become spiritually weak and useless in His service. He knew the necessity of their abiding in unbroken fellowship with Him.

The purpose of a branch is two-fold: to abide and bear fruit. Abide? What an ambiguous word! Does it mean you sit in a corner, bow your head and think of God all day? No, to abide is a lifestyle of relaxing in God's strength. It means "to remain or to stay in God"[3] on a continual basis, while you go to work, or while you cook hamburgers on the grill, or whatever you do. It's a command to "let the Word of God richly dwell within you,"[4] which requires mental activity, discipline, confession of sin, and cultivation. It's linking meditation with prayer and watching to see what happens. It's fertilizing the soil of your soul with His commands. It's relating in love to the community of believers, stripping off a life that revolves around your own interests. It's being ready to cooperate with God's gardening tools that prune worldly thoughts, which drain energy from your spiritual crop. It's to allow His joy to be in you so that your joy may be full. All these activities fetch in a fresh supply for a healthy branch. The core truth behind the vine and the branches is that the believer cannot enjoy his Christian life apart from an active connection with Jesus.

A branch has no use but to bear fruit. Apart from allowing the sap of the Holy Spirit to fill you, there will be no harvest. A carnal Christian can produce favorable works, but only an abiding Christian can produce transforming fruit. It's only in the abiding stage that fruit outlasts a season.[5] You need patience? Then abide in The Vine. You need self-control? Then abide in The Vine. If you want to observe the usefulness of your branch, then observe your fruitfulness. Have you been fruitful with your time? Your unwanted circumstances? Your spiritual gifts? Your wealth? Your branch's crop displays visible evidence of your invisible commitment to Christ. A fruit tree might be visibly enticing, but it's measured by what it produces!

"I am the Vine, and you are the branches."

John 15:5

88. I am A Blessing

Who of us doesn't enjoy the feeling of blessing others? If you look closely, you will see an invisible sign around every human being's neck. It reads, "Make me feel like a person of value." I've discovered it doesn't take much to bring someone hope. It's alarming how far the tiniest gesture of kindness will travel.

Years ago I gave a tiny pearl to a single mom encouraging her to keep it in her coin purse as a reminder that God would someday work together her difficulty and heartache into a pearl of great beauty. Years later she called in an emotional alarm. "I lost my pearl! I lost my pearl!" It had rolled under the refrigerator; so with fervent gusto, she asked the neighbor to help her retrieve the lost treasure. After much filtering through the dust and lent, she found it. A few years later I received a letter and a picture taken at her recent wedding. She commented, "See the tiny silver bag under my bouquet of flowers that I carried down the aisle with me? In it contained a tiny little pearl, the one you gave to me." Indeed, God has placed His Spirit in us that we might extend His love and light to others. What does it mean to spiritually bless someone? What mind-set do you have when you perform a kind deed?

To bless is to bring the Spirit of Christ into another's presence. You are the carrier of His goodness, depositing His favor into others' atmosphere. Such an act of benevolence might come through a prayer, a deed, a spoken word, or a forgiveness extended. Have you considered that your very presence can impart a blessing? When you demonstrate goodwill toward someone with the conscious motive of delighting God, then He uses your kindness as a mirror for others to see the character of Christ. Notice the ways you can exercise your role as "A Blesser."

You can bless God. Most of us can't even comprehend how our presence before the Lord brings Him joy, but it does. He thrives on our praise. I often envision what that feels like for God. What if your children came into your room, kneeled down before your feet, and began verbalizing specific ways you had been gracious to them. "Mom, thank you for always being there for me, for not judging me, or always having my best interest at heart. Mom, you are amazing, compassionate, trustworthy, unselfish," and on and on. How would that make you feel? Meditate on that image, and then take time to sit at His feet reciting His miraculous goodness. You'll be amazed at the joy you receive from blessing Him!

You can bless your family. How do you respond to the uniqueness of others in your household? In Genesis, Jacob commissioned favor onto his sons: "He blessed them, every one with the blessing *appropriate to him.*"[1] Who in your family needs an appropriate blessing? Have you taken time to consider specifically how you can bring the life of Christ to each one by your attitude or deeds? After all, who can grant respect and appreciation toward a spouse more than you? Or who can establish the atmosphere in the home to turn one's heart toward God more than you? While it's true that sometimes the door remains shut in granting a verbal blessing, the gift of prayer always stays open. And, of course, the most premiere blessing of all is a godly example.

I still recall a favor passed on to Jason when he was six years old. When I took my children to school, I would give them an invisible blessing, an expression of my prayer coverage over them. I'd say, "Here's your blessing!" and they'd reach out to grab it from my outstretched hand. One morning Jason hurried back to the car. Surely he had forgotten his lunch or something very important! I rolled down the window as he panted, "Mommy, you forgot my blessing!" That was twenty years ago. Never underestimate the impact of speaking God's favor over another!

You can bless your enemies. The Apostle Luke instructed, "Bless those who curse you and pray for those who mistreat you."[2] Who in your life has brought injustice against you? Is Luke's request even possible? For years it was hard for me to formulate the words on my lips for God to bless my former husband. But God knew my heart, my struggles, and my desire to please Him, and in time genuine prayers began to flow. Loving those who have hurt you is not to act out of your affection but to act out of your will. Luke gave seven instructions in loving others: love your enemies, do good to those who hate you, bless those who curse you, pray for those who mistreat you, do not retaliate, give freely, and treat others the way you want to be treated. God will never give a commandment without His enablement to perform it.

You are a blesser. Your new nature patterned after the likeness of Christ finds its greatest fulfillment in doing what He did. Christ blessed His Father, family, and foes. Who's God calling you to bless today?

> "Consider how to stimulate one another to love and good deeds."
>
> Hebrews 10:24

89. I am A Spring of Water

Dr. Dwight L. Moody was scheduled to preach at a crusade in England. Many were elated about the possibility, but one elderly man protested to the committee: "Why do we need this Mr. Moody. He's uneducated. Who does He think he is, anyway? Does he think he has a monopoly on the Holy Spirit?" A wise younger pastor rose and said, "No, but the Holy Spirit has a monopoly on Mr. Moody."[1]

What happens when the Holy Spirit exclusively possesses a believer? What does it look like when one is filled to overflowing with the Holy Spirit's control? Jesus wonderfully told us, "He who believes in Me, as the Scripture said, from his innermost being shall flow rivers of living water."[2] Christ was speaking of the Holy Spirit that would indwell His followers after His ascension.

At conversion, three invisible, instantaneous acts of God took place. You were regenerated, given a new supernatural life; you were sealed, secured with the assurance of God's ownership; and you were baptized, placed in a new union with Christ and fellow believers. All of these lay hold of your position in Christ, but God gives you opportunity on a daily, moment-by-moment basis to yield your thoughts and choices to the Holy Spirit. When you surrender and ask Him to enthrone your life, He fills you with spiritual power and service. To be Spirit-filled is to live in a spiritual state where the Holy Spirit is fulfilling all that He came to do in you.

What happens when something is full? Ask The Old Faithful Geyser in Yellowstone National Park. Every 45 to 120 minutes the geyser bursts forth with jets of hot water spewing up to 180 feet releasing a display of God's wonder in nature. Jesus said when you are filled with the continual flow of Christ's satisfaction within, you will bubble up and overflow into the lives of others, indeed, a display of God's wonder of the Spirit's filling.

Do you ever wonder why others seem to have a special anointing from God in releasing the flow? The truth is all believers are anointed, but not all believers liberate the power. Why is that? The power you possess to impart the energy of Christ's life is directly related to how much control you give to the Holy Spirit's filling. When your life's needs are drawn from the reservoir of the resurrected life within, then from your innermost part will overturn streams of the lifesaving spring of Jesus.

God's placed you around the lives of others in order that you might be their water fountain or spiritual geyser. Who do you know that needs a drink of the thirst-quenching Word of Life? Your mist induces a spiritual hunger drawing others to your spring for a drink: a sip of hope, a sip of a prayer, or a sip of a word fitly spoken. In the Old Testament, Zechariah spoke of "a fountain that would be opened for the house of David, and for the inhabitants of Jerusalem."[3] A river of living water would flow from the temple in The Holy City to all the earth bringing regeneration, joy, guidance, and empowerment to all who would drink. Jesus became that fountain testifying, "If anyone is thirsty, let him come to Me and drink."⁴ And from His fountain you would in turn "become a well of water springing up to eternal life,"⁵ serving as a channel of His fullness passing along the river's spiritual blessings. You would become a source of new streams for others. Are you able to say, "If anyone needs refreshment in their walk with Christ, come to me and I will dip from Christ's well within me and give you whatever you need?"

How's your channel flowing? Is it more like a trickle or a torrent? Have you tasted it lately: sweet, stale, bitter? Never can you expect a spirit-life of infectious joy until you empty your self-life of contaminating conceit. Christ didn't intend for His water to lie in a stagnant cistern bringing discontent and unfulfillment, rather to flow like a spring bringing His life-revitalizing power. Christ fills you that you might point others to your water source. What thirsty saints or parched sinners lay in your river's current?

"And you will be like a spring of water whose waters do not fail."

Isaiah 58:11

90. I am The Salt of the Earth

It was likely a breezy afternoon on the Sea of Galilee, one of those days when the winds from the north cooled the atmosphere over the waters. Finally, Jesus sat down under the umbrella of a shady tree, a welcomed spot from the great multitudes that followed Him that day from Judea and areas beyond the Jordan. Indeed, a rest was in order, and what better way to improve the afternoon than for the disciples to join him. Disciples, fishermen, no one of particular notoriety, just your run of the mill Israelites. But with x-ray vision, Jesus saw beyond the ordinary, beyond the ripple effect of these men's influence in the Palestian world. He saw the remnant of believers that would follow them, men and women who would carry on their legacy, seeing themselves equaled to the value Jesus would assign to them that day. And what was that value? Jesus summed it up in seven words: "You are the salt of the earth."[1]

Salt? Of what value is salt? We'd be a lot more impressed if He had said, "You are the diamonds of the earth." We understand jewels! But who knows anything about salt? To us salt is nothing more than seasoning, packed granules in a shaker on our dining room table. But Jesus knew the immeasurable worth of salt:

- In ancient civilizations, salt was minted into coins.
- In the eighteenth century salt was a gift to the groom's parents.
- Phoenicians traded salt, ounce by ounce for gold.
- Except for the sun, nothing was more valuable than salt.
- Wars were fought over salt.
- Newborn babies were bathed in salt.
- Covenants between individuals were sealed in salt.

That's exactly what Jesus was saying: "You are of great value, worth more than gold, honored gifts or minted coins!" Do you see yourself as salt, immensely useful in the service of God, impacting your sphere of influence?

Like salt, you season others. Who would eat popcorn without salt? Just a little pinch seasons the entire bag bringing out the best! Does "just a little pinch of you" bring out the best in others? When you walk into a room, do others capture the richness of God's savor? Does your presence elevate their thoughts? Are your words palatable and appetizing or compromising and flat? Colossians 4:6 encourages, "Let your speech always be with grace, as it were with salt, so that you might know how to respond to each person." In other words, let your words be flavored with God's seasoning, serving as a purifying agent in every conversation. Salty words last a lifetime!

Like salt, you preserve. To preserve is to retard from corruption, to slow down the process of decay. In the early 1700s when ships from England carried the settlers to America, their meat provisions were preserved in barrels of salt, delaying spoilage. Like salt in the barrels, you are God's activating salt agent fighting against the decay of sin in the world. By the indirect influence of the way you live, you can impede the corruption of sin around you. Is it possible that your presence in the room holds back someone from using the Lord's name in vain or acting out in some dishonoring manner? Why is it that when the pastor walks up, your countenance changes?

Like salt, you heal. I always knew that salt was a healing agent, but never was it more real to me than when I swam in the Salt Sea in Israel two hours after I had shaved my legs. It's true. Salt in a wound creates a sting! Could it be that Jesus meant for us to exercise boldness in our witness, unafraid to sting others with the salt of truth? Is that why Paul asked for others to pray "that utterance would be given to him in opening his mouth in boldly making known the mystery of the gospel?"[2] God's servants of salt should courageously speak the truth knowing their words from God speak a language all their own in penetrating the hearts of men. Your words have great power in bringing both conviction and blessing.

So consider your value of salt, and the next time you're out to dinner and someone across the table says, "Pass the salt," maybe you should get up and go sit next to them.

"You are the salt of the earth."

Matthew 5:13

91. I am A Light of the World

The tradition of the Olympic flame began during the ancient Olympic games over 2,700 years ago in Greece. Today, every four years the flame begins its Olympic torch relay by first touring Greece. From there, it travels around the country to the sight of the games by a variety of people running, riding horses, and even scuba diving!

I have always enjoyed the personal stories of the people who were chosen to carry the torch in their parts of the world. To be *the person* carrying the flame must be an exhilarating endeavor. Stephanie Materese, a junior from the University of Maryland, found her dream come true when she was selected as one of the 11,500 participants in carrying the torch across forty-six states to its final destination. She said, "I never realized ordinary people could be chosen for such an honor."[1] Oh, the ecstasy to be a torch-bearer carrying the flame!

Friends, as a child of God, you are a torch-bearer. You've been entrusted with *The Flame* from on high, the Holy Spirit who ignites in your heart the Light of Jesus Christ, the one True Light who's come to enlighten every man.[2] God could have chosen anyone to carry His torch, but He chose the ordinary, like you and me, to transport His light to a darkened world. What an honor! You are a light of the One True Light of the world! You've been selected by Him to communicate His light in your family, neighborhood, grocery store, and everywhere your feet carry you. In Acts 13:47 God says, "I have placed you *there* as light." Where is your *there*? Has God purposefully placed you in a situation to be His light amidst the darkness? Do you see yourself enflamed with His mission, an assigned torch bearer?

A torch bearer represents his heritage. In the original Olympic games, the flame carried by a torch bearer symbolized the death and rebirth of Greek heroes. Carrying the torch identified them with their origin whose legacy they intended to pass on. As a follower of Christ, your hero, you lift up His flame, whose death and resurrection has given you a new life. Do you run in such a way to pass it on?

A torch bearer shines. The Greek word for shine is to be enlightened, to borrow the rays of another. As a light radiator, you cannot shine unless you place yourself under the True Light that is always shining, Jesus Christ, thereby allowing your human light to be charged by His. To shine is to borrow His light. Have you ever attempted to shine in your own strength, causing spiritual burnout? No matter how hard *you* try, you cannot rise above your dim attempts to feel better? Your shining comes from His infusing.

A torch bearer remains conspicuous. Your light represents a city set on a hill that cannot be concealed. In order for light to be valuable, it must be visible. A redeemed heart cannot be hidden. It sits on the pinnacle of a hilltop during the day and at night it shines brilliantly. Indeed, the light of the righteous shines brightly for all to see.[3] It's an illustrious light that collectively joins others' lights serving as a beacon to curious onlookers.

A torch bearer enlightens others. Sometimes our light flickers but is rekindled into a flame by another human being. The nineteenth century Englishman William Farrar pictured every man's soul as a *cavern full of gems.*[4] The relaxed observer glances into it and all seems dim and useless. But let light enter into it and behold, something changes. It will sparkle with crystals, effervescent and alive. If souls do not shine before you, maybe it is because you bring them no light to make them shine. Light them up with the light of love, and they will perk up, arise, and shine.

You are a light of the world. Who do you know that needs the candle of a hug or the candle of a warm meal or the candle of a phone call? You carry the torch, the enflamed power to totally revolutionize a life. You make a difference! Indeed, there's a candle in every soul longing for someone to light it.

> "You are the light of the world, a city set on a hill that cannot be hidden."
>
> Matthew 5:14

92. I am An Instrument of Righteousness

Let's review previous entitlements and add the cherry on top. "Evenso, consider yourselves to be dead to sin, but alive to God in Jesus. Therefore, do not let sin reign in your mortal body that you should obey its lusts,…but present yourselves to God as those alive from the dead, and your members as instruments of righteousness to God."[1]

At the Cross Christ broke sin's power over every born again believer! Praise God! You are dead to sin's grip and enabled by the Holy Spirit to respond to sin in the same way a dead person would react; and though it's true that you are dead to it, it's not dead to you. (Remember? It frequently sneaks up on you in the sheep's clothing of temptation!) Nonetheless, the truth gloriously remains: you are separated from its position of rulership and free to live for Jesus. And for what purpose has God declared your corpse to life? "Therefore if any man cleanses himself from sin, he will be an *instrument* for honor, sanctified, useful to the Master, prepared for every good work."[2] An instrument? God assigned His servants a new description. Speaking of Paul God said: "He is a chosen *instrument* of Mine to bear My name before the Gentiles, Kings, and sons of Israel." You are, indeed, dead to sin, alive to Christ, and now appointed and anointed as His megaphone before your own world of influences: your family, neighbors, and friends.

You give God praise in many ways: you present yourself to Him as a worshiper; you present yourself to Him as a Bible student, but have you ever presented yourself to Him as an instrument? When's the last time you sought the Lord in prayer and visualized yourself approaching His throne dressed in the costume of a trumpet? You are His righteous tool whose purpose is to live in such a state that your life is conformed to His standard, indeed, a condition that's acceptable to Him. You serve as a means or a supernatural passageway through which God can be honored by the sounds you produce.

How useful is your trumpet in the advancement of God's Kingdom? Has it been tucked away in its velvet case stored in the attic too long? Do you feel like you're not worthy to play it anymore? Has it broken a key and been tossed in the dump pile to be given away to the next charity who will be in your area soon? My friend, bring to life what God has mandated about your purpose! No one has an instrument like yours! No one! So remove it from its case and play it!

You are his chosen instrument, divinely designed to extol His greatness. Your circumstances are uniquely your own; no one can praise Him for what He has done, is doing, or will do quite like you. Remember the Little Drummer Boy: "Shall I play for Him pa-rum pum pum pum." Pluck your strings of thanksgiving and strum the harp of your heart in melodious praise. Such an offering releases a transcendent lullaby into His presence and brings festivity and joy into your own. God inhabits the praise of His instruments.

You are His chosen instrument, divinely designed to blow encouragement into the lives of others. God placed you in your environment to be a channel of hope to someone. Who is that someone? It doesn't take much to restore a down-trodden spirit. To encourage means to come alongside another in order to strengthen the foundation of their faith. Just like the Word of God is oxygen to the spirit, encouragement is oxygen to the soul.

You are His chosen instrument, divinely designed to appropriate Christ's righteousness in thwarting off Satan's darts. Years ago in the midst of a Latin American revolution, an American citizen was captured and sentenced to death. But an American officer rushed before the firing squad and draped an American flag entirely around the victim. "If you shoot this man, you will fire through the American flag and incur the wrath of a whole nation." The revolutionary in charge let the prisoner go.[3] Likewise, Isaiah claims, "You are wrapped in His righteousness."[4] As you drape the garment of Christ about you, Satan's forces collide with your instrument, standing as a weapon against his destructive regime. You are one powerful means through which God performs His sovereign rule. So go blow your horn!

> "…and present your members as instruments of righteousness."
>
> Romans 6:11

93. I am Enabled to Abound in Good Deeds

Generosity—it's the golden thread weaved between every verse of Scripture, God's plentiful love unveiling the giving of His Indescribable Gift, Jesus Christ, the most gracious gift of all. And what is God's heart? He is first and foremost the Supreme Giver of the universe, and how greatly He demonstrated His benevolent passion: "For God so loved the world that *He* gave!"[1] He gave His Son. And The Son gave as well, for He was the grain of wheat that fell into the earth and died, and by its dying, it bore much fruit.[2] God, in a unique fashion, planted Jesus as a seed and from Him came a redeemed 'much fruit' crop, a new race regenerated with a nature patterned after God through Christ. It all started from the seed of giving: God gave, Jesus gave, and today the Holy Spirit gives that we might imitate and follow suit. God loves a cheerful giver. We are never more like God than when our lives exude with the luscious fruit of generosity.

> Give strength, give thought, give deeds, give wealth,
> Give love, give tears, give thyself,
> Give give be always giving
> Who gives not is not living
> The more you give, the more you live.
>
> Author Unknown

It was Paul who encouraged the Galatians to exercise a benevolent heart: "So then, while we have opportunity, let us do good to all men, and especially to those who are in the household of faith."[3] The internal goodness Paul spoke of was an act produced by the Spirit when one lives to sow the seed of kindnesses and multiply His field of caring deeds.

Do you ever feel like a poor harvester? For some reason you seem to lack the confidence in trusting God for any effective work: you fail to take a bold stand for Christ in the workplace, or you lack the courage to carry out some seemingly impossible task God asks you to do? Believing yourself to be totally incompetent, retarded in any effectiveness in the cause of Christ, the only kind of giving you feel like doing is giving up?

Then join the host of saints in Corinth. They, too, needed a lesson in God's power of sowing generously in them. So Paul encouraged, "And God is able to make all grace abound to you, that always having all sufficiency in everything, you may have an abundance for every good deed."[4] My friend, you were born of God, given a new nature that you might abound in serving others, and not just abound, but super abound! Look at the reaping benefits in that promise:

- God brings to you His might when you have none. He will always enable the disabled. *God is able.*

- God gives you excess in all that causes joy and gratitude, with His only motive being a desire to express His bounty...*He makes all grace abound to you.*

- God grants adequate resources within you, a God-given means of self-sufficiency in Him, independent of any other external resource. Jesus Christ is your perpetual inside Source...*always having all sufficiency!*

- God supplies an overspill, granting affluence for any useful work He assigns...*in everything you have abundance for every good deed.*

What deed has God delegated to you? You possess an overflowing supply in Him! Observe *God's Six Step Process of Grace Giving* in 2 Corinthians 9. Notice what generates God's cycle of generosity, ultimately bringing Him glory:

1. God extends full power toward you.

2. God grants an excess of grace, always rendering you capable of every valuable work He calls you to perform.

3. God supplies the ability and multiplies its effectiveness. God continuously provides the generous giver with the means of expressing more generosity, having been enriched in everything for all liberality.

4. God allows your seed of enablement to meet the needs of the saints, causing them to overflow with thanks.

5. God moves others to awe by His extravagance in you, and they, in turn, give Him glory.

6. God induces in those touched by your generosity the desire to lift you up in prayer, thereby, enriching your harvest, until ultimately, your earthly labors cease, and you enter Heaven's glory escorted by your good deeds. And so the abounding catapults deeper, wider, and higher.

> "God...makes all grace abound in you that always having all sufficiency in everything, you may have an abundance for every good deed."
>
> 2 Corinthians 9:8

Chapter Ten

My Eternity

What propels my eternal destiny of hope?

94. I am A Victor on a White Horse

I have never been much of a horse lover, but there is coming a day when I will experience a horse ride of a lifetime! It won't be a horseback ride from Texas to Kansas, or Nevada to Oregon, but from heaven to earth. Won't you fast forward the events of your own life and step into the drama with me because you'll be on horseback, too.

Often when I read spectacular events in Scripture where God has displayed His glory, I have thought, *If only I could have been there, like the all-night water works marathon when Moses parted the Red Sea!* But there's another event on the calendar of God's "Top Ten," and the saints of God will partake in the episode.

The Bible speaks of an actual event when Jesus descends from heaven to earth. "For just as the lightning comes from the east, and flashes even to the west, so shall the coming of the Son of Man be."[1] Ultimately, His entrance will culminate at the Battle of Armageddon, a much prophesied event at the second coming of Christ. John recorded what God showed him in a vision, "And I saw the heaven opened, and behold, a white horse and He who sat upon it is called 'Faithful and True,' and in righteousness, He judges and wages war...*And the armies of heaven* clothed in fine linen, white and clean, were following Him on white horses."[2] Christ returns to earth in the clouds of heaven in a procession accompanied by all the saints and His angels. Though some believe the horses only to be symbolic in nature, the point is this: Christ is coming and will continue to establish His sovereign rule! Can you imagine being a part of that entourage? Do you suppose it will take hours or even days for the millions upon millions upon millions in His army to enter earth's atmosphere?

Upon His victory at Armageddon, Jesus will usher in the Millennium Kingdom, a 1,000-year reign with His saints where Christ Himself gains His long-awaited title, King of Glory. He'll set up His earthly monarch and regather Israel to her Promised Land, and all God's people, both Jews and Gentiles, will celebrate the defeat of Satan and sin.

You may be thinking, *What difference does it make to me? I have enough to think about in the here and now!* Dear friend, when I consider that so much of what encumbers me today is only temporary, I well up with excitement to press on until that day. The Millennium should serve as a great encouragement to God's children. It will be earth's finest day, an era in which John instructed us to pray for its hastening! "Amen. Come, Lord Jesus."[3]

Observe what God has in store for that day! It is Jesus, the Sharp Sword, who will rule the nations as the supreme political leader. Worldwide peace will prevail. "Nation will not lift up sword against nation and never again will they train for war."[4] Israel's old enemies will submit to her supremacy and the "sons of those who afflicted her"[5] will bow down and place their soles at Jesus' feet. The newly theocratic political government will be run "with the rod of iron,"[6] where all those who go against Christ will be punished. Satan will be bound and his demons will be rendered inoperative. Peace in the animal kingdom will be restored, and the wolf will dwell with the lamb and "a nursing child will play by the hole of the cobra."[7] Can you imagine befriending a poisonous snake for your baby's pet?

But most glorious of all, it will be a time of universal adoration to the long-awaited Messiah! You will have an increased desire to worship the King of Kings! "Israel's gates will be open continuously and men will bring wealth to her with their kings leading the procession."[8] Praise God! I can already hear the melody of joy in our hearts as we sing the Christmas carol we once knew, "*Joy to the world, the Lord has come; Let earth receive her King.*"

Rejoice, yes, rejoice, for you have reason to live from glory to glory! You belong to Jesus, Yeshua, "God saves," the Christ, "Anointed One!" So take courage, take hope, take heart, fellow horsemen, and lift your head in glorious anticipation, for there's more ahead of you than behind you!

"And the armies which are in heaven, clothed in fine linen,
white and clean, were following Him on white horses"

Revelation 19:14

95. I am The Bride of Christ

The wedding motif has been ringing since before time. The theme flows throughout the entire Bible. In the Old Testament Israel was chosen as the wife of Jehovah, whose unfaithfulness broke the heart of God. In the New Testament, the wedding bells again chime with the church being revealed as the virgin bride waiting for her coming Bridegroom, Jesus Christ.

What image comes to your mind when you think of a bride? I'm certain men don't respond the same way women do, but whether male or female, no matter what portrait comes to light, it fails in comparison to what Christ Jesus sees when He gazes at you, His beloved Bride!

The position that the Church holds in eternity landscapes the beauty of glory. She will reflect Christ's own image, perfect, without blemish, a holy bride suitable for a holy Bridegroom, united with Him in wedded bliss. At the marriage supper she will be seated with her Bridegroom upon the throne of the universe, ruling with Him over the ever-expanding

Kingdom. The feast's gaiety will be a time when all the other saints from all time will celebrate with Christ and His marriage to His church.

If ever you have wondered about your present purpose as His fiancé, viewing the wedding's tapestry from God's perspective will provide blessed insight into the magnificent honor you carry in your role as His bride.

Paul Billheimer's book, *Destined for the Throne*, provides expansive insight into this biblical truth:

> As the Lord of history, God is controlling all of its events, not only on earth but in all realms, to serve His purpose of bringing to maturity and eventually to enthronement the union of His Son with His chosen Bride, the Church. From all eternity God purposed that His Son should have an Eternal Companion.... This Bride would share the Bridegroom's throne following the Marriage Supper of the Lamb. All events from all eternity were ordered and directed for one purpose–the eventual winning and preparation for the Bride. All that have ever been born are included in God's all embracing redemptive love, but God knew that only a select remnant would accept this universal provision. If God knew from all eternity that the net result of all His creative activity, including the plan of redemption, would be only this tiny minority, then it may be presumed that this small group was the object of all of God's previous plans, purpose, and creative enterprises. Therefore, it follows that it was for the sake of this small remnant, His bride, that the universe was originated.[1]

Have you ever considered the significance of your role as the bride in light of your remnant status? How should that truth weave itself into the fabric of your day? In Revelation, John records the voice He hears at the marriage feast: "Let us rejoice...for the bride has made herself ready."[2]

What are you doing to make yourself ready? You will be adorned at the marriage feast in white linen whose fabric will be the manifestation of your earthly obedience. Do you live in a state of readiness and preparedness for that day? Or would its opposite meaning, to neglect, paint a sharper image? How can you make yourself ready?

The translation for the word ready (*hetoimazo*) carries with it the idea of an oriental custom, that when a king was making a long journey, a person would go before him and level the roads making it passable. In your daily life, do you see the Holy Spirit as the One who goes before you making a passable trail in your journey to the throne? Could it be that His way of making you ready is by quickening your heart and mind in sold-out obedience to His Holy Word? Are you mindful that it is God's inborn Spirit that leads the way to the wedding reception? Do you yield to His leading? Are you purposely asking Him to weave the fabric of your wedding gown? Oh friends, we don't have to toil in preparing! If we will yield our lives to God's wedding planner, He will do the weaving for us!

I praise the Lord Jesus for His perfect eternal plan for us, the remnant, His church! Indeed, God's love is at the heart of redemption! Just listen to our Bridegroom's song: "Here Comes the Bride."

"Come and I will show you the Bride, the wife of the Lamb."

Revelation 21: 9

96. I am Rewarded

What do these people have in common: Jaxson, a three-year-old earning stickers for his good behavior; Ann, a teenage girl washing dishes to get an allowance; Michael, a contestant on "The Price Is Right" game show? Winning! Winning! Winning! Yippee! Who doesn't love to win? Built into the fabric of every human is the desire for reward. Where did such an inborn aspiration come from? For, indeed, it's not just a popular concept to our generation only.

From the beginning of time God assured Abraham and his descendants that He was their reward and through Him their recompense would be great. And we remember Christ's concluding statement: "I am coming soon, and my reward is with me."[1] It's a fact. The prize mentality finds its origin in this truth: God created the institution of reward ultimately for one purpose: to bring Him glory. When you received your new identity in Jesus, you gloriously entered into the Kingdom of His upcoming awards assembly, a future date when rewards would be rendered to the people of God according to their acts of righteousness. As a recipient of His indescribable merits, you've stepped into the winner's circle, a victor of heavenly proportions!

Speaking of the winner's circle, one of the champions I interviewed on the television show was Josh Davis, the three-time Gold medalist in the 1996 Olympics. When his presence graced the stage with one of his gold medals, my immediate thought was, *Wow! Gimme that! Can I wear it?* And yes, he must have read my thoughts because the next thing I knew, he was draping the grand prize over my head! How many get the opportunity to model the gold, even if it is for only the length of a TV show? I just had to ask him, "How did it feel stepping up to the platform of unimaginable adulation in receiving your reward?"

In the Greco-Roman world when athletes completed a race, they stood on the bema, or platform known as the stand of judgment, receiving their wreath of honor.[2] The Bible says there's coming a day when the believers will take their place on a similar platform: the Bema of God. It's here at the Judgment Seat of Christ where all believers individually will account for the quality of their works while on earth. It's not a hearing concerning the indictment of eternal damnation because believers' sin is no longer held against them, but it is a time when each one will step onto the platform of God's x-ray machine as He tests the quality of our works on earth. For some the reward will be minuscule to nothing; for others, medallion-size! I must admit, when Josh put the gold around my neck, my immediate thoughts fast forwarded to the moment I would stand on the Bema Seat of God. What will that feel like? I loved Josh's response of how it felt stepping onto *The Champion's Throne* at the Olympics. He said, "Unbelievable, but the most surreal moment came when I laid eyes on my parents."

Can you visualize the moment of impact when you see Christ at your awards debut and face your heavenly parent? What will take place when your eyes meet with His and you give an account of your life's service? You'll receive imperishable crowns, or acknowledgements, that bring to life His most celebrated attributes. For example, with the Crown of Righteousness He will grant you eternal righteousness because you longed for His appearing, and with the Crown of Glory, He will grant you joy for your faithfulness in serving the body of Christ. And you'll receive the Crown of Life because you endured and the Crown of Rejoicing because you saved souls. Who can imagine such a climatic ceremony?

As a reward recipient, how can you increase the pleasure of that day when you see Him? I often play a little game with myself where I pull behind me an invisible red wagon. All day long, I notice opportunities to praise God, not to get a reward, but to give Him glory! With each get-well card I write for Christ's sake, or with each control of the tongue for Christ's sake, or with each ungodly thought brought to God for Christ's sake, or with each praise received for Christ's sake, I put a reminder card in my wagon of my heart's desire to bring God glory in whatever I do. Day by day, week by week, I'm building a pile in my wagon, and one day when it's my turn to take the Bema Seat of Christ, and I see Him eye to eye, I will wheel my little red wagon right up to Him as a reminder of all the wondrous ways He worked in me. My wagon will stand as a monumental tribute of His spectacular power and grace!

You may not be an Olympian for this world, but you can be an Olympian for God. Didn't I hear you say gold's your best color?

"For we must all appear before the judgment of Christ, that each one may be recompensed for his deeds in the body according to what he has done, whether good or bad."

2 Corinthians 5:10

97. I am A Benefactor of a White Stone

I am Grammy Pammy to two precious grandchildren, Karsen and Reed. Like all children, they love surprises. Just the other day, I was compelled to buy two $1.00 grab bags at the convenience store. On the outside of one was written the words, "For a girl" and the other, "For a boy." Oh, the joy to watch them hold their grab bags wondering what mysterious treasures lay inside: a sticker, candy necklace, a toy action figure? You are no different. You love surprises, too. You perk up every Christmas morning when someone lays a wrapped package on your lap! What valuable treasure lies inside? "Hummm! This gift in not simply a present but a personal reflection of what this person feels about me." Often we will look at the gift under the tree for weeks and wonder what's in it, only escalating the joy of finally opening it! Jesus has a unique, one of a kind gift for you. I wonder how often you contemplate what's inside. It's been exquisitely fashioned as a valued treasure that will forever remain a symbol of God's insatiable love and His brilliant plan of eternal favor. Revelation 2:17 reveals the nature of this mystifying and dazzling gift. And the angel revealed the Word of Christ: "*And I will give to him a white stone, and a new name written on the stone which no one knows but he who received it.*"

You hold in your hand a grab bag from Jesus with an outside inscription: "A white stone!" What sticker, candy necklace, or toy action figure lay inside? What love expression could be tucked in Christ's spirit that is so consequential that He could only give it to you in person? It's a gift so intimate that your grab bag lay hidden in Christ at the Cross until the day He could give it to you. It's true: some gifts can only be delivered heart to heart!

This promise of Revelation 2:17 gave a message of warning and hope to the church of Pergamum, a church on the west coast of Asia Minor. Toward the end of the first century, members of this assembly were compromising their Christian teachings with the pagan practices of the state religion. The angel of God delivered a blessing for those who would remain true to Christ's words until His return. They would be granted a personalized white stone symbolizing their union with God and Christ for all eternity. What does this white stone mean? What treasures did Jesus have in mind in describing such a puzzling gift? I suppose you will actually never know until you see Him and He grants eternal permission for the opening of your grab bag. What might Christ say to you that day when he gives you His long-awaited white stone?

In the first-century Roman culture, either a white stone or black stone was put into a vase by a judge signifying his vote for a person on trial: a white stone, acquittal; a black stone, condemned. Will Jesus seize your hand and whisper, "Beloved, I have found you innocent of all sin and shame? You are emancipated from all charges against you because of your faith in Christ. I love you, precious one!" Or will He say, "You are graciously granted the victory of eternity." For, indeed, in the ancient society of Jesus' day the winner of an athletic race was awarded the white stone as a symbol of triumph. It served as an entrance ticket into the halls of an awards banquet. Will Jesus beckon, "Come and dine with me and me with you."[1] Or will He remember the glory of the high priest in the Old Testament temple and remember his breastplate of jewels and the white stone that glistened like a diamond. It was *that* stone that God used in a strange way to enable the priest in the knowledge of God's will. Maybe Christ will enumerate, "Beloved, I placed in you the diamond of the Holy Spirit whose brilliance exercised divine spiritual insight! Oh, how I have loved watching Him resonate in you."

Rejoice, friend! The white stone assures you a new name, one so resplendently astonishing that its meaning can only be embraced face to face in the glittery setting of eternity. Oh, the joy of anticipating what treasures lie inside your grab bag. I suppose some packages will just have to remain tucked under the tree until resurrection morning!

"...and I will give him a white stone."

Revelation 2:17

98. I am An Overcomer

No other word more accurately describes the insatiable desire of a believer to prevail over hardship than this one: *overcomer*. The reality that God has granted you His power to overcome life's most difficult trials should hoist in you great hope. You don't have to remain trapped in a never-ending battle of despair. You are not a victim, but a victor.

An overcomer is one who is reinforced by God's Holy Spirit to win through opposition, to conquer impossibilities, and to secure the victory against all odds. God's given you everything you need to persist through formidable obstacles that break down your fortitude of faith. Remember, you are in Christ, made new in your nature, given divine enablement to obtain the triumph. Believe it! Say it out loud: "I am an overcomer obtaining continuous victory because Christ, The Overcomer, lives in me." But sometimes our position as victors grows dim.

When the World Trade Center was attacked on September 11, 2001, confusion exacerbated the tragedy. One aspect of the bewilderment occurred after the structures were altered by the impact of the two planes. The movement in the two towers caused many doors to seal up due to the pressure created on doorframes. People literally became prisoners in their own offices. Survivors told of being locked in the office with no hope of survival, when suddenly rescue workers knocked holes in the walls. They felt trapped because the walls were painted to look like concrete, and they thought they were doomed to suffocate. In reality, the walls were nothing more than sheetrock, and they could have easily escaped much earlier had they only known. Many of life's obstacles are no different. We believe we are staring at impassable walls, but they are not as impregnable as you might think.[1]

What sheetrock stands in your way of obtaining release from what binds you? What painted walls of discouragement loom before you as an impenetrable foe? How can one know God's power to deliver if there's never an obstacle to overcome? Jesus affirmed, "In this world you will have trouble, but take courage. I have overcome the world."[2] Did you hear that? He admonished, "You can overpower the difficulty with abiding confidence; so relax and reinstate your trust in Me." There is no obstacle big enough to destroy you unless it first destroys Jesus. Take an aggressive stand and pronounce the truth out loud:

"As an overcomer, I know my destiny."

> The victory's already been won. It was solidified when Christ overcame Satan at the Cross. You obtained that victory by placing your faith in Him. Ron Dunn encourages, "You work from the victory, not to the victory."

"As an overcomer, I know my enemy."

> Study Satan's tactics. Acquaint yourself with your weaknesses. He schemes with a strategy in mind to disarm your reliability in God faithfulness. Activate the Word of God and remain strong, for "greater is He who is in you than he who is in the world."[3]

"As an overcomer, I know my weapons."

> Though your victory is a continual victory, so is your battle. God has granted two armaments for the fight: "And they

defeated Satan because of the blood of the Lamb and the word of their testimony."[4] Testify of what God has done in your life.

"As an overcomer, I know my strength."

"You are my strength, Oh God, for I wait for you to rescue me, for you are my place of safety. In your unfailing love, oh God you will help me" - Psalm 59:10

As an overcomer you've been granted God's favor in combating spiritual warfare. But the blessings of God don't stop at the end of life's journey. For all eternity you will wear a victor's crown for emerging as a conqueror over Satan's forces. You've been promised rewards for persevering as an overcomer! You will share in the glory of the Messiah's throne: "He who overcomes, I will grant to him the honor to sit down with Me on My throne, as I also overcame."[5] What? Do you suppose you'll actually sit on the throne? Who knows! Indeed, glorious unveiled benefits await those who enter His Kingdom as overcomers. Your name will be individually highlighted by Christ Himself to His Father and the Hosts of God: "and to him who overcomes I will confess his name before My Father and the angels,"[6] thereby, confirming Christ's delight over you. And in return, you will partake in a spiritual feast of seeing Jesus Christ like you have never seen Him before, the King of Glory in all His fullness, for on earth you only knew Him in part. Paul exhorted, "We enter heavens glory through many tribulations."[7] But praise God, we do enter, not as beat up soldiers, but victorious conquerors!

"Whatever is born of God, overcomes the world, and this is the victory that has overcome the world - our faith."

1 John 5:4

99. I am A Dweller of the Celestial City

Who in the world would read a number one best-selling novel and put the book down without reading the last chapter? Yet many Bible readers cruise right up to the last book, Revelation, and stop right there at their own invisible sign: No Trespassing. Yes, please do trespass, and enter into the celestial zone of Revelation chapter 21. It's God's climatic, indescribable celebration of a never-ending festive gaiety. It's the Oscars of eternal glory where the saints of all ages, Abraham, Moses, Paul, you, and I will attend wearing the apparel of our glorified bodies. Together we will exalt the Lamb of Glory and give praise to our God! Hallelujah! I'm preparing my gown now! How can one even begin to grasp what God, the architect and builder of the heavenlies, has prepared for those who love Him?

It'd been almost sixty years since John had seen his beloved friend. Oh, how he missed Him. And to make it worse, he sat imprisoned in a dungeon cell on the southwestern coast of Asia Minor. It's one thing to be homesick for someone, but quite another to be confined to four walls with one's friend's laughter and love plastered in a mirage everywhere. Unremitting thoughts of how his friend patted the children on His lap and healed the royal official's son at Capernaum replayed like a broken record in his mind. Then it happened! The musty prison hole encountered a collision with a vision. An angel appeared and there stood his friend, Jesus Christ, not in person, but in a dramatic play, unveiling the events of the believers' destiny. Can you imagine how shocked and frightened John must have been? I imagine John, the disciple whom Jesus loved, fell flat on his face in inexpressible joy and adulation at the unfolding of God's blueprint concerning the climax of history! Most precious to John, I'm sure, was envisioning his friends of the past in heaven strolling the streets of gold shining like transparent glass. Perhaps he saw his buddies on earth who had been martyred for their faith: Simon sawed in two or Andrew Mithius tied to a tree and eaten by vultures, or maybe he saw a few other new acquaintances, you and me. Oh, the joy to have seen the city dwellers traipsing about the Holy City, the New Jerusalem.

What do you think John did when the angel disappeared? Do you think he went back to sleep, or do you suppose He feasted on eternity's glory, marveling over the graphic images of the celestial capital city that had unfolded before His eyes? How often do you leave this world in thought and dine in the banquet place of your future abode? Followers of Christ are commanded to focus on heaven "setting their minds on *the things above*, not on the things that are on earth."[1] John recorded *the things above* that were revealed to him that you might intentionally let its reality propel you onward and upward in your journey to the throne!

The Holy City, the handmade "tabernacle of God among men"[2] awaits your daily visitation. Won't you halt your busy pace and bring to mind heaven's paradise? It's a place where there is no pain, death, sadness, sickness, or sin. Can you imagine an atmosphere where there is nothing to worry about or even a twitch of discontent? You will serve the Lord with exalted gladness of heart where your capacity for heavenly service will reflect your faithfulness in this life. The Lord Jesus himself will bless you and *even* serve you![3] God will manifest His full glory, illuminating His light throughout the recreated universe. No longer will God be distant to you, for He has promised that the pure in heart shall see Him face to face. No human has even seen the face of God and lived, but you will peer into His eyes, enjoying rich, intimate, personal fellowship. Heaven's spectacular images are far beyond our imagination, aren't they?

How can we envision such a place of perfection and illustrious joy? Perhaps a six-year-old captured the magnificence of such a place. She was taking a lovely evening walk with her grandfather. Wonderingly she looked up at the stars and exclaimed, "Oh, Pawpaw! If the wrong side of heaven is so beautiful, what must the right side be?"

"And I saw a new heaven and a new earth."

Revelation 21:1

100. I am Heaven Bound

I recall one of the most tantalizing moments of my young life! It happened at 5:30 a.m. in the foyer of my aunt and uncle's house. It was a snowy morning and there on the inside porch squirmed my sister Vicki, my cousin Rusty, and me. The anticipation of the grandiose display inside the other room teased our hearts in shear bliss! It was Christmas morning! We waited for the command that would call forth, "Children, come and see!" And with wide-eyed innocence, we bounded into the room of shimmering lights to receive what lay beyond our fondest childlike dreams.

I love to translate my childlike memories of Christmas morning's glory into my own adult anticipation of the day that God opens the gates of His Holy Habitation and beckons, "Children, come and see!" My focus, my desire, my drive in this life revolves around all that lay "in the next room." Jonathan Edwards encouraged, "It becomes us to spend this life as a journey towards heaven."[1] Friends, God has "set eternity in our hearts!"[2] We should be the most becoming people in the entire world testifying, "Come and see! Come and see all that God has promised for those whose destination awaits the outpouring of The King's highest favor!" We're on a sacred quest to the throne of The Almighty! Praise God! Heaven's glory!

Heaven! It's the longing of the human heart, the goal of the believers' pilgrimage on earth. Heaven, it's the eternal and transcendent dwelling place of God and His angels, a new order of life distinguished from our physical earthly existence. Heaven, it's the final destination of all who, through faith, have become God's children. Heaven, it's God's handmade temple where the purest of praises celebrate the greatness of the King of Glory. Heaven, it's a celestial hotel with many rooms specifically prepared by Jesus Christ for His followers. Heaven, it's the address of the Holy City, the New Jerusalem, whose brilliance, like a costly stone, reflects images of pearly gates and gold-laden streets. Heaven, it's a colossal symphony of glory resounding with one unified love song to the King of Zion, where even the monstrous wings of the angels swish like the sounds of abundant waters, dropping their wings in hallowed allegiance. Heaven, it's the abode of the redeemed, the place where they have become "a pillar in the temple of God."[3] Heaven! It's your future home, your destiny! Oh friend, if we could catch a glimpse of our perfect satisfaction in heaven's glory, abounding in God's goodness, we would hold the ties that bind us to this sin-infiltrated earth with an open palm, eagerly anticipating our homecoming into resurrected life.

We get so excited about a family getaway to a sandy beach where our worn-out souls can find rest. Yet, how often do we live in the spirit of vacation concerning our future heaven-bound resort? Can you imagine such a spot where the barriers between redeemed humans and God will forever be removed and through God's lens you experience His unveiled spectacular glory? What thrills might await you when the curse you've lived under lifts itself? Who can indulge in the reverie of God's blessings of perfect peace, entering a place where one never droops, weakens, toils, or dies?

But most glorious of all, calculate God Himself living in your presence face to face! Yes! God's pleasure in your face! He will talk to His creation like in the original Garden of Eden. His unfolded greatness will permeate the celestial air where His people will continually frolic in unhampered fellowship with Him. Along with every nation, tribe, people, and language, you will exalt in one melodious voice extolling God for His most lavish gift of all: your ticket into heaven, Jesus Christ, the Sacrificial Lamb! You will inhale His presence, exploring and serving His Kingdom as a delegated king, enjoying His graces of friendship, assigned work, and unconstrained joy! Can you imagine reveling forever in God's most breathtaking labor of love for His creation: heaven in its entire splendor! Oh, beloved, please do imagine! Glory to God in the Highest! You're heaven bound!

"We are looking forward to a new heaven."

2 Peter 3:13

Friends, I pray these entitlements have opened your eyes to the inexpressible value of you! May these truths given by God in *Will the Real Me Please Stand Up* enrich your journey to the throne, and may you rejoice in His immense love. You're redeemed by the Lamb's blood. Glory to God, the Father, for His excellent mercies extended to you!

You've been created *new* in His likeness
granted a new identity and a *new* standing before the Father
given a *new* heart in which to relate to Him
with a *new* nature marked with a desire for holiness
celebrating a *new* song in which to offer Him praise
headed for the *new* heaven and *new* earth
in order to inhabit the *new* Jerusalem
For it is Christ Himself who promised He would one day
make everything *new*!

Now, will the *real you* please stand up and celebrate
The King of Glory...
Jesus Christ!

If you've enjoyed *Will the Real Me Please Stand Up,* check out the study guide accompaniment and additional media resources at www.ariseministries.net

Index of the
100 I Am Blessings

Endnotes

Part I—My Spiritual Ancestry

Chapter 1 - My Authority

1. Paul Lee Tan, *Encyclopedia of 7700 Illustrations* (Rockville, Maryland: Assurance Publishers, 1979) #1680, 442.

2. Matthew 25:21

3. *The Oprah Magazine*, March 2007, p. 217.

4. Colossians 1:16–17

5. John 1:3

6. Hebrews 1:2

7. Genesis 1:26

8. Jeremiah 17:9

9. Matthew 7:13–14

10. John MacArthur, *The MacArthur New Testament Commentary* (Chicago, Illinois: Moody Press, 1985), 449–458.

11. 1 Kings 18:21

12. James 1:8

13. James 4:4

14. Ephesians 4:6

15. Hebrews 1:3

16. Ephesians 3:16

17. 1 Corinthians 3:11

Chapter 2 - My Salvation

1. Genesis 5:3

2. Philippians 2:12

3. Titus 3:5

4. Strong's, G4409, p. 1176.

5. Titus 3:5

6. C. L. Barnhart, Webster's The American College Dictionary (New York, NY: Random House, 1961), 284.

7. Spiros Zodhiates, The Complete Word Study Dictionary (Chattanooga, TN: AMG Publishers, 1992), #2537, 804.

8. members.tripod.com/ahrens/serial/serial.html

9. Jeremiah 13:23

10. 2 Peter 2:22

Chapter 3 - My Arising

1. Strong's Concordance, H183, p. 9.

2. Psalm 19:12

3. Ephesians 4:22–24, Message

4. Philippians 4:10–11

5. John 5:23

6. Spiros Zodhiates, The Complete Word Study (Chattanooga, TN: AMG Publishing, 1993), #1843, 605.

7. John 3:20

8. Psalm 105:1-6

9. Psalm 9:6

10. Acts 7:2

11. Psalm 105:1–6, Message

12. Dwight Edwards, Experiencing Christ Within (Colorado Springs, Colorado: Waterbrook Press, 2001)–Week One, 11–30.

13. Hebrews 9:1

14. Roman 6:6

15. Isaiah 30:31

16. Philippians 4:19

17. William MacDonald, Believer's Bible Commentary (Nashville, TN: Thomas Nelson Publishers, 1990), 1907.

Chapter 4 - My Reservation

1. Billy Graham Association. Steps to Peace With God, World Wide Publications.

2. Romans 10:12

Part II—My Divine Inheritance

The 100 I am Blessings

Chapter 5 - My Foundation

Delivered / Redeemed

1. Strong's Concordance, G1805, p. 29.

Elected

1. Warren Wiersbe, Be Decisive (Wheaton, ILL, Victor Books, 1995), 61.

2. Holman Christian Standard Bible- Everyone Can Receive the Gift (Nashville, TN, Holman Publishers, 2005), 398.

3. Romans 1:6

4. Colossians 3:12

5. Romans 8:29

6. Titus 2:14

Accepted/Appeased

1. 2 Corinthians 5:21

2. Strong's, G1344, p. 23.

3. Romans 3:22

4. Romans 5:1

Transferred / Secure

1. Colossians 3:3

2. John 10:29

3. 1 John 2:2

4. Lewis Chafer, Major Themes of the Bible (Grand Rapids, MI: Zondervan Publishing, 1953), 225.

5. Ephesians 1:13

Holy

1. The Complete Study Word Dictionary New Testament, #40, 70.

2. The Complete Study Word Dictionary New Testament, #299, 139.

3. John 17:11

4. 1 Peter 1:19

5. Ephesians 5:26–27

Legalized by Adoption

1. Ephesians 1:5

2. Romans 8:15

3. J.I. Packer, Knowing God (Downers Grove, IL: InterVarsity Press, 1973),195.

Heir Calling My God 'Papa'

1. Strong's Concordance, H3810, p. 58

2. Ibid, G3962, p. 56

3. Galatians 4:6

Indwelt by the Holy Spirit (Part 1)

1. John 16:7

2. 1 Corinthians 2:10

3. Complete Word Study New Testament, # 2397, 775.

4. P.L. Tan, Encyclopedia of 7700 Illustrations, (Chicago, ILL: Assurance Publishers, 1979), #2232, 555.

Conduit of the Holy Spirit's Release (Part 2)

1. Strong's, G1411, p. 24

2. Strong's, G3594, p. 51

3. Ann Graham Lotz, Just Give Me Jesus (Nashville, TN: Word Publishing, 2000), 160.

4. John 16:13

Filled with the Holy Spirit (Part 3)

1. John 17:13

2. 1 Peter 1:8

Forgiven

1. Today in the Word, March 1989, p. 8.

2. Mark 2:5

3. Strong's, G918, p. 1692.

4. Hebrews 9:22

5. Micah 7:19

Eternally Glorified

1. John Ortberg, "Ultimate Hope," Menlo Park Presbyterian Church, 3/27/5; Toonopeida. com.

2. 2 Thessalonians 2:14

3. Philippians 3:21

4. 1 Corinthians 15: 42−44

Chapter 6 - My Position

In Christ

1. Romans 6:30

2. Galatians 3:28

3. Romans 12:27

4. Isaiah 46:9

5. Philippians 2:7–8

Hidden with Christ in God

1. Ephesians 2:6

2. Colossians 3:3

3. JD Lightfoot, Colossians and Philemon, The Crossway Classic Commentaries (Wheaton, IL: Crossway Books,1997), 94.

4. William Barclay, The Letters to the Philippians, Colossians (Louisville, Kentucky; Westminster John Knox Press, 2003), 172.

5. The NIV Exhaustive Concordance, G3221, p. 1745.

6. John 10:29

7. Jeremiah 29:13

Sanctified Saint

1. Wuest's Word Studies in the Greek New Testament, Chapter One from Romans 1:5.

2. Revelation 20:1

A Worshiper

1. Job 40:10

2. Acts 16:25–40

Glory Giver

1. Jerry Chafer, Major Doctrines of the Bible (Grand Rapids, MI: Zondervan Publishing House, 1953), 29.

2. Geoffrey Bromiley, Theological Dictionary of the New Testament (Grand Rapids: Eerdmans Publishing, 1985), 178.

3. 1 Peter 2:9

4. Dwight Edwards, Experiencing Christ Within (Colorado Springs, CO: Waterbrook Press, 2001), 39.

5. John 17:20

6. Edwards, 39–40.

Living Stone Being Built Up in Him

   1. 1 Peter 2:9

   2. Isaiah 28:16

   3. Strong's, G 1588, p. 45.

   4. 1 Timothy 3:15

   5. Ephesians 2:19–22

Temple of the Living God

   1. Revelation 3:12

Ambassador

   1. 2 Corinthians 5:15

   2. Raymond, McHenry, In Other Words, August 2006, Issue 3.

Child of Light

   1. Strong's, G3473, p. 49.

   2. Ibid, G516, p. 13.

Eternal Plan of God

   1. 1 Corinthians 2:9

   2. Job 38:4–8 NLT

   3. Ephesians 3:18

   4. John 15:16

Dead to Sin

   1. Romans 6:12

   2. The Complete Word Study Dictionary, New Testament, #3049, 922.

   3. Luke 4:4

Alive to God

   1. P.T Tan, Encyclopedia of 7700 Illustrations (Chicago, IL, 1996), #53, 121.

   2. Barend Klass Kuiper, Martin Luther: The Formative Years (Grand Rapids: Eerdmans, 1933), 198.

   3. Galatians 2:20

   4. Matthew 16:16

   5. Wiersbe, The Bible Expository (Colorado Springs, CO: Victor Books, 1989), 652.

   6. NIV Exhaustive Concordance, G2409, p. 1728.

   7. 1 Peter 1:3

A Member of a Kingdom of Priests
    1. Romans 12:1–2
    2. Hebrews 13:16

Abraham's Seed
    1. Genesis 12:2

Hated by the World
    1. John 15:18
    2. Romans 12:19
    3. John 15:19

Enemy of the Devil (Part 1)
    1. 1 Peter 1:13
    2. Isaiah 14:14
    3. Revelation 12:7–9
    4. Revelation 12:4
    5. Barna Research, 2005–www.barna.org/FlexPage.aspy
    6. 2 Corinthians 2:11

Alert to the Enemy's Schemes (Part 2)
    1. 1 Peter 5:8
    2. 1 John 4:4
    3. The NIV Exhaustive Concordance, G3497, p. 1751.
    4. Ephesians 2:2
    5. Ephesians 6:12
    6. 2 Corinthians 4:4
    7. Luke 22:31
    8. Strong's, G1465, p. 25.
    9. 1 Thessalonians 2:18

Armed Against the Enemy (Part 3)
    1. Encyclopedia of 7700 Illustrations, 1234.
    2. Ephesians 6:10
    3. Ephesians 6:10–16
    4. 2 Corinthians 12:9

Dangerous Threat to the Enemy's Domain (Part 4)
    1. Luke 10:18
    2. Luke 10:19a
    3. Luke 11:20b

4. Luke 11:20

5. John 14:12

Led in Christ's Triumph

1. Colossians 2:15

2. F.B. Meyer, Paul the Life of Christ (Lynnewood, Washington: Emerald Books, 1995), 74.

Spiritually Circumcised

1. Deuteronomy 7:7–9

2. Colossians 2:11–12

3. Philippians 3:3

4. Deuteronomy 6:5

5. Deuteronomy 10:16

6. Jeremiah 4:4

Crucified with Christ

1. Galatians 2:20

2. 2 Corinthians 4:10

3. Galatians 2:20

4. Ibid

Citizen of Heaven

1. Dr. Raymond McHenry, In Other Words, August 2006, Issue 3.

2. William Barkley, Daily Study Bible Series: The Letters to the Philippians (Louisville, Kentucky: Westminister John Knox Press) 2003, 81.

Alien and Stranger

1. Acts 7:6

2. John McArthur New Testament Commentary, 1 Peter; (Chicago, ILL: Moody Publishers, 2004), 137.

3. 1 Peter 13:14

4. Revelation 11:15

5. 1 Peter 2:11 Message

Assigned to the Age of Grace

1. Lewis Chafer, Major Bible Themes (Grand Rapids, MI: Zondervan Publishing House, 1953), 127.

Called Out

1. The Complete Word Study Dictionary, #1577, 541.

2. Mark 16:15

3. Hebrews 3:13

4. Strong's, G4182, p. 59.

5. Psalms 19:1

6. Ephesians 2:6–7

Member of the Body of Christ

1. Ephesians 4:4–7

Chapter 7 - My Significance

God's Delight

1. Ezekiel 16:25–27

2. Isaiah 62:3

3. Ibid, 2:4

Adequate

1. Judges 6:12

Confident

1. Strong's, H7965, p.116.

2. 1 John 4:4

3. Adrian Rogers, The Power of His Presence (Wheaton, ILL: Crossway Books, 1995), 75.

Inseparable from God's Love

1. 2 Peter 1:12

2. 2 Timothy 1:12

3. Encyclopedia of 7700 Illustrations, #170, p. 143.

Friend of God

1. Warren Wiersbe, The Bible Exposition Commentary (Colorado Springs, CO: Victor Books, 2001), 357.

2. John 15:15

3. Exodus 20:16

4. John Mark Ministries, article "Prayer, Friendship with God" -rcc-roucher@optusnet.com.au

Free From Condemnation

1. Romans 8:31

2. Galatians 5:1

An Expression of the Love of Christ

1. Philippians 1:21 NLT

2. Ibid - NAS

Valued
  1. Isaiah 61:10
  2. Strong's, H559, p. 14.
Enlightened
  1. Ephesians 2:6
  2. William MacDonald, Believers Bible Commentary (Nashville, TN: Thomas Nelson Publishers, 1995), 1913.
  3. John 11:43
  4. MacDonald, p. 1913.
  5. Ephesians 1:17
Clean
  1. John 8:1
Loved
  1. Hosea 1:2
  2. Ibid, 3:1–3
  3. Romans 5:8
Complete
  1. Max Lucado, Six Hours One Friday (Portland, Oregon: Multnomah, 1989), 36–38.
  2. 2 Peter 1:3
  3. John 1:16

Chapter 8 - My Benefits
Trustee of God's Promises
  1. Psalm 84:11
  2. 2 Corinthians 1:20
  3. The New Encyclopedia of Christian Quotations, 834.
Beneficiary of God's Perfect Timing
  1. Strong's, H3303, p. 50.
  2. Luke 24:29
  3. Luke 24:31
  4. Job 23:14
Cultivator of a Grateful Heart
  1. Luke 1:13
  2. Colossians 2:7

3. Mark Water, The Encyclopedia of Christian Quotations (Grand Rapids, MI, Baker Books, 2000), 449.

4. Job 1:21

Granted an Intercessor

1. Hebrews 7:25

2. The Complete Word Study Dictionary, #1793, 595.

3. Hebrews 10:21

4. John 17:20

5. John 17:9

Participant in Prayer

1. James 5:16, Amplified Version

Attended by Angels

1. Hebrews 1:7

2. Genesis 1:1

3. Billy Graham, Angels, God's Secret Agents (Garden City, NY: Doubleday and Company, Inc., 1975), 36.

4. Psalm 91:11

Rider on the Heights of the Earth

1. Isaiah 40:29

2. Isaiah 40:31

3. Ibid

Well Content with Difficulties

1. 2 Corinthians 12:10

2. Strong's, G2106, p. 33

3. 1 Peter 4:13

4. John Piper, Suffering and the Sovereignty of God (Wheaton, ILL: Crossway Books, 2006), 89.

5. 2 Timothy 2:12

6. Matthew 26:39

7. Colossians 1:24

Afforded Sabbath/Salvation Rest

1. Internet website–www.english.pravda.ru/society/family

2. Internet website: www.cdc.gov/nccdphp/dnpa/obesity

Abounding in Hope

1. 1 Peter 1:3

2. 1 Peter 3:15

3. Hebrews 6:19

Enriched in Speech and Knowledge

1. 2 Peter 1:3

2. Exodus 4:10–12

3. Matthew 10:15

Grace-Filled

1. Ephesians 2:8

2. The New Encyclopedia of Christian Quotations, 447.

3. Philippians 4:19

4. John MacArthur, The Quick Reference Guide to the Bible (Carol Streams, IL, W Publishing Group, 2001), 242.

Empowered

1. Philippians 4:13

2. Warren Wiersbe, The Bible Expository Commentary, Volume 2 Philippians (Colorado Springs, CO: Victor Books, 2001), 98.

Assured That God's in Control

1. Romans 8:28

2. The Complete Word Study Dictionary, p. 1341.

3. The John MacArthur New Testament Commentary on Romans (Chicago: Moody Press, 1991), 472.

4. The Complete Study Dictionary, #4903, p. 1341.

5. The John MacArthur New Testament Commentary on Romans (Moody Press Chicago, 1991), 473.

6. Ephesians 1:3

Disciplined

1. The NIV Exhaustive Concordance, G4082, p. 1769.

2. Hebrews 7:5

3. Galatians 6:7

4. Hebrews 4:11

A Receiver of Eternal Life Now

1. John 10:10

2. John 17:3

3. Strong's, G1097, p. 20.

4. Mark Water, The New Encyclopedia of Christian Quotations (Grand Rapids, MI: Baker Books, 1984), 312.

Recipient of God's Cleansing

1. 2 Samuel 24:10

2. 1 Samuel 13:14

3. 1 Timothy 1:15

4. Romans 3:23

5. Richard Foster, Celebration of Discipline (New York, NY: Harper San Francisco, 1998), 151.

6. The New Encyclopedia of Christian Quotations, p. 863.

Renewed

1. Job 5:9

2. Jeremiah 37:17

Blessed with Spiritual Blessings in the Heavenly Places

1. Galatians 3:9

2. James 1:17

3. Ephesians 2:6

4. Warren Wiersbe, The Bible Expository Commentary (Colorado Springs, CO: Victor Books, 2001), 10.

5. Revelations 7:10–12

Compelled to Walk in God's Statutes

1. John MacArthur, New Testament Commentary (Chicago, ILL: Moody Press, 1983), 105.

Afflicted but Not Crushed

1. Acts 14:22

2. John 17:33

3. Chambers, My Utmost for His Highest (Grand Rapid, MI: Discovery House Publishers, 1982), August 2.

4. Genesis 39:23

Lavished with the Riches of God's Grace

1. 1 John 3:1–2

Bestowed with the Mind of Christ

1. 1 Corinthians 2:13

Favored

1. Luke 1:42

2. Luke 1:48

3. Matthew 5:3–10, Message

Comforted

1. Strong's, H3068, p. 118.

2. Strong's, G2424, p. 47.

3. Isaiah 40:11

4. Strong's, H2637, p. 101.

5. Ibid, H7257.

6. Ibid, H5095.

7. Ibid, H7725.

8. Ibid, H8034.

9. Ibid, H6757.

10. Ibid, H3962.

11. Ibid, H5162.

12. Ibid, H6186.

13. Ibid, H1878.

14. Ibid, H7291.

15. Ibid, H3427.

Carried

1. Matthew 11:28–29

Chapter 9 - My Service

A Servant

1. Philippians 2:3

2. The Complete Word Study Dictionary, #1401, p. 483.

3. Doug Fields and Bret Eastman, Experiencing Christ Together: Serving Like Jesus (Grand Rapids: Zondervan, 2006), 46.

4. Dr. Raymond McHenry, In Other Words, Newsletter, November 2006, Issue 1.

Gifted Gift to Others

1. Ephesians 4:7–8

2. 1 Corinthians 12:18

God's Workmanship

1. Strong's, G 4161, p. 59.

2. Ephesians 4:8

3. Strong's, G 2938, p. 44.

4. 2 Corinthians 9:8

5. John 15:8

Repairer of the Breach

    1. Strong's, H8934, p. 1637.

    2. 2 Corinthians 5:19

Fruit Bearer

    1. John 15:16

    2. John 17:4

    3. Raymond McHenry, In Other Words, January 2007, Issue 2.

Witness

    1. Dr. Raymond McHenry, In Other Words, weekly publication, 8/06- Issue 2. www.iows.net

    2. Acts 1:8

    3. Strong's, G3144, p. 46.

    4. Matthew 28:19

    5. Acts 16:7

    6. 1 Peter 3:15

Branch

    1. John 15:5

    2. Bruce Barton, Life Application Bible Commentary (Wheaton: ILL: Tyndale House Publishers, Inc, 1993), 308.

    3. Spiros Zodhiates, The Complete Word Study Dictionary (Chattanooga, TN: AMG Publishers, 1992), #3306, 959.

    4. Colossians 3:16

    5. MacArthur Commentary on Matthew 1-7, 470.

A Blessing

    1. Genesis 49:28

    2. Luke 6:28

A Spring of Water

    1. Adrian Rogers, The Power of His Presence (Wheaton, ILL: Crossway Book, 1995), 56.

    2. John 7:38

    3. Zechariah 13:1

    4. John 7:37

    5. John 4:14

Salt of the Earth
  1. Matthew 5:13
  2. Ephesians 6:19
A Light of the World
  1. Http. www.newsdesk.umd.edu/archive/release
  2. John 1:9
  3. Proverbs 13:9
  4. "cavern full of gems" - Frederic William Farrar, source unknown
Instrument of Righteousness
  1. Romans 6:11–12
  2. 2 Timothy 2:21
  3. Romans: God's Freedom (Grand Rapids: Eerdmans, 1961),118.
  4. Isaiah 62:2
Enabled to Abound in Good Deeds
  1. John 3:16
  2. John 12:24
  3. Galatians 6:10
  4. 2 Corinthians 9:8

Chapter 10 - My Destiny
Victor on a White Horse
  1. Matthew 4:7
  2. Revelation 19:11–14
  3. Revelation 22:20
  4. Isaiah 49:2
  5. Micah 4:3
  6. Revelation 19:15
  7. Isaiah 11:6–8
  8. Isaiah 60:11
Bride of Christ
  1. Paul Billheimer, Destined for the Throne (Bethany House Publishers, 1975), 23–24.
  2. Revelation 19:8
Rewarded
  1. Revelation 22:12
  2. NIV, #1037, p. 1694

3. 2 Timothy 4:8

Overcomer

    1. In Other Words, Dr. Raymond McHenry, 9/Issue 2.

    2. John 16: 33

    3. 1 John 4:4

    4. Revelations 12:11

    5. Revelation 3:21

    6. Revelation 3:5

    7. Acts 14:22

A Dweller of the Celestial City

    1. Colossians 3:1–2

    2. Revelation 21:3

    3. Luke 12:35–40

Heaven Bound

    1. Ola Elizabeth Winslow, Jonathan Edwards: Basic Writings (New York: New American Library, 1966), 142.

    2. Ecclesiastes 3:11

    3. Revelation 3:12